"Powerful, pragmatic, and direct, this book is a compassionate pathway to freedom through mastery."

—SAKI SANTORELLI, EdD, MA, Associate Professor of Medicine, Director, MBSR Stress Reduction Clinic, Executive Director, Center for Mindfulness in Medicine, Health Care, and Society, University of Massachusetts Medical School

"In this generous, clearly written book, Larry Peltz makes a compelling case for mindfulness practice as an antidote to addiction. It is an authoritative, nondogmatic guide through all phases of recovery, challenges to recovery, and available treatment options. Chock-full of illuminating stories and essential mindfulness exercises, this book is a doorway to freedom for people struggling with addiction and those who love them."

—CHRISTOPHER GERMER, PhD, Clinical Instructor, Harvard Medical School, author of *The Mindful Path to Self-Compassion*

"Larry Peltz gives a unique and enlightening view of addiction and provides a very clear way to change one's destructive habits. I highly recommend it."

—SHARON SALZBERG, author of *Lovingkindness* and *Real Happiness*

"A mindful and compassionate attention is the very ground of recovery from addiction. In this book, Lawrence Peltz offers a penetrating understanding of the nature of addiction, and the meditation practices that can help us find freedom from this suffering. Drawing on his rich clinical experience, Dr. Peltz shares the struggles of people who have found great healing on this path of recovery and transformation."

—TARA BRACH, PhD, author of *Radical Acceptance* and *True Refuge*

"Addictions are rooted in distress and suffering. Dr. Peltz shows us how practicing thoughtfulness, awareness, and acceptance can bring solace, relief, and happiness without resorting to addictive solutions."

—EDWARD J. KHANTZIAN, MD, Clinical Professor of Psychiatry, Harvard Medical School, Associate Chief Emeritus of Psychiatry, Tewksbury Hospital

"A thoughtfully and beautifully written journey that guides the reader through the recovery process, integrating theory and practice of mindfulness and traditional addictions treatment. Dr. Peltz is exquisitely sensitive to the human experience; he addresses real-life situations with interventions that are informed and practical. He offers acceptance of the chaotic existence of those suffering with active addiction and hope that effective interventions can support the patient regardless of their motivation to change."

—JANICE F. KAUFFMAN, RN, MPH, LADC, CAS, Vice President, Addiction Services, North Charles Foundation, Inc., Assistant Professor of Psychiatry, Harvard Medical School

"Dr. Peltz writes with empathy and expertise about addiction, combining psychological savvy with mindfulness. The wisdom and humanity here can benefit us all."

—ELANA ROSENBAUM, MS, MSW, LICSW, faculty and senior teacher, The Center for Mindfulness, University of Massachusetts Medical School, psychotherapist and mindfulness coach at Mindfuliving, and author of *Being Well*

"This is a really helpful and important work."

—JACK KORNFIELD, PhD, author of *A Path with Heart*

The Mindful Path to Addiction Recovery

The Mindful Path to Addiction Recovery

A PRACTICAL GUIDE TO REGAINING CONTROL OVER YOUR LIFE

LAWRENCE A. PELTZ, MD

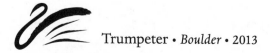

Trumpeter • *Boulder* • 2013

Trumpeter Books
An imprint of Shambhala Publications, Inc.
4720 Walnut Street
Boulder, Colorado 80301
www.shambhala.com

Grateful acknowledgment is made for permission to reprint the following material:
"Kindness" from *Words Under the Words: Selected Poems* by Naomi Shihab Nye, copyright
© 1995. Reprinted with permission of Far Corner Books, Portland, Oregon.
"Weathering" by Fleur Adcock, from *Poems 1960–2000* (Bloodaxe Books, 2000).
"Wild Geese" by Mary Oliver, from *New and Selected Poems* (Beacon Press, 1992).
"You've Really Got a Hold on Me," words and music by William "Smokey" Robinson.
© 1962, 1963 (renewed 1990, 1991) Jobete Music Co., Inc. All rights controlled and
administered by EMI April Music Inc. All rights reserved. International copyright
secured. Used by permission. Reprinted by permission of Hal Leonard Corporation.

9 8 7 6 5 4 3

Printed in the United States of America

♾ This edition is printed on acid-free paper that meets the
American National Standards Institute Z39.48 Standard.
♻ This book is printed on 30% postconsumer recycled paper.
For more information please visit www.shambhala.com.

Distributed in the United States by Penguin Random House LLC
and in Canada by Random House of Canada Ltd

Designed by James D. Skatges

Library of Congress Cataloging-in-Publication Data

Peltz, Lawrence A.
The mindful path to addiction recovery: a practical guide to regaining control over your life
/ Lawrence A. Peltz, MD.—First edition.
Pages   cm
Includes bibliographical references and index.
ISBN 978-1-59030-918-6 (pbk.: alk. paper)
1. Addicts—Rehabilitation. 2. Substance abuse—Treatment. 3. Self-care, Health. I. Title.
RC564.P456 2013
362.29—dc23
2012036974

To Nancy,
Miles and Haley,
Harriet and Marvin,
Selma and Willie,
Susan and Les,
and the thousands of patients who taught me most
of what I needed to know

Contents

PART FOUR Authority amid the Full Catastrophe

Foreword

We're all addicts. Even if we don't become hooked on alcohol, cigarettes, or other drugs, we rely on different things to avoid pain and cling to pleasure. Whether it's eating, sleeping, gambling, shopping, exercising, reading, watching TV, surfing the Internet, or having sex—almost any activity can become an addiction. While some of these can have dire consequences and others may even be healthy, they all share a common dynamic.

What turns an activity into an addiction? As Dr. Larry Peltz clearly illustrates in the following pages, all addictions involve being enslaved by our desires. The wish to feel good and avoid emotional or physical pain is very natural and deeply rooted. Activities that feel good to us (and to other animals as well) were in our evolutionary history associated with survival and passing on our DNA: drinking when thirsty, eating when hungry, avoiding pain, being comforted, having sex. Difficulties arise when things that feel good in the short run cause problems in the long run. And, unfortunately for us, the ancient, pleasure-seeking parts of our brains are quite powerful—so powerful that the newer parts that can anticipate the consequences of our actions are often no match for them. To make matters worse, these newer, thinking parts of our brains are easily impaired by addictive substances, and before long the intoxicants themselves can become a source of distress.

Luckily, by using the newer areas of our brains during clear-headed moments, people have developed ways to address our evolutionary problem and free ourselves from addictive habits. While some of these techniques come from modern scientific advances, others are thousands of years old. One of the more exciting developments in addictions recovery blends ancient wisdom traditions with recent psychological and neurobiological discoveries. This new approach teaches *mindfulness*—a deceptively simple way of relating to experience that has been successfully used to alleviate suffering for thousands of years. Rather being compelled to rush toward pleasure and run from pain, scientific research is showing that through mindfulness practice we can learn to open to whatever is happening in the present moment, embrace what is, and live freer, more fulfilling, healthier lives as a result. And this book will show you how.

One of the reasons addictions can be so hard to overcome is that they become self-perpetuating, vicious cycles. Even if they have disastrous long-term consequences, addictive behaviors initially feel good. This good feeling becomes *positively reinforcing*—we have a natural tendency to repeat those behaviors that are followed by a good feeling (or the removal of an unpleasant one). So having done something addictive once, the next time we're faced with the opportunity to repeat the behavior, we're likely to do it again. And again, and again, and again.

We learn through mindfulness practice that we don't have to be controlled by these sorts of conditioned responses. Rather than feeling compelled to fall into our addictive behavior whenever we feel the urge, we discover that we can create a gap between impulse and action—we can take a breath, feel whatever is behind our urge, and decide whether or not to act on it. In this way, mindfulness practice helps us learn to make wise choices.

As you'll see throughout this wide-ranging book, mindfulness practice can also help us to get at the difficulties that may have led us into addiction in the first place. It can help us to effectively work with physical and emotional pain, difficulties with others at home or work, and even the effects of past traumas.

Despite having much in common, everyone's addiction is also different, so no single approach is best suited to all people. That's why having detailed guidance, from someone who knows the territory well, is so important.

This book provides that guidance. Dr. Peltz, a psychiatrist with many years of experience with both mindfulness practice and substance abuse treatment, offers in-depth guidelines for working with a wide range of addictions. He gives clear, real-world accounts of how many different sorts of people fell into and were able to overcome their addictions. Since complex problems require complex solutions, this book addresses the psychological, biological, and social aspects of addiction, along with diverse treatment modalities that can be effective along with mindfulness practice—including 12-step programs (such as AA), various forms of psychotherapy, and psychiatric medications—providing insights into the advantages and disadvantages of these different approaches for different people.

Dr. Peltz also presents a deep understanding of mindfulness—the kind of understanding that can only be provided by an author who has had years of personal and clinical experience with the practice. The book's blend of personal and professional insights is both instructive and inspirational, providing a path anyone struggling with addiction can follow to awaken to a freer, healthier, richer life.

RONALD D. SIEGEL, PsyD
Assistant Clinical Professor of Psychology,
Harvard Medical School,
author of *The Mindfulness Solution:*
Everyday Practices for Everyday Problems

Introduction

This is a book about personal authority, the process of gaining control of our lives. Addiction and mindfulness are both strategies toward that end. We will see that addiction leads to greater suffering and mindfulness to wisdom and well-being, but if we are addicted to a substance or behavior, we must see the nature of the problem before we can solve it.

One of my teachers, Hal Stone, has said that as human beings we are running many "businesses." There is the literal business of career or earning money, but we also have businesses around primary relationships, parenting, family, friendship, community, interests, physical well-being, appearance, religion, spirituality, and many others. Life keeps coming at us with all of its attendant pulls and stressors. We are fortunate, or we are not. Time goes by too quickly or too slowly. We are all dealt good and not-so-good cards around our strengths, parents, country of birth.

At times we are grateful for our circumstances, for all we have, even for bad luck or interpersonal conflict that eventually turns out well. At other times, we feel stressed, challenged, even overwhelmed by the enormity of our burdens and emotions. Our lives can feel disappointing, frightening, confusing, unfair—and they are.

We all do the best we can to manage. Our strategies combine elements of confronting, avoiding, and taking refuge from our experience or feelings. Jim works for the electric company and does a lot of overtime in order to support his family. He gets home late to find his wife, Karen, asleep after her day of working and caring for the kids. Jim is tired, depleted, and wanting contact with Karen but is not willing to wake her. He needs to be up again in seven or eight hours but also needs some time to recover and experience some pleasure without any demand. So he turns on the TV, has a beer, eats too much, and stays up too late. Jim wakes up exhausted and repeats the process the next day and the next.

This may sound familiar. Our attempts to be successful, earn enough money, and be good partners, parents, and caregivers all take time and energy. We have homes to take care of, errands, medical appointments. All of our efforts may fulfill our role requirements but often neglect our well-being. Once we slow down, the body calls out to be comforted, relaxed, satiated. Like Jim, we have all used food, sex, work, exercise, or substances at some point to feel better. Is that a problem? Not necessarily. The problem begins when we think we have found a strategy to repeatedly control or escape difficult experience whenever we want to. Alcohol and drugs have provided a source of power, however false, or protection, at least in the short-term.

Addiction is a pervasive pattern of attachment to these short-term benefits. There is a saying that goes, "If the only tool you have is a hammer, everything starts looking like a nail." At different times, Jim feels sad, anxious, resentful, or lonely when he gets home. A beer might take the edge off, so why not two or three, he is only going to sleep? If he is feeling upbeat, what better way to sustain that feeling? Eventually Jim looks forward to that drink as his refuge from stress and inner turmoil. This is a discovery that works for him, and he can do it on his own. It is a reward and an escape.

We can see that Jim is on a slippery slope, but he cannot. Alcohol seems to help him. When Jim is around the house with the family or working in the yard, he also has a few beers. Initially, this is to deal with the little annoyances of family life, and later it becomes a habit. He is now glad to come home to find his wife asleep, and in a largely imperceptible way, he begins to withdraw from her and the kids. Jim tells himself that they have enough problems, so why worry them with his? There is also a guilty sense of relief in hiding his worry that he is not measuring up as a provider, husband, and father and that Karen will leave him if he cannot pull it together soon. Karen is actually genuinely concerned and tries to have an exchange, but Jim angrily fends her off.

He is particularly irritated if she raises his drinking as an issue, a screen for the fear that he pushes away and his wife experiences.

Jim can glimpse what is going on. He is sad and ashamed but often drinks to keep those feelings at bay. In fact, his capacity for dealing with his emotions and the simple stressors of life is beginning to diminish. Jim hates what he is doing to himself and his family but feels at a loss as to what to do. His strategy for relaxation has created a vicious cycle of stress, drinking, relief, shame, more drinking, shutting down, self-hatred, more drinking, and so on. Health, work, and relationships all begin to deteriorate, with predictable outcomes if help is not sought.

It is possible that Jim can stop drinking on his own, but more likely he will need to go into the hospital for detoxification or intensive outpatient treatment to prevent an alcohol-withdrawal seizure. To sustain his sobriety, it will be advisable for him to go to Alcoholics Anonymous (AA) and to have a therapist with whom to discuss his personal issues and concerns. He may need medicine for depression or anxiety. This course of action will give Jim a chance to recover from alcoholism, but it will not be easy. As we know, many people relapse repeatedly.

Each year approximately one hundred thousand people die in this country of alcohol-related illnesses. In 2006 the overall cost from excessive drinking in the United States was $223.5 billion. Nearly 75 percent of this was related to loss of workplace activity, along with expenses related to health care, law enforcement, criminal justice, and motor vehicle crashes. Many involved in auto accidents, violent crime, and suicide are likely drinking as well, which may go unreported. Alcoholism is a costly and deadly disease.[1]

Mindfulness practice is a powerful accompaniment to the recovery, psychotherapy, and medicine an alcoholic or addict needs. In essence, mindfulness is the quality of awareness that sees without judgment, shining a light on each moment just as it is. This includes physical sensations, feelings, thoughts, and the nature of our experience continually shifting and changing. With practice, it is a skill that can be developed by anyone.

This book explores the place of mindfulness in the recovery from addictive processes. As I noted at the beginning, we must clearly see a problem before we can solve it. Mindfulness is an investigative technique that can help illuminate our difficulty so that we can look into it. Once there is some interest in the problem and the obstacles to recovery, a new path is created, and if that path is more interesting than escaping in the usual ways, it will likely be pursued. I have found mindfulness skills to be a key to this process of addicts' taking a greater interest in their well-being than in avoiding their experience. So much of addiction is like living in a tunnel, screening out much of life in the quest for relief or escape. Mindfulness gives us the capacity to open up the field and do it at our own pace. Greater vision leads to greater choice and the ability to deal with problems previously thought to be unapproachable.

The first section of this book is an introduction to addiction, mindfulness, and meditation practice. This is followed by sections about approaches to treatment and challenges to recovery and finally some thoughts on bringing wisdom and compassion practice into our busy lives. All sections incorporate case examples, clinical perspective, and practice in the attempt to both show and tell. (Case examples either are composites or have sufficient changes in identifying information to protect confidentiality.) My main goal is to encourage you to try the practices presented at the end of the first few chapters and gradually build your repertoire from there, based on where you are drawn, applicability to your particular situation, and time available on a given day. I believe you will discover that it is time well spent.

Is it possible to recover from addiction, take charge of one's life, and become an adult without practicing mindfulness? Yes it is. But a life-threatening problem requires a number of tools, and many have benefited from the simplicity of being aware of their breathing or their feet on the ground in the midst of a challenging moment or situation. It may be obvious that these skills are not only for addicts and mental patients but for all of us. In treatment groups, it often feels as if we were all growing up together, learning how to experience a greater sense of freedom and power over our lives. Many people have said, "Thank God I am an alcoholic, because otherwise I would never have discovered who I really was." For those struggling with addiction, mindfulness practice can open up new possibilities for contentment, joy, self-efficacy, growth, and compassion. Many have been encouraged by just glimpsing this potential.

PART ONE

Addiction and Mindfulness

1

Addiction

I don't like you, but I love you.
Seems that I'm always thinking of you.
You treat me badly, I love you madly.
—SMOKEY ROBINSON

THE ESSENCE OF ADDICTION is an attempt to manage an intolerable experience that we cannot avoid any other way. As we will see, people use drugs to change consciousness, which does work. However, once this mode of operating becomes a habit and then a way of life, changing consciousness transforms into avoiding suffering. This happens outside of awareness. Before long, addiction is causing suffering and eventually *is* suffering. It is also, ironically, an attempt to heal, to seek relief via getting high, medicating feelings, escaping how things are right now. It is a process that attempts to change reality and control experience so that it is more acceptable, palatable, bearable.

Addiction can be a container for fear, disappointment, confusion, grief, or anger. It allows us to move forward in life with some hope that we might actually feel pleasure, even happiness. Of course, the happiness never materializes and the pleasure is more anticipated than realized. The addict becomes increasingly discouraged, unable to stand his experience as he digs a deeper hole. Abstinence, if considered, is quickly rejected. "I'm a total loser," he tells himself. "Fuck it. My life is going nowhere anyway."

Roger completed day treatment after an alcohol detox and many years of drinking. He was committed to recovery and was able to stay sober until he became involved with a much younger woman he had met in the program. He relapsed with her, they ended badly, and he was back for another round of treatment, during which he learned something about his vulnerability in romantic relationships.

When Roger came back for a third time, it was not about drinking but gambling. He had been playing the slot machines regularly and, as a retiree on a fixed income, was courting financial ruin. Driving to the casino, Roger experienced the excitement and anticipation of winning, the fear of losing even more, the dread of facing his creditors, and a wish to escape what he eventually was able to identify as loneliness and desperation. His foray into gambling had begun much like his relationship with the young woman, his drinking, or any addictive process. Initially, he had a sense of power, a rigged game in which he felt in love, one up on everyone, no limits, totally in control of the situation.

Let's focus on the experience of falling in love. At the outset the lover is perfect in looks, reactions, speech—a missing piece to complete us and fill us with the miracle of life and of our amazing fortune to have found this person. In fact, we often do fall in love with our opposite, or what Hal and Sidra Stone have called our "disowned part."

Think of the attraction between the hard-driving, successful, somewhat obsessional man and the free-flowing, flirtatious woman. He loves her openness, creativity, ease with her sexuality, and she is drawn to his confidence, power, and organization. All is well until the honeymoon is over and it is necessary to engage in the business of life with the other person. Then, she or he is less perfect, annoying, and even impossible to communicate with at times. If mutual judgment proceeds unchecked, the couple will get further apart—not an uncommon outcome. But with time, patience, and maturity, differences can be accepted and love deepens. It is no longer fantasy driven and is far more enduring and workable.

When we fall in love with a substance like cocaine or alcohol, there is also a sense of feeling complete and perfected. Addicts have repeatedly described an experience of infinite power and of being "un-stoppable." Once the glow is gone, however, there is no negotiation and, suddenly, significant constraints. The drug, in a true bait and switch, now demands enormous attention and time. As the addiction proceeds, it brings diminishing returns in terms of pleasure and costs increasingly more in money, relationships, health, and safety.

Of course we know there is no hope of discussing or bargaining with a drug, but there is more here than meets the eye. A disease process has begun that is progressive and takes over our ability to think clearly. Much as HIV infection attacks the immune system that is needed to defeat it, addiction compromises our brain and emotional capacities. As the addictive process evolves, there is a progressive atrophy of maturity and clarity.

Responsibility

Roger is an intelligent man. He was in serious debt and understood the futility of his actions. However, once he entered a relationship with a woman who was not committed to recovery, began driving to the casino, or took the first drink, he no longer had the capacity to make a reasoned judgment or a choice.

This is the flaw in Nancy Reagan's famous call to "just say no." As the disease advances, the part of the mind that might be able to abstain is less functional and there are so many conflicting agendas that a reasoned judgment is nearly impossible. The heart closes, and the addict is living with blinders or in a tunnel. The capacity for responsibility, the *ability to respond* intelligently and decisively toward well-being, has been seriously impaired.

The process is insidious, almost imperceptible at first. Getting high on opiates for manageable money becomes getting high for a lot of money, then just getting straight for even more. An obese person does not come to weigh four hundred pounds in a few weeks. It occurs over a long period and depends on much denial and rationalizing. The pursuit of pleasure or relief becomes an end in itself, and other consequences are pushed away until it is no longer possible to do so.

Even then help is often not sought. Addicts wind up broke, alone, in prison, mentally ill, physically sick, or dead. I often tell our patients in the Bournewood-Caulfield Partial Hospitalization Program (who come for the day while living at home, a sober house, or residence) that they are a select group. These people either choose to come to day treatment following hospitalization or come because their outpatient therapy has not adequately stabilized them. Clearly, there are patients who are coerced to come by the legal system, their spouse, their boss, or financial circumstances, but they still have to be willing to be there. There is no locked door. Many addicts would never come to treatment, preferring to withdraw, hide, escape as long as possible.

Why is that? Why not seek help as an alternative to prison, illness, or death? I will give five possibilities, with considerable overlap among them:

- The person has lost the mental or emotional capacity to think clearly about his or her circumstances.
- He or she has become insulated from health-promoting information from the body or relationships.
- It is too painful to face the physical discomfort, fear, shame, or grief.
- There is a history of unreliable health providers or caregivers in general.
- There is a deep sense of unworthiness to accept or receive help.

Addiction progresses toward an absence of emotional intelligence, receptivity, and self-compassion. It promulgates the delusion that we are alone in a unique engagement with emotional pain and alienation. It is a hole that has no bottom. As the addiction to a substance or behavior becomes the only game in town, self-judgment and guilt increase, with only one mode of relief, however transient. The addict moves through discouragement, despair, self-hatred, resignation— and the stories that emerge from these mind states only reinforce a sense of unworthiness of caring or help.

Many just die—in a hospital, a prison, alone, and via accident, violence, or suicide. Beyond the one hundred thousand alcohol-related deaths, there are half a million from nicotine each year in the United States. I have seen patients with chronic lung disease die on respirators, and it is not pretty. Did they know this would happen?

The answer is yes and no. I once encountered an ex-patient that I had cared for as a medical student outside the Hines VA Hospital in

Chicago. He was finally being discharged after recovering from extensive surgery. As I chatted with him and his wife, I was aware of smoke coming through the fist of his right hand. As it became clear that he was hiding his cigarette from me, he smiled sheepishly, and I wished him well. All he was doing was enjoying a cigarette and his freedom after several weeks in the hospital. But somehow he was ashamed, caught by the "doctor."

Who is the doctor really, in this case? I believe it is his mature energy that takes responsibility for his own self-care. That part wanted to experience a robust sense of well-being and knew that smoking was not moving him in that direction. Another part just wanted to feel relief, whatever the cost. These were clearly in conflict and underscore the problem of addiction. It is "normal" to want to relax and feel better. We do it all the time by reading the newspaper, having a cup of coffee, turning on the TV, calling a friend. How is smoking a cigarette different from these? When does "having a snack" turn into overeating or bingeing on food?

Why Do People Use Drugs?

If you are considering or coming to treatment for addiction, you are likely feeling some combination of exhaustion, confusion, powerlessness, despair, and shame. But what is good about using cocaine, for example? With some encouragement, people will say things like "The euphoria," "I like the energy," "I get focused," "Sex is so much better," "I am the man," "I really don't know, it's pretty stupid," "I think I am going to get high, but I just get paranoid." Highlighting the initial motivation for using a drug is the beginning of a conversation on the pluses and minuses and the presence of a conflict. This will be discussed in more detail in the section on the recovery process. There are many reasons why people use drugs, but all of them fall into three categories:

- To get a feeling
- To get rid of a feeling
- To escape

Let's look at these one at a time.

Get a Feeling

Generally we want the "positive" feelings noted in the cocaine example above—euphoria, energy, self-esteem, power. Some of these come directly from the use of the drug and can be particular to the individual or setting. Alcohol can facilitate a buoyant mood or a simple calming; opiates can bring deep relaxation or energy; cocaine provides intense stimulation or focus; marijuana can be experienced as a buzz or an enhancer of experience; hallucinogens can be speedy and a means to radically shift our perceptions.

Other feelings can come from the setting surrounding the drug. Heroin addicts come to methadone programs (and more recently buprenorphine providers) sick and depleted from years of hustling. Like professional athletes, many run out of gas in their mid- to late thirties, and the risks begin to outweigh the rewards. As medical director of a methadone program, I offered a deal —"We give you methadone, you come to treatment"—that was readily accepted. However, within three to six months, a significant number got depressed. This was partly because, for so many years, much of their energy, ingenuity, and creativity had gone into the street. It was a source of self-esteem and effectiveness, possibly providing an identity as hero, renegade, or desperado. Often the addict stayed in treatment to face the guilt, grief, and wreckage of her life. But there was a sense of loss at times manifesting in war stories glorifying the lifestyle or drug. People became attached to the adrenaline rush, the risk, the experience of efficacy, the needle, or any aspect of the experience.

Often teenagers begin to use drugs and alcohol in their peer group in order to feel part of something. It seems to me that there are two universal human needs: to feel good about ourselves and to belong. Some kids have never had either experience, and substance use, in one fell swoop, can appear to provide both. On the plus side, using together can create a bonding experience of fun, going outside the rules, and exploration or self-discovery. However, at some point the party is over, and if the person has not explored more mature modes of operating, he or she will either be alone or connect with another group of users.

In either case, the drug is likely to be the new vehicle for comfort, despite the fact that the original goal was to have friends. Sadly, addicts can also become quite attached to "negative" feelings of shame and alienation. Though these feelings may not appear to be much fun, they can become the new hiding place or refuge.

Get Rid of a Feeling

Attempting to get rid of a feeling is what we have come to call "self-medication," a term popularized by one of my early mentors, Edward Khantzian, a psychiatrist and researcher at the Cambridge Hospital. Dr. Khantzian's clinical experience demonstrated the association of certain drugs with particular intolerable mood states—opiates for rage, cocaine for depression, alcohol and benzodiazepines for anxiety. One important discovery was that a number of cocaine users were treating poor attention and were actually able to focus and calm down on cocaine. Nicotine has the ability to either stimulate the mind or reduce anxiety depending upon the smoker's level of arousal. Appetite can be suppressed with nicotine and stimulants, enhanced by cannabis.

We do not like being bored, disappointed, agitated, depressed, angry, or in pain and want to change our consciousness. This is normal, and substances have been used for this purpose for millennia. (It is notable that for some diseases, drugs are all that Western medicine has to offer.) Also available to us are food, sex, shopping, gambling, work, exercise, and many other modes that can alter an experience that feels intolerable.

Escape

Escaping has some similarity to getting rid of a feeling but is more global and possibly more unconscious. Did you ever not know what to do with yourself and either open the refrigerator or turn on the TV? Again, it is normal to take refuge in an ice-cream cone, a movie, a book, a bath, a nap, or a beer after a long day. There is a fine line between a moment of pleasure that makes life feel livable and a pattern of dissociating or checking out.

A good high, a good low, adrenalized or lethargic states transport us to another realm away from our fear, boredom, or self-doubt. In one astonishing example, a heroin addict was unable to tell me almost anything about the decade of his life between twenty and thirty. He had literally dissociated from his experience for ten years as he went about his business of acquiring and using the drug.

Escaping our feelings has pluses and minuses. I have noted a tendency in myself to leave just enough time to get to my destination. This gave me the opportunity to get one more thing done and to experience some adrenalin as I drove. The downside was that I felt stressed, was late at times, and got a couple of speeding tickets. If I leave plenty of time, I am more relaxed and do not miss my plane, but I lose the sense of efficiency and of being on a roll. I also might have to wait for someone or be aware of unpleasant feelings.

The heroin addict I mentioned above took a radical approach to changing consciousness with enormous cost. However, the costs of not using may have appeared greater. These two examples, using heroin to escape vs. scheduling my life too tightly, while quite different, I hope suggest a continuum between a bad habit and an addiction, which we will now explore.

Habit, Substance Abuse, and Dependence

Tom is a college student who smokes marijuana on Friday and Saturday nights with his friends. He enjoys the camaraderie and laughter; the enhancement of music, movies, and conversation; as well as the eating that seems to happen every time. Tom is a serious student who works hard and looks forward to his weekend ritual, which he will skip only at crunch time, late in the semester. He will also get high during the week, but sporadically and never jeopardizing his work or his ability to get up in the morning for a class. Invariably on Sunday, Tom is able to hunker down with his studies, reestablishing his rhythm and producing good-quality work.

Tom has a habit. He would likely agree and say he is enjoying it for now, with an idea that he would change this behavior at some point after college or graduate school. For now, he is having fun, not hurting himself or his future prospects. If asked if this was substance abuse, he might acknowledge that it is technically illegal but otherwise not a problem. His parents would likely disagree, but Tom could counter that his behavior is no different from their having a few drinks and getting tipsy.

The most recent diagnostic manual for psychiatry, the DSM-IV, would back him up. According to its criteria, the diagnosis of substance abuse requires recurrent use resulting in one or more of the following:

- Failure to fulfill major role obligations in work, school, or home
- Physical hazards (driving a car or operating a machine when impaired)
- Recurrent substance-related legal problems
- Persistent or recurrent social or interpersonal problems caused or exacerbated by the effects of the substance

Now, if Tom began not getting out of bed on Sundays, rationalizing that he only had enough energy to watch football games, not studying, and getting poorer grades, he would qualify for the diagnosis of substance abuse. His parents would now be more justified in reading him the riot act, stating that he could watch football at home and attend a community college for a lot less than $50,000 per year.

In either case, Tom is in a good position to change. His marijuana habit will likely shift with maturity, having a girlfriend who does not want to use, having a job where he will be drug tested, or merely moving on to a new place and group of friends. If it had gotten more serious, the wake-up call from his parents might have been sufficient for him to give it up. Once he stopped smoking pot, Tom would likely miss the drug and the good times, rationalize using again, and wonder if he were an addict. However, there is little evidence that he is at this point.

Louise is a young woman in her midtwenties who came to our day treatment program following a "devastating" break-up with her boyfriend. Though nearly forty, he was fairly immature, and Louise knew the relationship was likely not to work. But they smoked weed together and watched the Red Sox, which felt cozy. Louise had a history of daily use since the age of sixteen, largely to control her anxiety. Over the years, she needed to get high more often in order to relieve her symptoms. At the time of admission to the program, she was smoking three to five times per day, getting increasingly withdrawn and depressed and calling in sick to work.

Louise's parents divorced when she was five, and her childhood was hectic, with frequent moves, little opportunity to develop stable friendships, and limited contact with her father. Smoking weed had been a way to have a peer group and experience a sense of inner stability via numbing her chronic tendency to worry. There were times when Louise knew she should stop, but when she tried, the anxiety was disabling. Her relationship, however problematic, had a routine she found soothing. With the breakup, troubling thoughts threatened to frighten and overwhelm her, leading her to use more frequently, perpetuating a vicious cycle of increased anxiety, depression, and marijuana use.

Louise is clearly dependent upon cannabis for her functioning. The diagnosis of substance dependence according to DSM-IV criteria requires "a maladaptive pattern of substance use, leading to clinically significant impairment or distress, as manifested by three (or more) of the following in the same twelve-month period":

- Tolerance (a need for increased amounts of the substance to achieve intoxication or the desired effect)
- Withdrawal (a substance-specific syndrome due to cessation [or reduction] of substance use that has been heavy and prolonged)
- The substance is often taken in larger amounts or over a longer period than was intended.
- There is a persistent desire or unsuccessful efforts to cut down or control substance use.
- A great deal of time is spent in activities necessary to obtain the substance or recover from its effects.
- Important social, occupational, or recreational activities are given up or reduced because of substance use.
- The substance use is continued despite knowledge of having a persistent or recurrent physical or psychological problem that is likely to have been caused or exacerbated by the substance.

Louise meets the criteria, but what is most notable is her sense of desperation in the face of her anxiety and worry, and the need to escape it.

Substance Dependence and Addiction

It is clear that Tom is not dependent upon cannabis and Louise is. But is Louise also an "addict"? The term *addiction* was replaced with *dependence* by the DSM-III-R committee in 1987, the latter appearing to be more neutral. Dependence, however, is closely related (and limited) to the physical and behavioral manifestations of tolerance and withdrawal. *Addiction*, in my opinion, is a term capable of carrying psychological meaning as well.

Lance Dodes, in his book *The Heart of Addiction*, makes the distinction between "physical addiction" and "true addiction," which is emotionally driven. An example of the former is nicotine dependence. Although smokers can become strongly dependent upon nicotine, the revelation of serious health consequences secondary to smoking during the 1960s caused many to stop. Whether the ones who continued were "true addicts" or just physically dependent is not immediately apparent and would have to be understood case by case. Also, patients with postsurgical or chronic pain who are given opiates will become physically dependent if treated long enough. But most of these patients will never become psychologically addicted.

Dodes, who is a psychoanalyst, makes a persuasive argument that the addictive process, what he calls true addiction, is driven by helplessness and the rage against it. Addictive behavior is seen as a substitute action (or displacement) for the need to reverse or escape the experience of helplessness or powerlessness.[1] What the person experiences that directly leads to substance use—desperation (in Louise's case), loneliness, or grief—almost invariably has a sense of powerlessness at its core. We will see how treatment, including mindfulness practice, allows patients to hold these experiences without reacting and find other, more effective alternatives.

Once in treatment, Louise smoked pot less often and did initially feel more anxious. Her mindfulness training, however, helped her to feel more grounded, living more in the body, less in her thoughts. So she was able to experience anxiety as a physical experience independent of all of the stories associated with it. In other words, she could be anxious without "freaking out." This was a major step that allowed her not to immediately run with the first flicker of anxiety.

Then Louise was able to work more effectively with both her

physiological and psychological dependence on the drug. This raises the question of whether someone can be addicted without being physically dependent.

Frank owns a successful construction company. He is able both to be the boss and to be respected by as well as have a sense of closeness with the guys. He does, however, have more problems in one-to-one relationships where there is no clear hierarchy.

Frank comes home from work every evening and has three or four drinks. He never develops tolerance (needing more and more to get a buzz) or withdrawal (shakes or inner tension requiring a drink to stabilize). He does not appear intoxicated, but his wife, Marjorie, knows when he is over the line. She tries to speak to him around the time of his first drink, because after that he is largely inaccessible for the remainder of the evening.

Though he doesn't realize it, Frank's behavior is causing Marjorie to feel abandoned and alone. The driving force behind his drinking is the fear of intimacy, and his addiction (facilitated by alcohol) is the compulsion to escape that fear. Not everyone will agree with me, but I believe that Frank is an addict. If he does not face his vulnerability in relationship, his wife may leave him, though he left her first without knowing it.

Is Addiction a Disease?

The dictionary defines *addiction* as "a state of physiological or psychological dependence on a drug liable to have a damaging effect; to devote oneself habitually and compulsively." It derives from the Latin *addicere,* meaning "given over, awarded to another as a slave." This is clearly resonant with the experience of helplessness in the face of our desires, a theme that appears in the first step of Alcoholics Anonymous: "We admitted we were powerless over alcohol."

The addiction psychiatrist Richard Sandor, in his book *Thinking Simply about Addiction,* calls addiction a "disease of automaticity." Automatisms, he says, are developments in the nervous system that cannot be eliminated but can be rendered dormant. Sandor points out that *doing* something (using a drug) is often confused with *having* something (an addiction), that is, the behavior is confused with the disease. He goes on to say:

What begins as a choice to drink or use a drug may later become something else, something no one chooses—a psychological reaction that has a life of its own—an addiction. At that point, the addict's drinking or using behavior has become the manifestation of the disease, not the disease itself. He may look like he is making choices, but where it really counts, something else is in charge.[2]

The subject of choice is a complex one that is taken up in greater detail in chapters 2, 3, and 8. Some relapses clearly begin with a choice and others do not, as the addict operates more in the realm of reaction or reflex. Sandor's "disease of automaticity" and Dodes's "rage against helplessness" both speak to the issue of addiction as a disease, but they disagree about what sort of disease it is. How some of us have this mind-body tendency to develop an addiction and others do not is also a source of some mystery.

It may help to acknowledge that we are all flawed in some way, even those who seem to get more than their share of intelligence, talent, or beauty. Addiction is just one of the possible flaws, manifesting in a given human being via a combination of biological, psychological, social, behavioral, and possibly spiritual factors. A full discussion of this subject is beyond the scope of this book, but as suggested in the section above called "Why Do People Use Drugs?" some of us may have a particular vulnerability toward the compulsion to grasp on to feelings, get rid of feelings, or escape.

How much of that is hereditary? In clinical practice, it appears that addiction runs in families, but so does speaking Portuguese, rooting for the Chicago Cubs, or appreciating Beethoven. No gene has been discovered for alcoholism. However, studies of twins and adoptees, which have been able to separate the effects of genetics from those of environment, have overwhelmingly demonstrated that there are hereditary factors determining who becomes an alcoholic and who does not.

That being said, our clinical task with an individual is to make some sense of an overwhelming situation, and what we see in families is widely variable. In some families, "everyone" is an addict, but in many cases the manifestation of alcoholism and drug addiction is more sporadic. In other scenarios, family history of addiction is absent, and emotional, developmental, or sociocultural factors will predominate.

We are talking about human beings, and there is a lot we do not know. Our task is not so much to solve the puzzle of addiction as to open to the physical and emotional manifestations of whatever is causing a person pain and suffering. The truth is in the experience. Once it is seen, our path becomes clearer and we are able to move forward with greater vision and confidence.

A Brief Introduction to Mindfulness

However you are sitting, notice your feet touching the floor or wherever they are landing right now. Feel the backs of your legs and your thighs, buttocks, and back as well as your hands and arms making contact. Give your full attention to each one, one at a time. You might also be aware of contact points around your mouth (lips, teeth, tongue) or your eyes, if closed, or the touch of breath at your nose. Simply direct your attention to the touch points, slowly moving through them or coming to rest in one place. Stay with this for about a minute.

What did you observe? Often, people notice sounds, energy moving in the body, physical sensations, thoughts, or emotions. Were you thinking as much as usual? If not, what was that like?

The practice of regularly checking in with our touch points gives us an immediate gateway to the present moment and the experience of embodied awareness. You might like practicing this as you read and throughout the day.

2

Mindfulness

I HAVE DESCRIBED the addictive process as a means of changing reality via getting high, self-medicating, or dissociating from one's experience compulsively. It has the goal of alleviating suffering but invariably perpetuates a cycle of suffering. Why is this so difficult to change? It is obvious to anyone outside the situation that something is not working, but somehow the addict is stuck in an endless loop. Addiction, whether you think it is a disease or not, is an attachment to a way of operating in the world. It might appear that the drug is the problem, but more accurately it is the relationship to the drug as a means of escape that the addict clings to.

Addiction is an energetic presence that controls our lives by interpreting our experience in terms of fear and desire. It has its own internal logic that must be seen and understood if it is to be overcome. Think of a young single mother of three small children who uses cocaine every night after the kids are in bed. It is a reward for all of her hard work, a brief respite from stress and desperation, something to look forward to. Misguided? Clearly, but that little voice that convinces her to continue on this track makes some sense. Life has been difficult and will continue to be. And "the difficult" must be heard, not merely silenced. Then there is the urge itself, which is a palpable experience in the body, albeit often operating outside of awareness, automatically and mindlessly. If these phenomena can be seen directly, there is the possibility of taking another path.

How to see clearly? Mindfulness can be a counterforce to the addictive process by bringing awareness to it as it unfolds. Addiction is habitual and predictable; mindfulness is creative and spontaneous. Addiction thrives in dark places that mindfulness can illuminate. Like a camera lens, it is a means of opening the aperture very wide or focusing it down narrowly and with great clarity. Addiction creates suffering, and mindfulness has the potential to untie the knots of suffering. Addiction starts as a means of escape but becomes a prison with extremely rigid rules. Mindfulness brings an attitude of flexibility and openness, a vehicle toward freedom and possibility.

Mindfulness Defined

Mindfulness is a skill and an attitude. It could be seen as the capacity to be fully engaged with life just as it is. The *Big Book* of Alcoholics Anonymous addresses this in its comments on the subject of *acceptance* (about which I will have more to say soon).

> Acceptance is the answer to *all* my problems today. When I am disturbed, it is because I find some person, place, thing or situation—some fact of my life—unacceptable to me and I can find no serenity until I accept that person, place, thing or situation as being exactly the way it is supposed to be at this moment. Nothing, absolutely nothing happens in God's world by mistake. . . . Unless I accept life completely on life's terms, I cannot be happy. I need to concentrate not so much on what needs to be changed in the world as on what needs to be changed in me and my attitudes.[1]

Along the same lines, a mindful attitude contains the recognition of the fact that whatever we want, life keeps doing what it wants. This is fairly simple but clearly not easy to swallow. We tend to want things our own way and be upset when we lose, are criticized, or have feelings we don't like. Then we tell stories, feel victimized, and are miserable. As we have seen, with enough of this we will get despondent and either become depressed or develop some addictive pattern to escape the pain.

Mindfulness is an alternative to this sort of reactive functioning, a means of seeing more clearly and approaching our lives with more dignity and maturity. I think of mindfulness as having four elements: (1) awareness, (2) of the mind-body process, (3) in the present moment, (4) with acceptance.

Awareness is a broad-based capacity of our nervous system. We might see it as an ongoing background function monitoring our inner and outer experience without evaluation or judgment. It is a witness state, a nonattached, objective point of reference.[2] Awareness is happening all the time, even during sleep and in patients under general anesthesia or in a coma. I am currently typing but am aware it is a sunny day. I am also aware of feeling buoyed by this as well as a little sad that I am not outside. Meanwhile I pay attention, the best I can, to typing. Oops, now it is gray outside. I am now aware of feeling more comfortable being inside but not as upbeat. Every moment has pluses and minuses, and awareness silently records these without judgment.

Attention is related to awareness but has a somewhat different function. Awareness, as I am using it, combines the qualities of being conscious, alert, and watchful. Attention is defined as "concentration of the mental powers upon an object; a close or careful observing or listening." As I am washing the dishes, I am *aware* of warm water on my hands, but I am directing my *attention* to cleaning a pot thoroughly. I could notice the pleasure of the warmth and stay with it for a short while as my primary object of attention before returning to the task. Or I might be vaguely aware of being annoyed with this job: it wasn't my turn to do the dishes, or why is someone else not helping me with the dinner cleanup? My attention might be on this annoyance, on the story line around it, or on what I wish I were doing instead of washing the dishes.

I might be aware of these things or I might not. Often we are not. The small upset fades but then goes underground, becoming part of our story of how life is not fair or how overwhelmed and alone we feel. Add this to the countless slights and injustices in our families and in our lives and we can see how resentment and a sense of victimhood can build. Unchecked, this sort of process can lead to depression, even suicide. We can begin to glimpse the value of being aware of and directing attention to experiences like disappointment or annoyance as a means to greater effectiveness in our relationships and dealing with our emotional lives.

This raises the question of what we are actually aware of or attentive to. Our *mind-body* is our means of perceiving the world as well as our inner experience. In Buddhist psychology there are six ways information enters our mind-body, or six "sense doors." These are the five senses we all know—seeing, hearing, smelling, tasting, touching—as well as thinking.

The sense impression, a smell, for example, comes into awareness. We then have an immediate reaction: pleasant, unpleasant, or neutral. If it is pleasant, we are generally drawn to it or want more of it. This is why people bake cookies when they have an open house to sell their home. If unpleasant, we feel aversion and want to get away, as we might roll up our windows on the New Jersey turnpike. If neutral, we will ignore, space out, dissociate, or look for a more interesting object of attention. The key point is that we are bombarded by sensory stimuli and that this process is happening in every moment of our lives.

This is the third aspect of mindfulness, that it is happening *now*, in the present moment. In our day treatment program, the first group of the day has a check-in format lasting from sixty to seventy-five minutes. Every day a number of patients will come in upset or overwhelmed about something that happened yesterday or something that is about to happen later today or in the future. Many of them could tell a long story about their current concern as well as associations to the past; stuck patterns in relationship; and random, obsessive concerns. Since most of these patients are substance abusers in early recovery, their usual means of coping with intolerable experience, physical and emotional, has been taken away.

What we then see are the thought patterns or thinking addictions that they generally escape through drugs or alcohol. Since it is clear that we will not have time to hear a twenty-minute story from each person, the patients are accustomed to our stopping the narrative at some point and focusing on what is being experienced right now. Where in the body are you feeling this resentment (anxiety, depression, anger, sadness, or craving)? What is the quality of it? Does it change as you pay attention to it? Are there any other stories you are telling yourself about this?

Often with this line of inquiry, patients do not feel entirely better, but they begin to glimpse something. They begin to see the difference between living in the past or future versus living in the present.

Though they might not like letting go of the story or the justification for their misery, it is clear there is a choice.

I might say, "Take a walk and notice your body in motion, the contact with the ground, or the weather. When you start thinking, just notice that and return to the walking." Whether the person follows my suggestion or not, the painful experience will change. At some point, later that day or the next, he will feel better. He will also see the process of embodied awareness operating in others. Once someone realizes that he can take refuge in the present moment, it can become a new habit, replacing more maladaptive ones.

Acceptance is the fourth and most subtle aspect of mindfulness. Let's start with what it is not. Acceptance does not mean that you like it. Often we don't. If I plan a picnic and it rains, I am disappointed, what we might call "pain." If I am also angry, cursing my bad luck or timing, that is *suffering*—the experience of wishing it were different. Mindfulness would enable me to see the difference, directly feeling sadness, regret, or discouragement in the body. It would also reveal that *rain is happening,* period. It is not happening *to me.* I might also see that while I could not control the weather, I am now freer to consider other ways to have fun with people I care about. Acceptance is an attitude with the motto "Pain is inevitable, misery optional."

The treatment of addiction is, in a sense, a continuous meditation on the subject of acceptance. People seek help because their strategy of nonacceptance is not working. Moreover, they can finally see that it is the very holding on to this strategy that is now creating much more suffering than it is relieving. This awareness does not eliminate nonacceptance, but it allows a clearer evaluation of how avoiding experience through the use of substances works and does not work. Then, if the addict cannot accept sobriety at this point, that is just where she is— and that is what needs to be accepted.

For example, I might ask a new patient, "On a scale of zero to ten—zero being 'I am going to use as soon as I leave here today' and ten being 'I am totally committed to recovery and plan never to drink again'—where are you?" Whether he says nine or five is totally okay with me if I believe I am getting the truth. That's our starting point for bringing awareness and acceptance to how things are right now.

Acceptance also does not mean condoning behavior that is hurtful to yourself or others, being a doormat, or suffering in silence. In this context, what acceptance connotes is the simple noticing of the flow of moment-to-moment experience with openness, embracing present reality just as it is. An idea like this just rolls off the tongue, but it is a lifelong discipline. We are besieged by thoughts, agendas, feelings, bodily sensations in a relentless stream. Here is an idea to consider and check out: We cannot control our thoughts and feelings. We certainly cannot control what other people do and think (though we try). We can control two things—where we direct our attention and our own actions.

Largely what we are exploring here is how to relate to all of our experiences in a way that is graceful and life affirming. As this openness of heart and mind is gradually cultivated, we are able to see with greater clarity that everything changes, even ourselves and the sources of our suffering. We are able to solve problems to the extent that we understand them. The ongoing development of mindful acceptance creates a positive movement of seeing how we suffer and being free to choose to let go. If we are not ready, so be it. Just accept that.

Mindfulness Origins and Universality

My own introduction to mindfulness came through learning about Buddhist psychology in meditation centers. The Buddha was a historical figure, named Siddhartha Gautama, who lived more than twenty-five hundred years ago in northern India (near current-day Nepal). He was born a prince, and his father, the ruler of a small kingdom, wanted him to be a king and a warrior. As the legend goes, Siddhartha was surrounded from birth by opulence and sensual pleasure—flowers that were always replaced before they wilted and the finest food, clothing, and entertainments. As a young man, he likely had a harem. His father carefully controlled what Siddhartha experienced so as not to expose him to any pain or trouble.

As the story is told, the prince was eventually able to convince his driver to take him on a series of forays outside the palace without his father's knowledge. It was on these trips that Siddhartha saw in succession an old person, a sick person, a corpse, and a monk. These experiences demonstrated to him not only that illness and death were the fate of all beings, even himself, but that there was the possibility of looking more deeply into the matter of human suffering.

Siddhartha stole away, leaving his father, wife, and newborn son. Why he would make such a choice is something we all need to feel into for ourselves. He was twenty-nine years old and could have continued to access pleasurable experiences. But now he knew it would end, and besides, these pleasures had not brought him lasting happiness or fulfillment.

Siddhartha studied with two different teachers and developed great powers of concentration. But he was unsatisfied and left these teachers not having attained his goal of understanding suffering. He went to the opposite extreme of his previously pleasurable existence, performing severe ascetic practices. He did not care for his physical well-being or hygiene and suffered starvation, extreme pain, and heat and cold. Despite these travails and near death, he still felt no closer to understanding the nature of suffering.

Siddhartha realized that he would need strength to sit still enough to see into the nature of reality, so in a beautiful moment of connection, he accepted a bowl of rice porridge from a young girl. He resolved to sit under a tree and not get up until he understood why he and all human beings suffer.

As he sat, Siddhartha was assailed by many deeply troubling and frightening images as well as ones that were quite pleasant and seductive. He saw these to be transitory productions of his own mind, insubstantial and impermanent. If he believed the thoughts or visions, he would suffer; if not, he was free. When Siddhartha finally opened his eyes, he was the Buddha, the awakened one. He then proceeded to teach what he had learned to his followers over the next forty-five years. Since the Buddha's time, many have followed his teachings, but no particular beliefs are required. "Don't take my word for it, see for yourself," he effectively said.

The practices that we will learn here are quite simple and compatible with any belief system. In fact, mindfulness can be found in many Western, Eastern, and native religions and practices. In Judaism, for example, there are many blessings that are said around daily, weekly, and monthly cycles as well as on holidays. There are blessings before eating, washing the hands, lighting candles; upon awakening and going to sleep; for mourning; and many others. All of these are moments of mindfulness.

This well-known prayer was written by the Christian philosopher Reinhold Niebuhr:

> God, grant me the serenity to accept the things I cannot change, the courage to change the things I can, and the wisdom to know the difference.
>
> Living one day at a time, enjoying one moment at a time, accepting hardships as a pathway to peace. Taking, as Jesus did, this sinful world as it is, not as I would have it. Trusting that you will make all things right if I surrender to your will, so that I may be reasonably happy in this life and supremely happy with you in the next.[3]

The Serenity Prayer, which is equally adaptable to purely secular settings, is essentially mindfulness—knowing the difference between what I can and cannot change, whether to act or not act, speak or be silent. Can I stand firmly in the middle of my experience, see it clearly, and make a choice?

Mystics and poets from countless traditions have employed mindful awareness to bring attention to the preciousness of being still in the present moment. Here is one short, beautiful example:

> Ten thousand flowers in spring, the moon in autumn
> A cool breeze in summer, snow in winter.
> If your mind isn't clouded by unnecessary things,
> This is the best season of your life.[4]
> —WU-MEN

Embodied awareness is a critical accompaniment to peak performance in athletics, theater, music, dance, public speaking, and virtually any field of human endeavor. Mindfulness can be developed by and manifest in housewives, parents, auto mechanics, teachers, coaches, shopkeepers, farmers, anyone without any formal training in meditation—anyone who has learned the art of being still and listening without judgment. Those people are likely not reading this book. For me and the rest of us who need a bit more help, let's look at how mindfulness operates.

Mindfulness and Stress

Jon Kabat-Zinn founded the Stress Reduction and Relaxation Program (currently called the Center for Mindfulness) at the University of Massachusetts Medical Center in 1979. Jon is now well known and a seminal figure in the integration of mindfulness practice into health care, peak performance, and daily life. However, back then he was just a very smart guy with a PhD in molecular biology, a longtime Zen student, and yoga teacher who did not know exactly what to do with his career. He was teaching at the medical school and hit upon the idea of teaching meditation, yoga, and daily mindfulness to patients who had not gotten better with traditional Western medicine.

This included patients with chronic pain or cardiac, respiratory, gastrointestinal, endocrine, neurological, orthopedic, or other stress-related disorders. Eventually the clinic was referred patients with HIV infection, dermatologic issues, and psychiatric problems that had not responded to standard psychotherapy and medicine, as well as many others. You can imagine that doctors at their wits' end were glad to have a place to send their patients, who, with no other good options, were willing to go.

More than thirty years down the road, thousands of patients have benefited from mindfulness-based stress reduction (MBSR) training, and many have continued to practice long after the end of their classes. Thousands more have been trained as MBSR teachers, and hundreds of programs are now operating worldwide. At the Stress Reduction Program of the medical center, people got better not from the elimination of their symptoms but by changing their relationship to them.

Consider chronic back pain that is secondary to an injury, resulting in a disability. There is the pain itself, the fear that it will always be there, the anxiety about money, the stories coming out of not knowing what is going to happen, the anger, the self-blame, the depression, the victim mentality, more stories, more pain, and so on. The patient/sufferer is totally trapped in his or her head, in negativity, alone, not able to be open to the help or emotional support offered.

MBSR training begins to untangle all of this by focusing on moment-to-moment experience, presented in some simple exercises and homework assignments. Patients are asked to practice meditation or yoga exercises for forty-five to sixty minutes per day, and the home-work emphasizes mindfulness in daily life. These experiences gradu-ally help the patient to begin to deconstruct the experience of pain, which is now a series of sensations, many admittedly unpleasant but changing over time.

Thoughts and emotions are similarly seen as transient phenom-ena. The stories are now stories, not the truth. This type of seeing creates space around the pain, which is still there but is often dimin-ished because there is not nearly so much tension in the body. There is also less fear, negativity, worry, sense of being overwhelmed—and when these states do appear, they can be seen and worked with in a new way. Less tension allows families to relax, relationships to im-prove, and a greater acceptance of life as it unfolds.

Stress has been defined as "any stimulus, as fear or pain, that dis-turbs or interferes with normal physiological equilibrium of an organ-ism; physical, mental, or emotional strain or tension." Stress happens by virtue of having a mind-body that needs to be clothed and fed, that gets old and sick, that has attachments of the heart. In other words, if you have a mind-body, it is part of the deal. Our problems come not so much from stress itself as from stress reactivity. In the back-pain ex-ample, the pain is unpleasant, but much of the misery comes from all of the inner noise. There will be more on the subject of stress in chap-ter 11.

Addiction is both the antidote to stress and the cause—a complex insanity that precludes clear seeing and understanding. Mindfulness is able to observe and distinguish both the benefits of substance abuse in dealing with everyday stressors and the downside. When people are clean, stress does not end. However, similar to the patient with chronic pain who is able to see into his or her tension, storytelling, and victim mentality, the addict has a new set of tools. Anger is just anger, sadness just sadness, fear, cravings, discouragement, stress—all insubstantial passing phenomena that become more workable with moment-to-moment attention.

Steps to Mindfulness

In the midnineties, I spent two years with the UMass Prison Project, a federally funded initiative of the Stress Reduction Program, where we applied MBSR principles to working with inmates that had gotten into trouble with their impulses—mainly violence, stealing, and substance abuse. Ricky had been in prison before, where he had had a chance to reflect on his life, and he was determined not to repeat the same mistake. However, once released, he was out one night at a bar and felt "disrespected" by something that was said. Afterward, Ricky did not remember everything, but he had beaten the guy so badly that he wound up back in prison for another eight years. Clearly, there was something he needed to learn if he did not want to spend his life there. The four steps to mindfulness we taught the inmates apply to all of us who are frequently caught by our impulses and reactions.[5]

1. Stopping

My father once told me that time is more valuable than money because you cannot save it. Indeed, the clock is ticking and our experience is continually unfolding. Monday turns into Friday and then Monday again. Time may seem to move quickly or slowly, and we may like it or not, but we cannot control it.

When life is unpleasant, we feel stressed, irritated, or bored and want to react or escape. Often we are successful if we, for example, turn on the TV, eat, or smoke a cigarette. However, there are two problems with this strategy: (1) the benefit is short-term and we will need to escape again soon, and (2) we become attached to the tendency to run from experience instead of facing it. *Stopping* means that we direct our attention into the here and now. This is not our natural inclination, but we might consider trying it when what we have been doing is not working.

Gina was an alcoholic who came into day treatment extremely depressed. A manager at a biotech company, she had been laid off, had relapsed, and had to move back home with her parents. Gina's frustration and sense of failure were to a large extent directed toward her father, whom she did not respect. She saw him as "weak," as he had bullied her as a child but was never aggressive with her brothers or anyone who might one day be tougher than he was. Although he was now trying to be nice to her, she remained unforgiving.

During her first week in treatment, she began to work with breath awareness as a means of grounding herself and soon found herself to be generally less tense and angry. One warm afternoon, Gina was walking home from the program and began to imagine that her father would, yet again, not have opened the windows in the house as she repeatedly had asked him to. She noticed that she was getting increasingly upset and decided to stop and take four deep breaths. Although her anger did not go away immediately, she was no longer pouring gasoline on the fire.

2. Seeing

Stopping and looking allow us to actually see what is there, which is impossible if we stay in our heads or on automatic pilot. In the example above, Gina glimpsed something that caused her to stop. Since she had spent significant time during the past week not being so angry, when anger came up so strongly, it got her attention. As Yogi Berra said, "You can learn a lot just by watching." Gina saw that she was telling a story that was upsetting her and that it was fueled by her grudge against her father. She could feel herself revving up and looking forward to blasting him as soon as she got home.

Gina could see that she was creating her current reality from her past experience. To her credit, she was able to put aside the question of whether her prediction would be correct or not, and this allowed her to stop justifying her vendetta. As the cloud of judgment-fueled anger gradually passed, the tension in her neck and shoulders also diminished.

3. Self-understanding

As Gina continued to observe her body sensations, emotions, and thoughts, she calmed down even further and began to see something new: that she was playing out her childhood trauma with her father and that she was determined to win this time. His lack of cooperation with her, which she interpreted as disrespect, activated her vulnerability in the form of fear and then rage. As she followed the story, she could feel a sense of power in blowing up, followed by guilt or sadness—common triggers to alcohol relapse. Gina began to understand how her being tyrannical had both benefits and liabilities but had caused everyone a great deal of pain, particularly her.

Stopping and seeing create a natural interest to look further, though we might not be pleased by what we learn. Self-understanding or insight is often bad news about *me* but good news about my capacity to take responsibility for my life. Gina's ability to see the sadness under her anger freed her from continually acting out the old drama, which was more fantasy than truth.

4. *Choosing*

Making a choice is the crowning achievement of this process of mindfulness, which is much more than simple awareness. Rather, it is a means to skillful action and can be understood through knowing the difference between *reacting* and *responding*. Reacting is automatic, much like a reflex. Responding suggests the consideration of alternatives and making the best decision possible under the circumstances. There is an element of "look before you leap," but responding need not involve thinking and may happen very quickly.

Consider the difference between being spontaneous and being impulsive. Spontaneity (this word has the same root as *respond*) implies a freedom of action born of the rapid integration of data from cognitive, sensory, and/or motor sources, an ability to improvise. Impulsivity, on the other hand, is automatic or reactive, generally not leading to productive or creative outcomes.

Gina's experience, which I have described, unfolded over a ten- to fifteen-minute walk home, and it helped to ground her between two alternatives—mindlessly playing out the childhood scenario versus staying open to the truth. Her exploration allowed her to see the benefits both of fueling her grudge and raging and of centering herself. In choosing the latter, she felt quite sad but also calmer and able to see the situation more clearly, including:

- It is her parents' house, not hers.
- Her father was spacey, not trying to disrespect her.
- He had mellowed and was trying in his own way to make amends to her.
- In being tyrannical, she was retaliating, "giving him a taste of his own medicine."
- She was the one being poisoned.

When Gina arrived at home, the windows were not open. She calmly noted how warm it was in the house, and her father apologized, saying he would try to remember next time. When Gina was asked what would usually happen, she said, "I would yell at him and he would just get away from me."

One of the prison inmates, who had been openly contemptuous of the meditation practices, told this story: "They were shaking down my cell. There was no reason for it; I hadn't done anything. I could have killed those guys, but I have gotten into trouble with my temper before, so I just sat outside on my mattress. Then I lay down and started to do a body scan. I was still really angry, but it distracted me, and I think I knew I was doing a good thing. It took a while, but I did calm down. They were just about done, and I wasn't even mad anymore. That was a new one for me."

Mindfulness and Respect

Working in prison taught me many lessons, possibly the most important being the link between *stress* and *disrespect*. At times they appeared to be synonymous. I was hanging around one day after class, waiting to speak to the program coordinator, when an inmate and a correctional officer came into the room. The inmate was Ricky, who had been reincarcerated for assault and battery and for whom disrespect was an issue. He was doing his job, sweeping up and talking with the CO, who casually used the phrase "a maggot like you."

I should not have been stunned by this, but I was. This kind of thing was clearly going on all the time. Ricky, who was in my class at the time, just smiled and then gave me a look that said, "This guy is an idiot, but don't worry, I'm not going to do anything stupid." Indeed, he said nothing, went about his business, and maintained his dignity.

As stress is associated with disrespect ("to regard or treat with contempt or rudeness"), mindfulness can become a platform for respect ("to show regard or consideration for"). Assertiveness training, or mindful communication, is a means toward skillful speech and action. Initially this can be disorienting to a family member or partner used to disrespect, but in the day treatment setting, patients are encouraged to try and they are often surprised by the results.

One man, Rafael, detailed a pattern of nasty exchanges with his girlfriend, until one day when she said "You're such an asshole" in the heat of the moment. "You may not agree with me," he countered, "but you can no longer speak to me like that." This was the fruit of Rafael's mindfulness training: the ability to ground himself, to feel how painful these conversations were, and to have the clarity that he was no longer willing to live this way. His girlfriend's response was positive, but he could not have controlled that. What he could control was where he directed his attention and whether his speech conveyed respect for himself and for their relationship.

Mindfulness and Truth

As I have said, mindfulness is a skill and an attitude, a vehicle for seeing clearly, but not the end result. The goals of practice are wise choices that prioritize truth over deception. Lying, "the intent to deceive or create a false impression," is deeply ingrained in all aspects of the addictive process. It affects relationships with dealers, using buddies, family, partners, bosses, coworkers. What is most damaging in this pattern of intrigue is the lying to oneself.

In my experience, the best liars are the ones that do not even know they are lying. This sort of ignorance is effective for a while but is eventually disastrous. Often people come into treatment because they can no longer believe or trust what they think, which can be so confusing and scary that seeking help may be the only alternative, short of suicide.

Once one is sober and more clearheaded, mindfulness training helps create a larger perspective. Lying is still a possibility but no longer a reflex. If your mother-in-law asks if she looks fat in her new dress, lying may be the best alternative. Poker is a game about deception. In most cases, however, the truth works best. The addict discovers that lying creates enormous mistrust, tension, loss of contact with loved ones, and the need to devise ongoing strategies to cover one's tracks.

In early recovery, being more straight up with people brings some relief to the addict, but she often finds herself still "on probation," literally having to prove herself. This sort of oversight and limits on movement—for example, having to be home at a certain time—is often resented, particularly by young adults who are "not children." However, once the patient (often with some help) glimpses her own responsibility for the condition of probation, there is some relaxation and even interest in what is going to happen next.

One young woman, Julia, was living with her parents, who did not allow her to take the car because of her past history of driving drunk and lying to them about it. They were frustrated with her but mostly afraid to give her too much freedom. Julia complained bitterly about her parents' treating her like a child. "I'm sober and going to treatment, can't they trust me?" Apparently not. At home Julia was angry and sullen, accusing her parents of punishing her, which in part they were. She judged them as being "tight assed" and "rigid." Not only was this not working for her, but she was feeling even more helpless, angry, and distant from the people who most cared about her.

However, because she was regularly grounding herself and not escaping with alcohol or drugs, Julia was able to see her victim thinking operating. Then, when we looked more closely at her judgments, we saw that it was *she* who was rigid, in her insistence on getting what she wanted even at the cost of lying. Julia could see that her parents had no defense against her lying except to become more restrictive. They, too, felt helpless. I am not shy about informing these often quite bright young people that they have no idea how hard it is to be a good parent.

With this understanding, Julia was able to approach her parents with more humility. She acknowledged the pain she had caused them by lying. It was *she* who did not trust *them*. This changed everything. Just two weeks into her treatment, Julia was allowed the car at night and was driving her younger siblings around as well. She saw for herself that once she let go of the judgment and anger she was directing toward her parents, they could feel her maturity and a greater degree of trust.

What Julia had done was to become more honest with herself, in part by seeing her inner stories and returning to the truth of the present moment, where she was feeling scared, sad, and alone. As she slowed down and stopped blaming, she was also able to see the lawfulness of her behavior and its consequences. She was then encouraged to be even more open and transparent with her parents, which allowed her to access their wisdom as well as increase the experience of mutual respect. This is similar to what Gina was able to accomplish when she saw a bigger picture, spoke respectfully to her father, and softened the hard feelings between them. The truth does hurt for a while, but it is also the medicine that heals.

Mindfulness and Authority

Gina's experience is instructive here as well. The immediate "addiction" she was dealing with was the compulsion to blow up at her father as a protection against the childhood vulnerability underneath. In this scenario, she often drank as a means of handling the combination of rage, guilt, and desperation that would inevitably follow. When Gina responded to her feelings instead of reacting, she took charge of the situation in a new way. In effect, she was the author ("creator or originator") of a new reality. Her behavior was also authentic ("worthy of trust, reliance, or belief," from the Greek *authentikos*, meaning genuine or authoritative).

Authority is defined as "the power to judge, act, or command." For our purposes, this is an internal matter, but it may be useful to look at a concrete example of authority, a ship's captain. The commanding officer has a goal (a destination, winning a battle, transport, exploration, commerce) and personnel to do the job. There are senior officers who plot a course, steer, and consult about strategy and the ship's maintenance. There are also sailors who clean up, maintain the engines or sails, cook, and so forth, and midlevel officers who manage them and report to superiors.

In modern times, the captain is also getting radio and electronic communication from his superiors and consultants. The captain's quite daunting task is to observe all of this, listen with awareness of people's motivations and to what is not being said, decide where to direct his energy at any given time, and above all, simultaneously hold the goal of his mission and the welfare of all under his command.

The practice of mindfulness, both formally (for example, sitting or walking meditation) and informally (awareness of moment-to-moment experience), facilitates our capacity to make more informed choices toward our own life goals. This happens via the four-step process of (1) *stopping*, developing the inner stability to stay still in the face of multiple and shifting contexts, agendas, opinions, desires and needs; (2) *seeing*, clearly observing those parameters; (3) *building self-understanding*, evaluating the existing conditions based on those observations, past experience, and current capacities; and (4) *choosing,* applying the best wisdom, both intellectual and instinctual, that we have at the moment to the situation at hand.

Sound difficult? Clearly so, but it is also exactly what Gina did when she took four breaths. It is what Julia was able to accomplish by being more present with her body and feelings and less involved with her stories and justifications. It is what we see with countless patients in early recovery, who have been triggered by life circumstances to drink or use and are now making a choice instead of just reacting in the old ways.

Then there are actually two more steps: (5) *accepting the results* (whether they gratified an addictive urge or not) and (6) *bringing that understanding into the next moment.* This is a path to what I would call adulthood. It is quite challenging, because it entails taking charge of all that comes our way, including our mistakes and misfortunes that are not our fault. Among the baby boomers, adulthood was derided and delayed, but at this point in my own life, it clearly seems better than the alternative.

I have had many lessons on the subject of authority. For example, I had the theory that if you loved your kids enough, they would cooperate. That one did not quite pan out. So if it is not about being nice and not about being intimidating, what are the conditions that lead to cooperation and respect? The answer, I believe, is cooperation and respect. Authority that listens from a grounded place and is honest and respectful is effective.

Adulthood could be seen as the opposite of victimhood. A great athlete does not get derailed by an error, a bad bounce, or a bad call by an official. Instead, he or she refocuses on the next play and *never* trashes a teammate. The question for drug addicts and all of us is, can we accept our situation just as it is right now without whining or wishing it to be other? I know of no better means to this than living in our bodies one moment at a time. As we stay grounded in the midst of our feelings, impulses, desires, agendas, prohibitions, and rules and the shifting nature of our circumstances, we are in the best position to evaluate our situation. Then we can choose to speak or act or not.

This sort of authority not only allows each of us to live more skillfully but also naturally inducts those around us—whether they be partners, kids, friends, family, coworkers, bosses, fellow motorists, dogs, anyone—into a different energetic state. This could take the form of teaching one's kids to be less reactive; neutralizing disrespect, as in the case of Raphael with his girlfriend; or merely defusing a difficult situation at work or on the road with a simple act of courtesy or good manners. We know these things intuitively and from experience. As we practice mindfulness, we begin to increasingly create and manifest dignity, respect, and compassion in our lives. Seeing is believing.

Mindfulness of Sensation

Addiction plays havoc with the senses while attempting to control experience—which ironically leaves the addict increasingly powerless. Our goal here will be to be aware of sense perceptions, one at a time, without the usual labeling or commentary. This builds our capacity to be more fully present and alive. After you read the instructions, the meditation will take five to ten minutes.

Start by sitting in a chair with a posture that is relaxed, upright, comfortable, and dignified. Take three slow breaths into your belly. Notice the touch points where your body meets the floor, the chair, or itself. Allow yourself to feel the effects of gravity, touch, and pressure. Take a minute to notice the quality of the sensations as well as how they shift and change.

Next, bring your attention to the experience of the air around you—warm, cool, just right, still, or moving. Do your hands, face, and exposed skin feel different from the rest of your body? Are some areas more sensitive to temperature than others? Is there a preference for warm or cool? Just notice without judgment.

Now open your awareness to the world of sound. You can hear sounds emanating from your body, from inside the room, and from outside. Notice the sound of your breath, the heating system, machine noises, vehicles, birds. There will likely be a tendency to identify each one and enjoy some sounds while disliking others. You might notice some appreciation for a working furnace or annoyance at your neighbor who allows his dog to bark incessantly. As best you can, let these thoughts pass by and return to simplicity of hearing. How does it feel to accept what you cannot change?

Finally, look around. Notice the objects in the room. Again, see them as if for the first time, letting go of their story lines. Look out the window if there is one. Notice the light, colors, shapes, any movement or change.

How is it to simply be present with each sensation moment to moment?

3

Mindfulness and the
Treatment of Addiction

SOON AFTER FINISHING my psychiatry residency in 1985, I took a job as medical director of the methadone program at the Cambridge Hospital with almost no experience in treating addictive disorders. That same year, Cambridge Insight Meditation Center opened as an urban alternative for people to learn about meditation and sustain their practices without having to go away to a residential retreat center. I was in long-term psychotherapy at the time and realized that I wanted something to continue my own inner work once the therapy ended. What about meditation? One evening, without any instruction, I closed my eyes and began to follow my breath and about twenty minutes later jerked awake, disoriented. I knew nothing of the relationship among the arenas of psychotherapy, meditation, and addiction, but this was the beginning of my exploration.

I first glimpsed the connection between addiction and mindfulness very early on in my time at the methadone program. The program required that patients receive their daily dose, attend individual and group therapy, and not use outside drugs, which was monitored by periodic urine toxicology screens. If a urine sample was dirty, a consultation was required, which was why I was meeting with Dave, who had used heroin. I asked him what had happened, and he said, "I was on the phone and then I was nodding."

"That's it?" I asked. Indeed it was. I did not plan what was about to come out of my mouth, never having said anything like it. I told him that what I felt he needed to do was to see the whole process: the wish, urge, or thought to use heroin; the decision to make the call; the conversation; any mixed feelings about what he was doing; putting on his coat; walking to the car; driving to his destination; buying the drugs; coming home; preparing the heroin; injecting it. If he did this, he would see the entire progression, the costs and benefits of heroin use.

Clearly there was something good about shooting heroin, or he would not have done it for so many years. But he was also on a methadone program, which suggested that he had bumped into the downside of living as a street addict. By continuing to use heroin, he was risking discharge from the clinic, but he was still drawn to it. This is the dilemma of the addict in early recovery, his *conflict,* which we will discuss at more length in chapter 7.

As I have suggested, addiction is a problem that limits our openness to important information and feelings because we are confused, conflicted, or dissociated. It alters consciousness, gives us a false sense of security, makes us think we know things we do not know, impairs the ability to judge and evaluate situations, blots out memory, and stunts the maturity necessary for effective and creative functioning. In short, an addiction is a colossal blind spot.

Mindfulness is useful for blind spots, because it is open to exactly what is there. A Nobel laureate in biology was asked about his method. "I just look into my microscope," he replied, "and if I look long enough, I will see something." This is the attitude mindfulness practitioners are trying to cultivate. But where do we look?

Experience and Stories

Let us start with the body. It is always with us and is able to give us an enormous amount of information if we are open. How should I dress for the weather? Do I really want to eat that? Would I like to see people or be on my own tonight? Am I able (or wanting) to do this favor that is being asked of me? Should I go out with this guy? Is this job a good fit for me? Do I buy her yet another pair of jeans? I am a little sluggish after lunch: should I take a nap, take a walk, or turn on the ball game? Et cetera, et cetera. There are endless possibilities, situations, and choices we need to face, and our bodies can answer many of our questions, or at least be a guide.

One critical aspect of mindfulness is *embodied awareness*. The tasks of this book are to suggest that embodied awareness is a useful skill to cultivate, to convey practices that help develop this skill, and to look at the obstacles in the way. A major obstacle to the development of mindfulness is that whatever our experience, we have a story about it. Here are a few examples:

- Jerry's lawn is nicer than mine.
- I am getting old; I can't play basketball anymore.
- There is not enough time.
- What's wrong with him?
- What's wrong with me?
- Our program is better than theirs.
- I'm done with her.
- How could anyone do that job?
- Why did I marry him?
- I am not a very good parent.
- Thank God I was born in this country.
- I am pretty hopeless at tennis; why don't I just give up?
- My parents didn't give me the attention I needed.
- Boy, I did a great job there.
- If I had not been such an idiot, this wouldn't have happened.

There is no end to this, and the more we think, the more we think. In a sense our ultimate addiction is "How am I doing?" and it plays out in nonstop comparison, judgment, and analysis. Three of the examples above (appreciating our good performance or our good fortune) help us to feel better, but most do not. We are generally not aware that this is going on, but all of this thinking creates a sort of background noise, a subtle (or not so subtle) agitation. A closer look at any of the thoughts listed above would reveal a feeling or set of feelings underneath. One very dear to my heart is, "There is not enough time."

Can you feel the anxiety in that? Any of our story lines can be a screen for the fear, disappointment, confusion, disgust, anger, helplessness, shame, or grief we are trying to keep out of awareness.

It does work, but like any addiction, our storytelling has pluses and minuses. The big minus is that it often creates unhappiness. I know this right now because I just reread the list of thoughts above and I feel sad, though not all of them are my own. Even the ones in which we wind up on top do not really work, because they imply both a need to maintain our status and our fear that we are going to lose it. "Mirror, mirror on the wall, who's the fairest of them all?"

Mindfulness invites us to look beyond all of the smoke and mirrors at what is actually happening. Stories associated with anger, for example, have themes of outrage and the wish for retribution, but the body feels warm, tense, constricted, highly alert, eventually exhausted. These are all palpable experiences that can be located and followed. Part of our task here is to explore the benefits and downsides of both modes of operation—relating through our stories or through our moment-to-moment awareness. Working with our thinking and various mind states will be discussed at more length in chapter 16.

Psychotherapy and Mindfulness

I, like many therapists from the Northeast, was trained by psychoanalysts. Psychodynamic theory, as developed by Sigmund Freud at the turn of the twentieth century, is a rich window into human suffering and functioning. Freud was interested in how we manage in the face of our animal nature, the challenges of living and getting along in families and society, and the continually shifting demands of our lives. Psychoanalytically oriented psychotherapy tends to focus on past and developmental experiences and how they play out in the patient's current life as well as in the relationship with the therapist.

Many people have benefited from learning about themselves in this way, having the opportunity to explore many life scenarios in the context of a supportive relationship with a skilled professional. True emotional learning does occur in psychodynamic psychotherapy, as well as receiving support in living well, but what often passes for insight are connections made among the many stories that have been told. The downside of this aspect of the work is that it can foster dependencies both on getting yet another explanation for our problems and on the person of the therapist.

The insights that come from embodied awareness are not explanations but direct experience and can be a critical accompaniment to what is learned in psychotherapy. Let us return once more to Roger, the alcoholic gambler from chapter 1. Through all of his years of treatment, Roger had seen a relationship among issues surrounding the neglect of his childhood, his low self-esteem, his fear of close relationships, and his addictive behaviors. Unfortunately, this knowledge at times only served to remind him that despite all he had learned, he still repeatedly relapsed. This fueled his discouragement, leading him to drink, gamble, or pursue yet another fruitless sexual encounter to escape the pain of feeling like a failure.

The goal of mindfulness training was to help Roger experience his feelings without having to explain them. He started by noticing simple objects such as his feet on the ground and his breath to develop some stability of attention. Roger was able to feel his anxiety and irritation, and once he was a bit steadier, he saw the sadness underneath. As he became more familiar with the experiences of anxiety or sadness in his body, free of stories or commentary, he was less fearful of them. Also, he saw that the feelings did not last.

This observation brought two important and related benefits: (1) the ability to be with heretofore unacceptable feelings and (2) the sense of self-efficacy and self-esteem he got from having the courage to face them. Roger was then free as never before to pursue a true recovery, with close connections, initially to two women he met in the program and eventually to an entire community.

He came by the program months after being discharged, looking much lighter and happier. He still has issues around finances, intimacy, shame, and grief and is not ready for a committed relationship. Fear comes, disappointment comes, as do helplessness and desperation. The difference is that he is not running anymore. He is free to pursue addictive modes but is not choosing to, largely because he has the skills and self-regard to follow another course that appears to lead to greater personal satisfaction. He is not being "good," just wise. And mindfulness practice was an important doorway to his new understanding.

Addiction, Conflict, and Choice

In breaking down any addictive habit, there tend to be two sides and four factors. Take drinking, for example. Once one is open to looking at the problem, there is a part that wants to drink and a part that wants to stop. On one side are the positive aspects of drinking and the negative aspects of not drinking. On the other side are the benefits of sobriety and the downside of drinking. The task is to stand in the middle of these options and make a choice. This is the nature of conflict. There are two (or more) seemingly reasonable alternatives, and each has pluses and minuses. This is true about a decision regarding any relationship, job, house, part of the country to live in, and so forth. In the case of drinking, these are the two sides.

1. Wants to Drink

Pluses of drinking: gets drunk—self-medicates anxiety, avoids feelings, has fun, is funny, has sex, connects with friends.

Minuses of not drinking: no social life—feels tense, angry, anxious, bound up emotionally; has to face difficult realities and challenges of life.

2. Wants to Stop

Pluses of sobriety: feels better, able to sleep, saves money, family happier, connects with healthier people, sees more clearly; that is, one has better information about oneself and one's relationships.

Minuses of drinking: with sobriety, much less angry and erratic; not sick and missing work; sleeping better; spouse not so angry and disappointed; marriage not threatened; avoidance of fighting, medical issues, blackouts, legal issues.

In the usual case, these alternatives are not fully considered. The person will either impulsively drink, rationalize drinking ("I can have one"), or abstain because it is somehow wrong. While the latter option is preferable to families and professional caregivers, it is unlikely to be sustainable. This is because the impulsive or unexamined acting out of one side of a conflict will bring an equal and opposite reaction from the other side.

If the conflicted alcoholic drinks, there are a number of possible negative outcomes that are followed by much guilt and self-recrimination. The slap is harsh and immediate: "How can you be so stupid? What is it going to take for you to get this?" If one abstains reactively to be "good" or to please someone else, the experience is more subtle, as things are initially fine on the surface. Underneath, however, disowned wishes to drink or to rebel against being good are creating tension. At some point this tension will break through in the form of reactivity, anger, destructive behavior, or relapse. I tell my patients that I do not want to turn them into good boys and girls, and that is why.

It is only when we stop long enough to see the entire problem that we are in a position to choose. In the short run, we tend to gratify our habit because there does not seem to be a major downside and we feel better. This is true for the woman who repeatedly has "one beer" and relapses, who eats to manage anxiety, or who is promiscuous out of loneliness and desperation. Our slippery minds can easily deny, rationalize, and change the rules to justify our actions. These justifications can often masquerade as wisdom or compassion: "If God didn't want us to eat ice cream, he wouldn't have created it." "Don't I have a right to enjoy my life a little?" "The rest of America is doing the same thing." These are just a few possible examples. When the person is able to see the downside of having the beer, cake, or affair *and* make a choice, she is in the game.

Roger had repeatedly indulged his habits over many years. He had certainly had fun in the past, but now his body was breaking down. He saw only misery in his future and agreed that he did not want to be having the same conversation with me in five years. So he was motivated to stand still in the face of the fear, sadness, desperation, and grief that he had always run from. It was not easy, but he learned to distract, to accept, and to take an interest in the whole process. He also sought support and over time gained confidence that his feelings were tolerable. Drinking was still an option, but a less attractive one. The grief was painful but opened his heart and connected him with a new peer group that was getting well, not staying sick. He was on the right road.

Mindful Walking: Coming Back to Our Senses

Walking is a beautiful practice that can be done formally or informally. It is meditation in motion and a great opportunity for learning embodied awareness, since we do it so often. We amble, stroll, climb stairs, power walk. The slower we go, the more we notice about the body, but we can be mindful at any speed.

Sometime today, if possible, make some time for a walk

outside. As you leave, notice your feeling state—pleasant, unpleasant, or neutral. Find your pace; just feel for it. This may change as you go, based on energy, mood, or interest. See if you can notice these shifts.

As you walk, focus on your body. There are many possibilities. Notice your feet making contact with the ground and the different textures of pavement, grass, sand, or wood. Feel your arms swing. Notice your breathing and your posture. You can experience the sequence of *lift–move–place* or simply be aware of motion. You might appreciate the coordination of feet, ankles, knees, hips, and pelvis. There is no need to notice all of these things, just whatever keeps your attention and interest on your body. If your mind wanders, simply return to the walking without judgment.

Walking outside, there are countless sights, sounds, smells, and physical sensations. Allow yourself to see their comings and goings. Notice the difference between experience and stories (seeing and hearing a car drive by versus fantasizing about owning that car).

Each season and setting brings its own unique set of conditions and surprises. You might feel the wind on your face. You can also hear it; see its effects in the trees; smell the burning wood, gasoline, or freshly cut grass that it brings to your nose. Stand still in the wind for a few moments, feeling your feet on the earth. Experience the power of being fully present.

4

Waking Up: Mindfulness in Early Recovery

KEVIN WAS A twenty-nine-year-old man who came to our partial hospitalization program after an alcohol detox. He was not happy to be there, feeling forced to come by his mother and brother, with whom he lived. This is not atypical, as patients tend to feel some combination of agitated, emotionally unstable, ashamed, anxious, shy, and/or coerced to be there by family, work, or the legal system when they first arrive. Kevin was angry and shut down but also a wise guy, which allowed us to share a few laughs during his initial interview.

When I introduced the subject of mindfulness as a part of our program, however, he was openly contemptuous, stating that this was a ridiculous way for him to spend his time. Later that morning, I introduced a simple mindful breathing practice to the group. My eyes were closed, but I heard snickering and then loud guffaws as Kevin left the room. In subsequent meditation sessions, he refused to participate, and staff never pushed him to do so.

Over the next two weeks, Kevin felt increasingly comfortable in the program. He eventually spoke of his father's alcoholism, abusiveness, and death when he was fourteen. Under Kevin's drinking, bravado, contempt, and anger were enormous grief and confusion about how to be a man. In the simplicity of silently breathing, he had experienced feelings he could not accept or manage. Quiet contemplation was a frightening thing.

Unlike some of our patients, Kevin never meditated on his own to my knowledge. He did, however, begin to participate in the group sittings, comforted, I believe, by the instruction that this was not to be a "torture chamber" and that people were free to stand up, walk around, or leave if sitting was intolerable. The only request was that they change position mindfully, that is, make a choice as opposed to just reacting. If they did react, they were just to notice that and learn about the difference they felt between reacting and responding to a feeling or urge.

Over three different day treatment admissions, Kevin saw that his relapses were invariably triggered by the grief or shame he did not want to feel. In the brief group sittings, he was able to glimpse some of the anxiety that heralded unwanted feelings and begin to work with it. Once he saw that it was "just anxiety" (an experience in the body), as opposed to a signal that he was a "loser" (a story), he was able to begin not to fight it so much. He now had a choice of whether to just allow the experience to be there, which was the more difficult, or to shift his attention away from it to his breath, his body, walking, peeing, whatever. Kevin began to see that fear, sadness, anger, cravings, and stories all happen. Now he had tools that enabled him to be less of a victim of them.

Waking from the Trance of Addiction

Kevin's case illustrates the function of the addictive process, that is, to avoid unbearable experience. Addiction is a trance state, where the user repeatedly dissociates from painful emotions via getting high and self-medication. One major benefit is that the heroin addict, for example, knows exactly who he is and what he has to do when he wakes up in the morning. The downside is that he is on automatic pilot, operating with little awareness of his body, feelings, or thoughts and at the same time highly reactive to them. This results in lost jobs, ruined relationships, accidents, emergency room visits, and mishaps of all kinds. One of the inmates I taught was doing twelve years for vehicular homicide and did not even remember getting into the car.

Entering treatment is painful. It is generally avoided until the situation is dire, because treatment entails waking from the trance and admitting that living on automatic pilot is not working. It is about slowing down long enough to understand a problem. Addicts can see a relapse coming, even to the point of setting it up or planning it. However, most feel powerless to take another course of action. Mindfulness is a means of witnessing the tendency to live in a trance, both the pluses and the minuses. Then it is possible to be more aware of thoughts, emotions, cravings, and triggers and make a more informed choice. Like the exercises at the ends of chapters 1, 2, and 3, the meditations in this chapter will utilize awareness of body sensations as the door to a new way of living.

In this context, *meditation* refers to practices that develop mindfulness, the openhearted awareness of mind-body experience in the present moment. Meditation can be done from a sitting posture, lying down, standing, or in motion. There are many practices from many traditions, but what they all have in common is a movement toward stability of mind and clear seeing. When we focus attention on a single object, the mind will begin to settle, or perhaps more commonly, we see how unsettled our minds actually are.

This may not sound like good news at first and will likely seem to be a huge impediment as we try to meditate. Particularly because many who are new to the practice believe that the goal of meditation is to "clear the mind" or to "relax," our noisy minds can be quite frustrating. In feedback sessions, patients will report that they "couldn't do it" or will say, "I can't concentrate." That's right, it takes practice.

If these are obstacles to you, please know two things:

1. The goals of meditation are wisdom and compassion, and the means to those goals is mindfulness, not relaxation. Relaxation will happen as a matter of course, but as a primary goal, one's attempt at relaxation will often lead to disappointment. This is because the spirit of the practice is to accept things as they are as opposed to getting rid of them, and under these circumstances we are often not relaxed.

2. You are in good company. Some minds settle very quickly, but from my experience in speaking with thousands of people, that is the exception. In this context of addiction treatment, instability of mind,

reactivity, and impulsivity are the key reasons people are in trouble with alcohol or drugs. This is also true for the rest of us with behavioral addictions, thinking addictions, or simple bad habits we seem to be unable to change.

Mindfulness and Concentration

Meditation is a training ground for mindfulness practice. If you are building a house, you need a foundation, and concentration is the base of stability from which moment-to-moment awareness is possible. The analogy is actually not perfect, since we can be mindful without much concentration, just not for very long. In my experience, concentration, or the ability to focus on one thing at a time, develops from two sources: (1) staying with an object such as the breath, body sensations, a chant, or a phrase and (2) stringing a number of mindful moments together.

So concentration and mindfulness have a synergistic relationship. Awareness of simple moments builds some steadiness of attention, which then enhances our capacity to stay present for the next moment. As we notice more of our experience, we find we take a greater interest in it, which creates more energy, leading to greater concentration and greater capacity to be aware of present-moment experience with acceptance.

Here is exactly the opposite sequence, which unfolds as addiction develops: escaping or attempting to control experience leading to less reliable information, unwise speech and actions, messy outcomes, more escaping, greater reactivity in a downward spiral of mindlessness. Stopping this process and looking at our actual experience is clearly a useful beginning.

However, when we begin to try to follow our breath, we invariably see that the mind has other ideas. Particularly in early recovery, there can be great turbulence in the body (agitation, anxiety, craving, withdrawal, pain), emotions (fear, shame, guilt, anger, grief), and mind (impatience, storytelling, judgment). It can be challenging to sit still at all, let alone focus in any sustained way. So in the beginning, our task is to make space for these experiences and work with them the best we can.

To begin to cultivate concentration, the instruction is simply to direct your attention to your breath or body and return to it as soon as you notice your mind has drifted off. The willingness to return is itself an object of attention and facilitates staying with the breath in a consistent way. We can notice what drew us away, where we went, our attitude about returning. If there is frustration or self-judgment, we just notice. By building our capacity to return gracefully to the object, we are beginning to experience self-acceptance, a major task of addiction treatment.

It is very much like training a dog. The instruction "stay" is often not heeded immediately. The puppy is excited and impulsive. As trainers, we then give a gentle but firm tug on the leash. We do it with patience and kindness, and when the puppy complies even a little, we give praise. If we bring a harsh or punitive attitude, we may get obedience but will not have a dog that is flexible, fun, and loving. Since that is likely the kind of animal we would like to be, let's do three practices that encourage simple presence, embodied awareness, and concentration.

Body Scan Meditation

Addictive processes—to substances, behaviors, or thinking—lead further and further into the head, alienating us from the body. The addict progressively loses a sense of the body's internal workings, its contact with the earth, and its position in space. In early recovery, there is often great discomfort and physical pain. The body scan is a powerful technique for reconnecting with embodied awareness. We have seen at the UMass Stress Reduction Program at the University of Massachusetts Medical Center in Worcester, the UMass Prison Project, and in addiction treatment settings that although pain does not disappear, the relationship to it changes and it becomes more workable. In doing the body scan on a regular basis, we cultivate the ability to surrender to our bodies, allowing sensations and feelings to unfold naturally as opposed to having to control or avoid experience.

I prefer to do the practice lying on my back on a rug, mat, or bed, since that posture allows maximum release of muscle activity, but it can also be done on your side or sitting up. Initially, the body scan will take twenty-five to thirty minutes or more, but eventually it can be done more quickly, for example, when transitioning to sleep, to wakefulness, or to sitting meditation.

As you read the instructions, remember that these words are far less important than your experience. Feel free to vary your pace, sequence, or emphasis in ways that work best for you.

1. In the supine posture, place your arms, palms up, slightly away from your sides and let your feet fall out to the side. Notice your contact points—heels, legs, buttocks, back, arms, and head—and let go as much as you can, allowing gravity to hold you. You might become aware of the air on your skin, sounds, or thoughts. Take a moment to notice all of these experiences as they arise and fade. Here we are cultivating the *being* mode, opening to and accepting our experience as opposed to doing, planning, or worrying.

2. Focus on your belly as it rises with the in-breath and falls with the out-breath. Stay with this for several cycles, riding the waves of your breath and the motion of your abdomen, back, and spine. If your mind should wander, which it will, simply return to the touch points, breathing, or region of the body you are focusing on. Remember, our goals are to nurture both awareness and kindness.

3. Now direct your attention to the toes of your left foot. You might be aware of warm or cool, moist or dry, spaces between the toes, or contact of the toes. Is there any tingling or numbness? Notice how your toes connect with your foot, not so much visualizing as feeling for bones, joints, or muscles. Then the ball of your foot, the arch, and the heel. Continue to follow your leg upward—top of the foot, ankle, calf, shin, knee, thigh, all the way up to your groin and your left hip. You will be able to take an interest in how these parts connect with each other and make contact with the surface you are on.

4. At this point you might notice if there is a difference between your left leg and your right. Did paying careful attention to your left leg make a difference in how you experience it?

(There is no right answer.) Now proceed to notice your right leg and go through the same sequence.

5. Next, focus on your pelvis—lower spine, buttocks, genitals—as well as the connection of the trunk to the lower extremities. You might notice the breath sensations moving downward into your pelvis and even your legs, creating a sense of liveliness.

6. Moving upward, notice the movement of your abdominal wall and the cylinder including your lower back. You might become aware of energy moving deep in your belly, discomfort, or even pain. Breathe into whatever is present, bringing as much interest and acceptance as you can.

7. Follow your spine from your tailbone to the base of your skull. Notice how it moves with your breath along with your rib cage and sternum. You might like to watch your breath spread up, down, and across your back, particularly if there is tension or pain.

8. You can feel your lungs fill and empty. You may also be able to sense your heart between your lungs as well as the great vessels that serve your trunk and extremities, head and neck. Take a moment to stay in the region of your heart, accepting whatever is there right now.

9. Starting at your fingers, slowly move up through your hands, wrists, forearms, elbows, arms, and shoulders. Notice sensations and connections as well as any tension or discomfort.

10. As you move upward to your neck, experience the many links it makes between your head and body. Notice any feelings in your spine and paraspinal muscles as well as sensations associated with breathing and swallowing. As you breathe, see if you can allow your throat to rest.

11. Direct your attention to your jaw. Is there any holding or clenching? If so, you can observe the area of the temporomandibular joint, where the jaw meets the skull. See if you can let go, allowing your jaw to relax.

12. Notice the structures around your mouth—lips, teeth, tongue, palate—and any sensations that arise. Do the same for the muscles of your face and around your eyes and forehead. Allow your face just to be, without any obligation or demand, simply resting in the present moment, letting your eyes be soft.

13. Become aware of your temples, the sides of your head, the back and top of your head. Again, notice any tension that is present and let it go or let it be, accepting as best you can whatever is present right now.

14. Before concluding, let's take a few moments to experience the body as a whole. You can breathe in all the way down to your toes and out through the top of your head, like a dolphin. Or simply notice your entire body breathing itself. Nothing to do. You might appreciate the marvels of your body or may be struggling right now with illness, agitation, or pain. If you are practicing mindful acceptance, you will see that there is so much more good news about you than bad. See if you can appreciate that and honor your efforts to become increasingly aware and kind.

Walking Meditation

Walking meditation is a concentration practice emphasizing moment-to-moment awareness of the body in motion. This is similar to the exercise at the end of chapter 3, but here it will be done more formally. In addiction treatment, everyone seems to be either agitated or lethargic, and walking meditation can help balance energy. It is interesting to experiment with different speeds. A brisk walk might improve a sluggish energy, but very slow walking can also wake up the mind by applying very precise moment-to-moment attention. Both speeds might help a revved-up system idle down as well.

Coordinating the breath with the walking can also be useful in supporting your attention. For slow walking, you might lift and move your foot on the in-breath, then place it down on the out-breath. If you are walking more quickly, notice how many steps you take for each breath, knowing that the number may be different for the in- and out-breaths.

1. In a place where you will not be disturbed, choose a lane anywhere from five to fifteen yards in length. Standing at one end,

feel your feet on the floor or earth. Take a few moments to be fully present with those sensations. Also notice your posture, your breathing, and any sounds.

2. As you prepare to take your first step, slowly shift your weight to one side and lift the other foot. Notice the sensations of lifting, moving, and placing the foot down. Feel the action of your hips, knees, and ankles. Notice the shift of weight onto the foot balancing you. Is there a slight wobble?

3. When the first step is completed, begin to lift the other foot, move, and place it down. Bring as much interest as you can to the whole process. Find a pace that allows you to feel a sense of balance and flow. If your attention wavers or drifts off, simply return to the sensations of walking.

4. When you reach the end of your path, slowly turn around with full awareness of motion and contact. Stand for a few moments, orienting to your sensations and surroundings, before starting back in the other direction. Try a few laps at first, eventually building to ten or fifteen minutes.

What was your experience? People have expressed gratitude that they are able to walk and that they are alive. One guy appreciated his big toes for the first time. More-settled energy is quite common. So is waking up. I once led a group of therapists in walking meditation on a spectacular day in late September—brilliant blue sky, warm, with a wonderful cooling breeze. Sunlight sparkled on the Charles River, and we could see the leaves beginning to turn yellow and red. It was summer and fall simultaneously, oscillating, transitioning right before our eyes and senses. I asked the group to stop for a moment and asked, "What did you notice?" One young woman who had been very interested and active in our discussions said, "Wow! I never see any of that, I just go right to my car."

When we walk or do the body scan, it often appears that not much is happening. However, with regular practice we can train ourselves to be more fully present, living as though our lives really mattered. Clearly, this sort of experience is frequently available to us to wake us up, to inspire us, as an antidote to stress, as a means to move from our heads into our bodies.

Eating Meditation

Whether it be substances or behaviors, addicts consume reactively and without much awareness. In early recovery, people eat either excessively or erratically, with weight gain a common outcome. Since senses have become dulled and energy is unstable, choices are often confined to four basic food groups—sugar, salt, caffeine, and grease. Smoking suppresses appetite and further desensitizes the taste buds. What would it be like to actually be aware of what is taken into the body?

This is a simple exercise, for which you will need one raisin, which I will use in the instructions. An almond, a tangerine, a strawberry, or a dried cranberry is a good alternative.

1. Choose your raisin and bring your attention to it. Look at it as if for the first time, as though you were assessing what it is and what it would be like to consume such a thing. Notice whether your body has any reaction: wanting, hunger, aversion, or neutrality. There may be some thoughts about the object or the exercise.
2. Examine the raisin carefully. Notice the play of light and color over the surface. Is it smooth, rough, ridged, symmetrical—or not? Look at the ends of the raisin. Are they different?
3. Without looking, feel the raisin between your fingers. Notice its texture and pliability.
4. Bring the raisin up to your nose and smell it. Again, notice desire, aversion, or any sensations in your mouth or elsewhere.
5. Place the raisin against your lips and then on your tongue. Do not bite it yet, but roll it around your mouth and explore it. What happens? Now prepare to bite into it. Notice how your lips and tongue know exactly what to do. Bite the raisin one time. What do you notice? Continue to roll it around, assessing your desire (or not) to eat this object.
6. Chew the raisin slowly, noticing the tastes released and its changing texture. Follow the tastes as they emerge, change, and fade. Bring full attention to your intention to swallow and then swallow the raisin.

7. Take a moment to notice the raisin passing into your body. Notice also any thoughts or feelings about your experience.

People who do this exercise often comment that they never really tasted a raisin before and that the experience was quite interesting and powerful. They see that liking something leads to desire (and disliking to aversion), a relationship we usually take for granted. Eating frequently occurs unconsciously, on automatic pilot, driven by a wanting that is unrelated to the body's need for food. So, not surprisingly, we see impatience, impulsivity, and a number of raisins swallowed before the instructions are completed.

Of course, we know that it was once a grape, but seeing the little scar where the stem was reminds us that this raisin was once attached to a plant. It required earth, sun, and rain to come into being. Someone had to prepare the ground; plant the seed; and tend, harvest, and dry the grapes. They had to be packed, loaded, shipped, unloaded, and placed on shelves in the market. The act of choosing your raisins and paying for them is preceded by the work of many people, work that has often been done in families over many generations. Here is an opportunity to bring discernment and gratitude to everything we ingest. You will find more resources for mindful eating in the bibliography.

The raisin meditation is an invitation to slow down enough to taste our actual experience and with greater awareness. Seeing our own likes, dislikes, reactions, and storytelling reveals the information needed to make a choice in the context of triggers or strong emotion. Addicts who are able to live in slo-mo are more able to utilize their attention and intelligence to sustain recovery and avoid relapse. And if life brings more real satisfaction, the draw of alcohol or drugs is much less powerful.

Mindfulness in Daily Life

The real payoff of meditation is turning our lives into our practice. Any moment can be an opportunity to experience embodied awareness, gratitude, and self-acceptance. You might choose one simple activity—taking out the trash, doing the dishes, vacuuming—for a week. Notice the whole process in much the same way you do the walking or eating meditation. You might see yourself rushing or thinking, leading to impatience, annoyance, or carelessness. There might be some skill involved that you will appreciate if you, for example, brush your teeth or shave with your nondominant hand. If you plan or obsess while in the shower, you ignore what could be a pleasurable experience. Walking the dog can be just a chore or an opportunity for companionship in nature on a day different from all others. Dogs seem to know this.

Since our lives are composed of these simple moments, we have countless opportunities to appreciate them. We are also in a better position to see how we shut down to experience by eating, working, drinking, or zoning out in equally countless ways. Tobacco, for example, can stimulate the mind or quell difficult feelings. It can also produce holes in the lungs, mouth, and wallet. Users often have mixed feelings about smoking but then push them away with another cigarette. With greater awareness and acceptance of the pros and cons of any activity, we are more able to make conscious choices—a huge source of power and authority. Many of our patients have also discovered that as mindfulness becomes a new habit, there is a greater capacity to handle more challenging situations involving our bodies, emotions, and relationships. These will be discussed in more detail in part 3.

The practices in this chapter provide a foundation in concentration and appreciation of simple experience. Chapter 5 gives more detailed instructions toward further exploring meditation as a means of developing mindfulness in our lives.

5

Going Further with Meditation Practice

WITH ADDICTION THERE IS a loss of orientation to both one's environment and one's inner reality. Recovery begins with admitting that this is true, that the old methods of controlling or avoiding experience are no longer working. It is a journey toward stability and flexibility. Toddlers learning to walk fall down repeatedly before feeling solid on their feet. Ninety AA meetings in ninety days is a foundational experience that begins with structure and leads to compassion and a deeper sense of morality. Meditation practice is a means of developing concentration and wisdom through an investigation of the mind-body process. The following guidelines help promote a mindful recovery, a path to greater clarity, openness, and maturity.

Attitude

A meditation teacher once suggested while I was on retreat that I do an "attitude check." She likely saw elements of impatience, self-criticism, or trying too hard, all of which have been challenges for me. Since then I have found the observation of attitude to be extremely useful both on and off the cushion, providing information about how I am relating to the current situation.

It is not difficult to have a positive attitude when we are hopeful or inspired. We might read something, hear a talk, or get a hint from a friend that meditation is what we need. There is a certain brightness of faith, and we are willing to pursue the practice, much like embarking on learning a language or a musical instrument. On some level, we all want to grow and develop ourselves and are excited to begin.

Eventually, however, we will encounter experiences that we do not like, challenges to our ongoing energy or enthusiasm for meditation. We will discuss these in more detail later on, but they basically involve some combination of not enough happening and/or occurrences in the mind that are troubling or just unpleasant. Difficult emotions, thoughts, or energy states; agitation; lethargy; and boredom are among the experiences that cause us to consider abandoning the whole project.

I understood Kevin (from chapter 4) because I was just like him. I, too, at times questioned whether mindfulness was a valuable skill to cultivate. I would struggle, go up into my head, and then rationalize or avoid practicing regularly. I was well-meaning but could see only what I was able to at the time. Why I continued was some combination of interest, support, and perseverance. Once I could glimpse actual benefits in the form of decreased reactivity and greater clarity or understanding, it was a very different game. I now no longer had to take anyone's word for these previously potential benefits but had seen them for myself. This was the beginning of a faith born of actual experience, which I found sustaining through the difficult times.

Effort

An important paradox of meditation practice is the fact that we are mobilizing effort, focus, and determination in order to let go of control. It is true with any skill we want to develop: if we are to experience a sense of flow or mastery, we must ask the part of us that wants to control the outcome to step aside. So new meditators will practice concentration with one of two tendencies: to work too hard or to be too relaxed.

The strivers try to control the mind with more and more effort, leading to increased tension and discouragement. I discovered that regardless of how hard I worked to get rid of my thinking and follow my breath, my mind was going to win. It was only when I stopped struggling and just allowed thoughts to come and go that I was able to settle enough to sustain my attention. If the effort is too slack, we tend to drift pleasantly along with stories, planning, and fantasies, totally unaware of current experience. We then need to boost tension and focus slightly.

Regardless of our primary tendency, the other side is not far away. Substance abusers, for example, have a reputation for being pleasure seeking, selfish, careless, and lazy. However, what I often see are people who overextend, try to control events and relationships, become exhausted, and relapse. If we do not seek a more balanced effort, our bodies will.

The good news is that right effort can be felt in the body. We can feel ourselves straining or pushing for a result, clinging to expectations, floating aimlessly, having to figure things out, avoiding experience, judging ourselves. With an attitude of openness and inquiry, we can sense whether we are too tense or too loose. Then we can make subtle adjustments akin to tuning a stringed instrument. Few observations are as important to our ability to concentrate and to our well-being.

Posture

As meditation can be a foundational experience in our lives, posture is the foundation of our meditation practice. In the posture, we are seeking a balance between comfort and stability. An effective position will allow the body to relax yet maintain just enough tension to keep the mind alert. Check this out in any activity. Try doing some serious reading both lying down and sitting up straight and notice the difference in your level of alertness. In hitting a tennis ball or baseball or shooting a basketball, the stance or ready position is critical to executing the swing or release. This is also true in performing arts, where correct posture facilitates a dancer's or a singer's energy flow.

Sitting meditation can be done in a chair or on the floor. In our program, we sit in chairs that are comfortable but allow the back to be straight. If you sit back so that your tailbone touches the back of the chair and tilt the pelvis forward, the back will arch. This allows an erect posture that facilitates wakefulness and the flow of breath. Some people need to lean back in the chair, and that works as well. Feet are flat on the floor.

There are two basic floor postures, cross-legged and kneeling, which will require a cushion or a stool for optimal comfort. In the cross-legged postures, the knees should be grounded, either on the floor or with additional cushions. These positions can be quite stable, but not everyone's body is able to do them, and knee and back injuries have occurred from forcing them. I hurt my own knee before admitting the truth. We do watch bodily sensations, including pain, as we meditate, but excessive pain can be destabilizing to one's practice. I eventually gravitated to the kneeling or Japanese style, sitting on one or two cushions, with the knees grounded on a mat or carpet.

Breath

We take our first breath upon being born and our last when we die. The words *inspiration* and *expiration* clearly express this theme of life and death. They also capture the idea of spirit or the connection to something greater than ourselves. Breathing is automatic, and we take it for granted, but anyone who has had trouble getting air, even for a short while, appreciates it very quickly.

The breath is such a useful meditation object because it is happening right now and continues to happen moment after moment. It is portable and observable both while meditating and in daily life. Breathing is a means both to rest in the present moment and to return when we drift away. It is also a wonderful vehicle for becoming more embodied and less in our heads.

Breathing is nature in action. Watching the breath is very much like walking in the woods, where the terrain underfoot, the vegetation, the weather, and the light keep changing. The breath can be long or short, deep or shallow, coarse or fine, easy or difficult, feathery or jagged, pleasant or unpleasant. It can be affected by physical sensations, feeling tones, thoughts, and emotions. Notice how the breath changes when you are tense, fearful, or relaxed.

The breath is a vital means to link our mind and body in the present moment. As human beings we invariably have multiple scenarios and agendas operating at any given time: vocation, finances, health and physical well-being, family, relationships, drug or alcohol use, hobbies, skill development, spirituality, and so on. The businesses of our lives engage different perspectives or parts of our personalities. In turn, all of these pieces of who we are have stories attached to them. How in the world do we understand and prioritize all of this, all the while caring for our own well-being and being decent to other people?

Although it is not the entire answer, awareness of breathing can accompany us. Each situation has its own set of demands. A simple walk to the store, a critical job interview, and a conflictual situation around a family member pull at different feelings and tensions within us. Coming to the breath allows us to be fully where we are, embodied, deemphasizing the effects of other issues in the background that are not of immediate concern. The cloud of all of our thinking lifts to some degree, and we can be more fully here and now whether it be for the purpose of planning, making a decision, listening, doing our work, having fun, or just being.

A common experience of meditators is that the breath is monotonous or boring as an object of awareness. It may help to know that breathing is our lifeblood or best friend, as I have suggested here, but it may not. At times the breath may not be sufficiently compelling to capture our interest. It cannot compare to seeing a movie or getting caught up in all of the dramas of our lives.

The breath is much more like that walk in the woods where we notice a lot of trees and leaves underfoot but also a number of subtle changes in the environment and within ourselves as we go. At times we will come upon a deer, a butterfly, a brilliant patch of moss, a sense of wonder about our connection to all of life. Then the surprise visitor, the beautiful plant, the awe, recedes. We have left the mystery and are back in the mundane.

Mundane literally means "of the world," but it has come to suggest "boring" or "uninteresting." This underscores a major obstacle to our developing the clarity and peace we seek in meditation. That is, the need to be entertained at all times. We may be critical of our kids, with their dependence on technology and short attention spans, but we are the same way. Being mindful of breathing literally reminds us to return to the present moment. This is not an insurance policy against making an ill-advised decision, but it can help. In the case of a purchase we really cannot afford, we might tune in to a need to escape a painful feeling, a subtle misgiving, or just a familiar urge to buy something. With this additional information, we are in a position to make a wiser choice.

Awareness of breathing is no big deal. The question for all of us is whether it is an ability worth cultivating among all of the other possible things we could focus on or develop. If you are reading this, you are likely at least open to the possibility that breath awareness might be helpful to you in changing a bad habit or a destructive pattern. As you proceed in your exploration, allow me to repeat two things: (1) seeing is believing, and (2) it takes practice. Sitting meditation practice on a daily or nearly daily basis will strengthen the ability to stay with the breath for more sustained periods on the cushion and help you remember to use it as a vehicle to be fully present with whatever is happening right now.

Objects of Awareness

The next step in meditation is to sense our level of concentration. If there is sufficient stability of attention, it is possible to take an interest in other objects in the field of awareness. Noting the different qualities of the breath—long or short, easy or difficult, coarse or fine—can now be used to build mindfulness as well as concentration. There is no need to figure out the difference. If you are watching your breath, just allow it to come to you, noticing whatever you notice. The goal of meditation is to learn about our experience, not to control it. It is true that we begin with an intention to stay with our breathing until the mind is more steady, but if you open up the field and get lost, you can always return to your breath. We are just as focused and stable as we are. If we can be okay with that, we are also beginning to cultivate honesty, patience, and kindness.

We bring the same attitude to noticing the body. If it is agitated, exhausted, racing, nauseated, or in pain, we observe the experience, seeing if we can allow it to be there without reacting immediately. It can be extremely challenging just to sit still. In the early going, the breath is often a way to distract from discomfort in the body as a means of tolerating it, a refuge of sorts. Addicts have learned to leave their bodies and often do not know that they are anxious or tense. They are also unaware that the stress they experience is fed by all of their thinking about the past and the future, their resentments and self-judgments. Simple breath awareness allows us to detach from these thoughts, if only temporarily, and experience a lessening of tension or anxiety and greater acceptance of what is there. The experience of the breath conditioning the body in this way is often what first demonstrates the value of meditation practice.

As concentration develops, there is a greater ability to bring bare attention to the physical sensations of craving, stress, tension, or fear without immediately reacting. We see that these are energies in the body that are moving and not solid. Mindfulness is now a vehicle for investigation into how our minds turn pain (or pleasure) into suffering and how we might respond more creatively and kindly. In meditation, we approach feeling tones, emotions, thoughts, and the shifting nature of our experience with the same attitude. It is a natural unfolding that with practice brings even greater stability and clarity. In the beginning, however, it is the stability that I want to emphasize. The addictive process thrives on people's being reactive and dissociated from their bodies. Feeling embodied and grounded is our first priority.

So to summarize, the beginning practice of meditation includes the following elements:

- Stable posture
- Awareness of attitude
- Awareness of breathing
- Awareness of physical sensations
- Noting the mind drifting into thinking, fantasizing, past or future
- Remembering to return to the body or breath whenever the attention drifts
- A greater ability to investigate our experience mindfully as concentration builds

Sitting Meditation

1. As we begin, we are aiming at a posture that is comfortable, upright, relaxed, alert, and respectful. Plan to sit for fifteen to

twenty minutes at first. Using a timer, if possible, can allow you simply to focus on your experience. Initially, you can notice your feet on the floor and your buttocks, if you are sitting on a chair, or your knees and legs touching the cushion. Let your hands rest palms down on your thighs or palms up, right hand resting in the left. Elevating the chest a bit will help to straighten the spine. The eyes can be open or closed, but allow them to be soft and slightly downcast. You might rock your shoulders side to side and front to back until you feel balanced.

2. Take a moment to observe the energy moving in your body. Is it agitated, bright, drowsy, sluggish, or calm?

3. Focus on the experience of hearing. Notice any sounds coming from your body and from inside the room or outside. Just receive each sound, whether it be pleasant, unpleasant, or neutral, as though you were listening to a piece of music. Notice how the sounds repeat or change.

4. Now direct your attention to your breath as it flows in and out. You can follow the breathing at your belly or your nose or by watching the breath as a whole. See where you are drawn, choosing a place where your breath is the most vivid or interesting. Allow each breath to come to you very much like you received each sound, with about the amount of effort it takes to watch waves roll onto a beach one by one.

5. At this point, our job is to stay with the entire breath. You might notice the rise and fall of your abdomen or the different temperatures as your breath comes in and goes out of your nostrils. It may help to say to yourself "in" and "out" as a means of staying present. The in-breath has a beginning, a middle, and an end, as does the out-breath. You might also notice a slight pause between or after each cycle. Keep your attention on your breath as continuous as you can.

6. When your mind wanders, which it will, simply redirect your attention to your breath. It's no problem. You might want to make a mental note of "planning," "analyzing," "worrying," or "fantasizing." If there is judgment, just notice the tension and let go the best you can, relaxing back into the breathing.

7. The practice of staying with the breath helps to stabilize the mind and experience the mind-body connection. This may

be as far as you go today, which is fine. Even after your mind settles, you may be drawn to even deeper states of concentration and one-pointed awareness. Once you feel a measure of stability, however, you may want to allow your breath to recede to the background and observe other objects in the field of awareness.

8. One possibility is to sense your posture and your body as a whole, experiencing your body and breath as a unified field. You might do a gradual sweep, starting from the top of your head, revisiting the various energies present in your body, taking your time to watch as they move, change, go, and return. This can also be done with touch points and any number of sensations. You might silently note: "itching," "paining," "craving," "tensing," "hearing," or "settling." If you have an urge to shift your position, just take a moment to notice that. You can then choose to move with awareness or continue to observe the impulse and sensation.

9. As you follow these objects of attention, you may become aware of each having a feeling tone—pleasant, unpleasant, or neutral. Notice what your mind does when each of these arises. Is it possible simply to receive each one, noticing the tendency to move into desire, aversion, boredom, or spacing out?

10. As emotions and thoughts emerge, can you bring the same attitude of openness and friendliness to them? You might ask yourself: "Can I make space for this anxiety?" (or any other feeling, such as emptiness, fear, sadness, joy, calm, or anger). Where is the emotion in your body? Are you able to watch thoughts come and go, or is there a tendency to get swept away by them? If you feel scattered at any time, you can always return to your breath, allowing the difficult thoughts or emotion to recede to the background.

11. As you prepare to end your sitting, you might notice the effects of mindful breathing and moment-to-moment awareness on your body and overall well-being. With regular practice, you will have increasing confidence in your ability to stabilize your attention and direct your energies.

Remembering Kindness

I meet many addicts in early recovery. Most are likeable and admirable in their efforts to learn new ways to relate to their thoughts and emotions. However, because many of these patients either are trauma survivors or see themselves as failures, self-acceptance and self-compassion are in short supply.

The instructions to all of the exercises thus far aim toward spaciousness of awareness, stability of attention, and a moment-to-moment appreciation of experience in the body. They also deliberately emphasize acceptance of the facts that minds wander, that mindfulness is a skill we are not born with, and that we are doing the very best we can. Still, there is a strong tendency for us to be impatient, reactive, and judgmental with ourselves—and this is not just about drug addicts and psychiatric patients.

If we are having difficulty bringing nonjudgmental attention to our meditation or if it begins to feel too dry or striving, a wonderful alternative is the practice of loving-kindness or *metta*. Kindness turned toward pain is *compassion*, which is the balancing energy to the mindfulness or wisdom practice. (There will be more about compassion in chapter 17.)

In loving-kindness meditation, we repeat a series of phrases toward the goal of developing unconditional friendliness. The instructions often encourage us to begin with ourselves. However, if that is too difficult, you can start with someone or something that is easy to love without much ambivalence, say a grandparent, child, or pet. One teacher of mine envisioned a lake from her childhood summers. Whatever we choose, we direct kindness toward our experience, which feels very different from trying to escape or get rid of it. And as we make friends with our suffering, it naturally transforms.

Loving-kindness Meditation

Once you settle into your posture, you might begin by taking three slow, deep breaths. A few minutes of mindful breathing will help to stabilize your body and attention.

Say silently to yourself: "May I be protected and safe, may I be healthy and strong, may I be happy, may I have ease of well-being." Please go slowly, connecting with the phrases in a way that is natural to you, possibly using visual images or some felt sense of yourself. As you repeat each one, pause for a moment to feel its effects.

There is much room for creativity here and for varying the phrases to suit your personal situation. If you are struggling with a particular mind or body state, you might ask: "May I be free from fear" (or anger, grief, pain). Or if you are working toward self-acceptance, you might say: "May I be happy just as I am, may I be peaceful with whatever is happening, may I love myself completely."

Next, we generally choose a benefactor, which is often a beloved elder, mentor, or spiritual teacher but could be anyone who is easy to love or who loves you unconditionally. As you bring this person to mind, repeat the phrases: "May you be protected and safe, may you be healthy and strong, may you be happy, may you have ease of well-being."

From here, you can move on to close family and friends, coworkers, clients, people in your community or place of worship. If your practice starts to become mechanical, fill your mind with acceptance and forgiveness toward yourself or a loved person, animal, or object, reconnecting as best you can to feelings of warmth and friendliness.

Now include people in all directions, most of whom you don't know, all beings on this planet and in the universe: "May all beings be happy, may all beings be free from suffering, may all beings live with love and with compassion."

The metta practice can soften the mind and prepare it for mindfulness meditation, increasing our capacity to accept difficult emotions. It can also be used in combination with walking meditation as a concentration practice or to add a component of kind attention to the body scan. In daily life situations, we can direct loving friendliness to family members or friends who are suffering or to random people on the bus, in the mall, or in our thoughts.

As the practice deepens, we are even able to send metta to people whom we dislike, resent, or want to avoid. You can mentally or emotionally include difficult family members in small groups to signal your intention to keep them in your heart even if you are not totally able to at the time.

A deeper level of understanding is possible here, because annoying people often are expressing parts of ourselves we don't like. That is why we don't like them. Once we look in the mirror, we can begin to relate to these energies in ourselves with kindness and friendliness. This is not easy, but it is a real opportunity for self-knowing and healing.

Loving-kindness practice is particularly challenging when everything that is "not metta" emerges. We have all made mistakes, hurt people, and been hurt. We can repeat the phrases: "May I forgive myself for making mistakes, may I forgive myself for being imperfect, or may I forgive _____ for neglecting or hurting me." However, self-hatred, resentment, and a refusal to be kind or forgiving are energies that often arise. Our inner critic may mock our loving affirmations ("go ahead, make my day") in an attempt to derail our practice. This is just fear. We need to acknowledge these resistant energies, which are part of our practice and worthy of our care and attention.

Last Resorts

I learned a technique from my meditation teacher James Barase that you might try for relentless judgment of yourself or others. Place your hand very gently on your cheek. Now, as you hold it there, softly say, "Judging." This is a simple acknowledgment of what we do automatically when frightened or stressed—with the addition of a pinch of kindness. There will be more about judgment in chapter 16.

For powerful emotion, we can ask in the very same spirit: "May I have the strength to weather this storm of fear" or "May I find the courage to face my grief." Finally, a beautiful summary of mindfulness and metta practices has been created by Kristin Neff, a researcher in the field of self-compassion.[1] I wrote it down so many times for people that I eventually just put it on cards. At difficult times, you can simply repeat:

This is a moment of suffering.
Suffering is part of life.
May I be kind to myself.
May I accept myself as I am.

PART TWO

Recovery and Treatment

6

Chaos and Exhaustion: What's Bringing You?

AS THE PSYCHIATRIST at a partial hospitalization program for patients with dual diagnosis (in most cases meaning addiction plus a mood, thought, or anxiety disorder), I ask all who arrive what has brought them there. It may not be the first question. The patient is understandably nervous and uncertain, walking into a doctor's office in an unfamiliar setting, entering a portal that may change his or her life, a life that is clearly not working but one the patient has become familiar with. He appears tired, embarrassed, withdrawn, or she seems fearful, angry, shut down emotionally.

We might chat a little bit. "Have you ever done this before?" Often the answer is no, or the person may recall an experience from the hospital or another day program. I might then say something like: "Obviously, I don't know you at all, but I do know that your life is not going so well." We can invariably agree on this. It is also an opportunity to connect this human being to the many who are here now and have come before, attempting to transition into a life that works better than the one they were living.

I ask about age, marital and parental status, living situation. Sexual orientation may come up at this point or not. I want to know if the person is working, in school, or disabled, and regardless of the answer,

I am interested in any life path the person can feel proud of, that has some meaning to him or her. "Okay, so what's bringing you?" This is a question that I feel honored and privileged to ask. As a clinician in a hospital, a clinic, and in private practice, it is easy to feel embattled and overwhelmed by the onslaught of patients, paperwork, meetings, and insurance issues, but right now I want to put all of that aside. What is most important at this moment is to give my full attention and interest to what is causing this person to ask for help.

Here are a number of actual answers from patients:

"I relapsed six days ago."

"The social worker recommended some sort of structure until I take GED classes."

"Depression. It's getting worse."

"I had a lot of suicidal thoughts."

"Drinking too much . . . three DUIs."

"I've been getting stressed out and overwhelmed with life in general. Lately it's hard to push things away."

"My wife left me, took the kids and moved in with her sister."

"I'm an alcoholic and I've had a hard time staying sober for the last year and a half."

"I just came out of here and started right up again."

"I'm looking for a way to be okay with myself."

"Cocaine."

"I have substance abuse problems. I felt depressed all the time. I did not open up."

"I had a nice life. I used visualization and meditation for anxiety and panic. My twenty-year-old son passed away in February. Everything came back."

"I've got a problem with my dad in the nursing home. The people at work didn't respond the way I hoped to my being in treatment. I relapsed."

"I've been struggling. I haven't been able to work since August. My anxiety has gone up. I have a volatile relationship."

"I was at the hospital for an overdose of alcohol and heroin."

"I'm not sure. My therapist thought I needed to get rebalanced."

"I really can't say."

The patient does not know it, but her mindfulness training has begun. We have acknowledged her being here, her having taken a difficult step, her not being alone in this undertaking. We have made the beginnings of a relationship and of an exploration of why she is here. One of our goals will be to integrate mindfulness practice into her repertoire, but before that can happen, a disorganized or frightened mind must tell its story in the context of a relationship of some trust.

Michael is a forty-five-year-old man who arrives with his wife, Patricia, following a medical hospitalization, including a week in the intensive care unit on a ventilator. They sit down, an apparent strong bond between them. He is a bit tense but appears to be reasonably healthy and open to being there; she, clearly concerned and loving but quite worn. When asked what is bringing him, Michael says, "Alcohol." Patricia gives the same answer. It is not an uncommon response, but in this case I am moved to tell them that alcohol is actually not the problem, that it had never to my knowledge flown out of the bottle into someone's mouth. They laugh at my less-than-subtle point, and our subsequent conversation confirms that Michael is here to take responsibility for a pattern of behavior that threatens the integrity of his family by causing him to shut down and emotionally leave his wife and son. It had also threatened his life. And what is good about alcohol? "It gives me a warm buzz."

The story is superficially not very complicated. This is a regular guy, whom you might be sitting next to at Fenway Park, who had been drinking since the age of fourteen. In retrospect, Michael felt he had a problem immediately but did not acknowledge this to himself until his late twenties, when he realized that once he started drinking, he could not choose to stop. He also has peptic ulcer disease, clearly exacerbated by alcohol, but not enough to motivate him to seek help. Prior to his recent hospitalization, he had never been admitted for alcohol detoxification. He has worked in maintenance for twenty years at a local university and has been honored for his excellent service. Patricia is unhappy with Michael's drinking but sees him as mostly a good provider, husband, and father and is clear she would never leave him.

Michael grew up in a family of four kids that he initially describes as "fun." He was the youngest of three boys and particularly loved to play football with his dad and brothers. His father, however, was a heavy drinker, prone to intermittent bouts of verbal abuse and violent outbursts. By the time Michael was twelve, the current age of his own son, his father had stopped playing ball with his kids and was to a large extent gone from the emotional life of his family. This was a huge loss for Michael, causing a sadness that never found expression and, because his brothers just seemed to move on, a sadness he bore alone. Roughly a year later, Michael was raped while on a camping trip with the Boy Scouts, an experience he also kept to himself. A link between this event, the loss of connection with his father, and his subsequent drinking had not occurred to him. However, in his adult life, Michael's dad had not shown up to see him receive an award at work, and he recalls drinking to manage his disappointment.

We also learn that Michael and Patricia share an enormous legacy burden from the previous generation. Patricia reveals the stunning detail that both of their mothers were left on doorsteps as infants, one at a hospital and the other at a home where she was taken in. Also, Michael's paternal grandfather had run off, abandoning his family. Unbelievable, but now it is clear why these people are together and why leaving is not an option. Michael has performed better than his father, who had done better than his own father. The elephant in the room is grief, and Michael's choice is to face it in some way or to continue drinking, progressively leave his family, and die young. Patricia's dilemma is also clearer: How could she leave such a decent man who has already borne so much pain? She has complained about Michael's drinking, bargained and cajoled, but has never directly told him that it is unacceptable and must change. This is because she has not allowed herself to see how it was affecting her own body and well-being.

This was all very interesting and helpful, but we must remember one thing: alcoholics and drug addicts do not come to treatment for personal growth but out of total desperation. Michael needed nearly to die and Patricia had to be totally exhausted and at her wits' end before they were willing to sit down in my office. Twelve or even six months earlier, looking into the problem in this way was not a serious consideration. They were doing the best they could day-to-day with the many challenges couples face around earning a living, parenting, and enjoying some well-earned pleasure and relaxation. For many years, it was easier to deny or rationalize problems so they could just get on with their lives. As we saw in chapter 3, any addictive strategy has pluses and minuses. We will take this up in more detail in the next chapter, but this is the beginning of the conflict an addict has around getting well versus continuing with business as usual.

I often tell our day treatment patients that they are a select group. They may feel sick and as if their lives were going nowhere, but at least they are stopping for a moment to admit that. There are many addicts out there that we will never see, that will never address their stuck condition, fear, or grief. I am sure they would not be particularly enthusiastic about meeting me, with all of my nosy questions and thoughtful comments. Asking for help is like getting out of bed to face a difficult morning, into the pool if the water is cold, or onto the dance floor if you're shy. A part of us just does not want to do it. We do not move, out of fear or by telling ourselves a story that argues that we are better off staying where we are.

As the legend goes, God parted the Red Sea after one man took the first step. The first step of Alcoholics Anonymous states, "We admitted we were powerless over our addiction, that our lives had become unmanageable." Once that step is taken, everything changes. Somehow we get out of bed, feel the cold air, walk to the bathroom, pee, splash water on our face, stretch, drink coffee. Then we are able to move to the next activity and the next. We are almost invariably glad we got out of bed. Even if something terrible happens, from the point of view of someone out of bed, staying in bed to avoid life is not a viable option. However, addicts are staying in a cocoon or fantasy refuge in order to avoid that blast of cold air, too fearful to emerge.

The painter Georgia O'Keeffe said, "I have been terrified my whole life, but it never stopped me from doing anything." That is courage. Anyone who was ever courageous was afraid. Coming into treatment takes the courage to ask for help, to admit that we do not have all the answers and that our lives are uncomfortably out of our control. We might also notice that we are unhappy or that our body is hurting. We have rationalized these observations away so many times and regressed to old ways. What does it take for us to overcome our pride, fear, self-hatred, negativity, or unworthiness?

If the situation becomes chaotic or overwhelming enough or if we might lose everything, seeking help becomes a consideration. But even then, it may not feel acceptable in one's family or culture. At the risk of overgeneralizing, Irish families possess a lot of quick-witted spark and fun but do not tend to be strong around emotional exchange. Many northern European cultures share this feature. In Michael's family of origin, it was as though everyone were living in his or her own bubble. In contrast, Latinos may be highly emotional with family, feeling more connected, even merged at times. However, these cultures originating in Southern Europe may have attitudes around hierarchy, gender roles, and emotional sharing outside of the family that would limit their openness to psychotherapy as a mode of addressing issues of an emotional nature.

We live in a highly individualistic society, one that prizes self-reliance and solving one's own problems. Drugs and alcohol, as we noted earlier, are vehicles for the management of our emotional lives, but the benefits are distinctly short-term. The problem is that when there is only one method for dodging bullets, we will continue to use it even as the bullets come faster and faster. Only when we can no longer weather the barrage do we surrender. We can only hope it is not too late.

After Michael's evaluation, we review the problems presented. His alcohol dependence is related to a genetic vulnerability that became a problem in the context of adolescent grief and trauma. He likely has a component of depression or anxiety but has never directly experienced either, since he has self-medicated all feelings, pleasant or unpleasant, for as long as he can remember. This makes sense, since he has been totally alone with a problem he has not understood and has been doing the best he could to be a decent person, albeit at major cost to his family and to his own well-being. Patricia, for her part, knows she has been "enabling" Michael to drink, though it becomes clear that, for her own reasons, she is terrified of abandoning him or of being abandoned by him. We discuss the problem of codependence—born of trauma and often operating in alcoholic systems—a relationship addiction where the addict balances him- or herself by caring for others. Patricia has also been trying to do the right thing for Michael and her son but has been denying her own physical and emotional health in the process. If she does not begin to do something different fairly soon, she will likely break down, an outcome that would help no one.

Once they have some understanding of the problem, I discuss what the treatment would be—recovery, psychotherapy, medicine, and mindfulness practice. I ask them if they would direct their attention to their feet on the floor, their butts in the chair, their hands—just noticing the points of contact. Then I asked them to follow a few breaths into their belly or chest, wherever they felt them. That takes about thirty seconds. I ask what they notice. Michael is able to see how much tension he holds in his shoulders and some anxiety in his stomach. Patricia feels "relaxed" but could also feel some fatigue around her eyes.

Both are surprised. They have not been in their bodies at all, and it is a new experience. It is also, I point out, a new source of information they have not been accessing. For example, in the discussion about medication, it is not clear whether Michael should take something for anxiety, reactivity, or depression. He cannot say if he has any of those symptoms, and Patricia has a bias against and fear of medication. Well, here is the potential for actual data that could guide our decision, a decision based not on any of our ideas about medicine or how alcoholics should be treated but on what is actually experienced. Even Patricia could know that her husband was irritable or reactive, because she could feel it. Then, if the decision is for Michael to take an antidepressant—which eventually it was—the effects of the medicine could be monitored the same way.

The couple feels relieved and encouraged. Indeed, I agree that if they pursue treatment as we outlined it, their lives will change for the better. Not much has happened, but they are able to glimpse the idea that their chaotic, confusing, overwhelming experience does not have to be that way. By staying in the present moment, more in the body, less in the head, they will be better able to identify their experience and reactions and respond more effectively as partners and parents and toward their own health and happiness.

This is the whole point. How do we live a happy and fulfilling life? Epictetus, the great Stoic philosopher of the first and second centuries of the common era, gave a prescription based on three themes: mastering your desires, performing your duties, and learning to think clearly about yourself and your relations within the larger community of humanity.[1]

We have all fallen short of these goals, celebrated victories, been the object of praise and blame, had regrets. We can still be affected by these events as they color our present reality but can do nothing to change them. We can only live now. Mindfulness practice provides us with a technology to learn from our experience, develop self-acceptance, and move forward with openness and compassion one moment at a time.

7

Conflict in Recovery

MARIA WAS WORKING the drive-thru window at McDonald's when she heard a familiar voice ordering a Big Mac and fries. It was her cocaine dealer. Maria was currently coming to day treatment, had been clean for two weeks, and was feeling noticeably better. She was telling the story, which had ended in her using cocaine, to the group. This was her description:

"I got a knot in my stomach as soon as I heard his voice. I told myself, 'It's not worth it, look how far I've come. My family is finally happy with me, and I'll be a better mother to my kids.' Then he pulled up and I saw the bags on the seat. I said, 'What do you have?' and bought a thirty-dollar bag. Then I used all evening in the bathroom. . . . I hated myself afterward. I'm an idiot. You'd think I'd know better, growing up around a bunch of junk boxes. Now I could lose my kids."

Any slip in treatment is concerning, and Maria was understandably upset. In AA circles, SLIP is an acronym for "sobriety lost its priority." While this is clearly true in Maria's case, the news is not all bad. First, this is a new experience for her, relating her story to a community that she feels safe with, that she trusts will not judge her. Also, Maria's description reveals that she had been aware of her feelings and thoughts as the action unfolded. She regretted what she had done, but it was clear from her account that even as she made the "wrong" choice, she was using what she had learned in treatment.

Maria lost that one but was able to stop short of a full relapse and go forward. This had been a highly challenging episode, one in which harm's way suddenly presented, which does happen in the life of an addict but is also the type of trouble often avoided by planning or anticipating. She was also encouraged that with ongoing mindfulness practice, she might be able to manage such a trial more effectively.

Maria's experience in group was heartening to her and to others with similar problems. However, it also revealed that she has an inner conflict. Despite her best intentions, there is a part of her personality or an energy that still wants to use drugs.

Parts and the Addictive Process

It is a bit more complicated than a devil sitting on Maria's shoulder. Cocaine use strongly stimulates reward pathways in the brain that are easily triggered in situations where drugs are presented or even suggested. This is the classical conditioning demonstrated by the Russian physiologist Ivan Pavlov with his famous dogs. People, scenarios, songs, smells, and mental associations once associated with drug use can and will stimulate the desire for the drug. Also, Maria is a trauma survivor, growing up in an environment of poor boundaries, physical and sexual trauma, and rampant substance abuse. She would tend to be highly reactive generally and particularly in contexts that carry a sense of unsafety or emotional charge.

All patients in addiction treatment have their own complexities and peculiarities, strengths and obstacles. But they all have one thing in common: a part of them wants to be clean and a part wants to use. Generally, the part that is choosing physical and emotional health over addiction is stronger, but not always—especially in circumstances where the patient feels forced by his or her family, boss, or the legal system to be in treatment. Even in situations where the patient seems wholehearted in the wish to be sober, I feel it is important to have some familiarity with a part that has no interest in sobriety, organization, cooperation, or even sanity. And conversely, in treatments with a coercive component, we are invariably able to find a wish to be well and free of substance dependence.

We all have parts or selves, and the better we get to know and accept them, the less likely they are to blindside us and take over, much in the way Maria's "addict self" did. These parts all have something to say, and if we are willing to listen to them, much can be learned. Maria's part, for example, has the feel of a crisis worker that comes out in situations of emergency or danger. This was not an uncommon experience in her childhood, and when she found a partner (that is, this addict or rebel part) who helped her take refuge in alcohol and cocaine, she had it made.

Finally, here was an ally that took away all of the fear and confusion, that gave her a sense of power and obviated the need to seek help from other human beings. The addict self knows that drugs are reliable and people are not. Even in the face of contradictory information—for example, that drugs get Maria into trouble and do not work in the long run—this part sticks to its limited strategy. It is a protector of Maria's vulnerability and will not allow her to feel so frightened and alone ever again. This self likely evolved when Maria was quite young, thinks like a four- or five-year-old, and is furious and ruthless in its determination to prevent further hurt and pain. In the heat of the moment, she will act.

Energies like this can be worked with both in psychotherapy and with mindfulness practices, but it is critical to know they are there, that there are selves with conflicting ideas and agendas. As we discussed in chapter 3, one way we begin to engage addicts in the treatment and recovery process is to name the pluses and minuses of the addiction. I once asked a young man what was good about using cocaine. "Nothing," he said. "Not only do I not like cocaine, I don't even want to use it, and I do anyway."

Since as clinicians we are trying to help people stop using, I was glad he saw the futility in his behavior, but I persisted: "You seem like a smart guy. I suspect you got something out of it."

"Well," he considered, "at the beginning I had this soaring feeling like I was unstoppable. But that was only once. I guess I keep trying to recapture that feeling."

The value in this exchange is to suggest that what appear to be fruitless, even seemingly insane, pursuits like cocaine addiction actually have a point. They are about human beings trying to solve a problem around their anxiety, depression, energy, self-esteem, or sense of efficacy or importance.

Addictions are like any psychological defense, such as denial or rationalization—they both protect and limit us. Identifying both of these aspects is the beginning of framing the addict's conflict around how he or she wants to live. From the clinician's point of view, once there is a conflict, help is possible. If the patient is not at odds with himself, my tendency is to return to why he is coming.

As we saw in the previous chapter, the situation must get fairly dire before assistance is sought from the medical system. "What is bringing you?" With a little patience on both sides, we soon see that the addict has become confused as to how to proceed with his or her life, how to achieve goals, or why, despite good intentions, things always seem to go awry. That confusion is our entry point.

On inpatient units, I have seen staff lecturing patients about what they need to do in the future in order to succeed, for example, to go to AA meetings regularly. This often leads to either sullen agreement or a struggle, both resulting from the patient's feeling either patronized or misunderstood. Families and therapists also fall into the same trap. It is not our job to solve addicts' problems, tell them how to live, or turn them into good boys and girls.

Maria's addict-protector part, as we noted earlier, is motivated by danger and the need for safety. Drugs have been a vehicle for quelling the ongoing impulses toward fight or flight, but they also potentially get her into trouble with the authorities, the "protective services." Her conflict is effectively between safeguarding her living children versus her inner children. Using cocaine temporarily shields the frightened inner child but puts the custody of her actual kids at risk. While in treatment, Maria was committed to staying clean. Using drugs would only bring more suffering and jeopardize any chance she had for a satisfying life. The part that wanted to "be good" was winning until reality intruded.

It was not Maria's fault that cocaine was presented, though she does bear responsibility for buying it, albeit under duress. In other cases, the addict will consciously or unconsciously seek the drugs out or "find himself" in a vulnerable situation. These slips tend to be the result of some combination of stress, poor judgment, and going unconscious to the ongoing conflict around whether or not drugs really work.

Maria's treatment will require four components, which will be discussed in more detail in the upcoming chapters. She will need recovery, to be sober in order to think clearly and feel connected to a group of people who are getting well. Psychotherapy will be critical to disentangle the various agendas, energies, or parts operating in her psyche. She will need medicine to help stabilize her anxiety, reactivity, and moods. Mindfulness practice is the fourth aspect of her treatment, serving to allow her to live one moment at a time, to see when she is not doing so, and to support the effectiveness of the other components.

Mindfully Approaching Conflicting Energies

From the mindfulness perspective, Maria's conflict about whether to use drugs or not is happening in the present moment, regardless of her history and psychological issues. It is also occurring in the body. Maria felt a knot in her stomach, triggered by the voice of her dealer. She had some thoughts telling her not to use. Then she reacted, unable to bear what could be seen as either anxiety, a craving for the drug, or some combination. In the aftermath of using cocaine, she was thrown into a place of intense guilt, with a strong tendency to loop between her fear of losing her kids and her self-hatred for not knowing better, given all of her past experience.

We can see that this is not a particularly constructive place. We can hear in her "growing up around a bunch of junk boxes" the sadness and confusion of her lost and frightened child. However, these reverberations are only perpetuating the state of feeling alone and desperate, with the drug being the only answer.

Maria's task in the face of her craving and impulse to use is daunting but fairly simple, involving three steps:

- Get grounded.
- Feel both sides.
- Make a choice.

Let's look at what each entails.

Get Grounded

This is where every intention to feel the feet on the ground, the many ways the body makes contact, or the breath sensations pays off. Jon

Kabat-Zinn has likened developing the skill of mindfulness to weaving a parachute. You do not want to begin weaving it as you are about to jump out of the plane, he says, but if you do it a little bit each day, when you need it, it might actually hold you. The repeated returning to the present moment through the body will begin to develop a sense of stability and calm, fragile at first and more reliable with regular grounding practices like touch points, mindful walking, and the body scan. Then we have a platform of sorts, allowing us to weather the tension, anxiety, ambivalence, and pure impulse of a challenging situation like Maria's.

How does a basketball player shoot a crucial free throw in the closing seconds of a game with the crowd screaming and hundreds of arms waving in his face from behind the basket? A regular routine practiced for many hours in both quiet and noisy conditions is a foundation for the action. The player has two main preoccupations—one is focused on putting the ball into the hoop, and the other is on the fear of failure. Greater relaxation and balance, while not ensuring success, permits the player to focus more on the goal and less on the fear. The equilibrium gained from practice allows us to stand still in the eye of the storm.

Feel Both Sides

Having an embodied experience of alternatives is what the addict does not do, because he has no practice. The habit either to escape unpleasant or scary feelings or to be swept away by urge and impulse is strong. Mindfulness provides the means to feel the pull of the habit with acceptance and without judgment. Not easy but possible once there is some stability. Then the other side can be sensed as well, the part or energy that has no doubt that using drugs in this situation, however enticing, will not bring a positive outcome.

This is the moment of truth, the addict at a crossroads. She has achieved some steadiness of mind, but the experience is anything but stable, with elements of craving, aversion, agitation, restlessness, confusion. Stories are raging on both sides about why or why not to follow the old well-worn path to drug or alcohol use. These stories are a distraction from how it actually feels to use drugs, which in many cases do not deliver the promised relief and respite or do so for a very short time. Mindfulness practice increasingly develops the capacity to stay in the body, deemphasizing the stories and allowing the truth of the choice between slavery and freedom to manifest more fully.

Make a Choice

Once the addict has glimpsed the possibility of not relapsing and wasting energy, money, health, and so on, it is a different game. Many addicts begin to report, "I saw where it was going and chose not to use." They can then perceive both the benefit and the downside of *not* using, as well as using, which further develops their possible choices. As we noted in chapter 3, on one side are the positives of using and the minuses of not using, and on the other, the positives of not using and the negatives of using.

Once the choice has been made, there will be pluses and minuses to that. For example, if a woman chooses not to use, she will be pleased by her inner strength and life stability, but she also misses the chance to get high or escape painful feelings. Since the knee-jerk reaction to use drugs has happened so many times, with its benefits followed by regret and guilt, these outcomes can be compared. The exposure to and awareness of a range of choices and subsequent consequences will develop a firsthand knowledge of cause and effect. Then the addict is a much more informed participant in her own life and choices, which she makes not to be "good" but from the wisdom of her own experience.

I have often said to patients: "You are a lot more interesting than heroin [alcohol, cocaine, and so forth], but you just don't know it yet." In teaching mindfulness skills, our hope is that by actually feeling into these choices, life does indeed seem more engaging and challenging, far richer than the prison of the addiction. Once an addict is actually free not to relapse, that understanding will guide future actions. And if sobriety becomes more rewarding than addiction, the behaviors associated with recovery will be more frequently repeated.

Of course, the choices keep coming long after the addict leaves treatment. It may get easier over time to resist urges and choose sobriety. However, life continues to shift and change, and the mind is quite slippery. Addiction to a substance has conditioned the mind to pursue actions that lead away from peace and well-being. Once an addict is clean, these behaviors, however problematic, are still accessible given the right (or, more aptly, wrong) circumstances.

Routinely practicing the mindfulness skills from chapters 4 and 5 will begin to develop new habits of grounding oneself in the body and consciously reflecting upon the advantages of living one moment at a time. This sort of remembering, an essential aspect of mindfulness, will continually strengthen the habit of embodied awareness while weakening the older tendency to reflexively escape unwanted or painful experience. It also allows us to be softer and more forgiving when we make mistakes. As the practice progresses and refines, the conflict around drug use, while still present, becomes more workable and less of a threat to one's livelihood, family, and well-being.

8

The Path of Mindful Recovery

ROBERT IS A LEAN, intense man of thirty-four who looks much younger. He is just out of the hospital and comes into day treatment with the chief complaint of "I'm an alcoholic." Robert had been drinking a fifth of 100 proof vodka daily for longer than a year. Alcohol, he says, helps him to forget and numb out, giving him a cocoon-like experience that he enjoys. The downside of his alcohol use is that he cannot be honest with people and certainly is not in a position to have a relationship of any depth with a woman.

Robert lives in a basement apartment that his few friends call "the cave." He would go to his job at a deli, mainly keeping to himself until he could escape at the end of the day. His nature is to be clean and organized, but when he drinks he does not care about making his bed or taking a shower. Robert knows that if he stays sober, he will have a chance at the kind of life he would like to have, but when he does not drink he gets severe social anxiety, which he then invariably treats with alcohol.

He was admitted to the hospital intoxicated and thinking about suicide. This is not an uncommon story, the basic elements of which are (1) an overwhelming experience, (2) the use of a substance to medicate or escape from it, (3) continuing use despite clear evidence of an adverse outcome, and (4) a downward spiral. The cave metaphor is apt. Robert has gone deeper and deeper into himself to avoid his pain and in so doing compounds it with his growing desperation. Friends and family care about him, but he cannot reach them, which further adds to his discouragement and self-hatred. Suicide is an understandable option. What would it mean to recover from such a condition?

Recovery: The Hero's Journey

Recovery, in this context, is defined as a "return to normal, to a previous state of health, prosperity, equanimity; to get back something previously lost." It derives from the Old French *recoverer* and the Latin *recuperare,* meaning "to take back." This makes some sense if someone develops pneumonia or a gallbladder attack, gets appropriate medical or surgical treatment, and returns to some semblance of his or her prior health. However, in recovery from addiction, there may be no optimal condition to return to, only going forward on an unknown path to an uncertain destination.

This is much more akin to a personal journey or quest. The journey of the hero, as described by Joseph Campbell, comprises a departure following a call to adventure, an initiation along a road of trials, and a return. The hero must overcome numerous obstacles on the path to acquisition (of a magic elixir, for example), rescue, or self-knowledge, which can be used in service to the world.[1]

The story of the Buddha was such a quest. The young prince Siddhartha, sated with the enjoyments of music, drink, and women, was curious about other experience. As his eyes were opened—and he saw the old man, the sick man, the corpse, and the seeker—his father, the king, tried to multiply his son's pleasures in order to distract him from the goal of leaving the world as he knew it. Did the prince need to "recover"? Apparently he thought so. On his journey, he learned that only by fully opening to the impermanent nature of his body, feelings, and thoughts could he be happy. The Buddha's awakening was his recovery from self-created suffering.

The recovery movement and the birth of Alcoholics Anonymous are largely attributable to another hero, a man who was lost and sick and wanted to get well. Bill Wilson, a stockbroker from New York and an alcoholic, had been struggling to stay sober when he made a trip to Akron, Ohio, in 1935 on business. Knowing no one, he considered going to a bar and realized that he could abstain only with the help of another alcoholic. Through his research of church directories and the

Oxford Group, a forerunner of AA, he met Dr. Bob Smith, a surgeon and alcoholic of thirty years. Wilson had had a spiritual awakening, which he believed to be essential to recovery, and was able to help Dr. Smith to get sober. The two men founded AA on the basic principles of

- Acknowledging powerless in the face of addiction
- Opening to a power beyond oneself
- Admitting past mistakes with the help of a sponsor
- Making amends
- Living by a new set of principles
- Assisting others suffering with similar addictions or compulsions.

Recovery and Connection

Recovery is about being sober or not under the influence of a substance, but the story of Bill W. and Dr. Bob shows that it is much more than that. The essence of recovery is opening to one's own vulnerability or flaw and connecting with a similar vulnerability in fellow sufferers. William Alexander describes this in his book *Cool Water:* "Here was my core predicament. As active alcoholics, we suffer alone in a savage state of denial and rage. As recovering alcoholics we still suffer, just as everyone does, but we do so in the company of other alcoholics and thus participate in a mutual antidote to suffering. The fact of compassion is realized."[2]

Compassion, or feeling with, contains the qualities both of knowing the suffering of another firsthand and of wishing to relieve it. Addiction and recovery both begin with "selfishness," a wish to feel better and save oneself. Yet only through empathy and compassion can recovery be fully known and understood.

Beyond mere abstinence, recovery is about not being alone. This is easier said than done, since it goes to the paradox of being a human being. On the one hand, we clearly need each other. Infants in orphanages who are not held often fail to thrive. In aboriginal cultures, shunning is a punishment that can lead to death. In another sense, we are born alone, die alone, and are alone. Whether one believes in a divine being or not, the quality of recovery that gets people well appears to be a connection to something greater than themselves. This quality could be called *spiritual,* a reaching beyond oneself born of the wish to transcend the isolation and shame of addiction.

Robert's urge to isolate was strong, and the prospect of sitting in groups with a bunch of strangers was not something he looked forward to. The combination of low self-esteem, social anxiety, and depression was why he had withdrawn from loved ones. But he was desperate and saw that he had no alternative if he wanted to live. Robert walked through the door of the program because he was powerless over alcohol. Though he had not come to learn meditation, when I asked him to feel his feet on the ground, his butt in the chair, and a few breaths going into his belly, he was willing to do it. It did not hurt him, and he felt somehow more stable and in his body. When it was time to leave my office and join the group, I encouraged him to continue to ground himself as often as he could remember. This allowed him to sit there without having to flee or withdraw into himself. Robert was still besieged by anxiety, restlessness, cravings, and shame. It took a great deal of courage to sit there, but now he was part of something. And it was that experience of belonging that was the key to his early recovery. He was no longer alone.

Over time, Robert was able to speak up in the group, and he began to hang out with his peers in the program, who clearly liked him. He went to an AA meeting with another guy in our program and soon connected with a regular group. His social life was still largely limited to his family, but he was engaging with them in a new way. He also began having some fun with his coworkers and saw that they accepted him even though he had been distant for years. Robert was experiencing the pleasure of belonging, and it was not complicated. That is not to say that it was easy, but this positive chain of events toward recovery began with the simple act of directing his attention to his feet on the floor.

One Moment at a Time

AA has many slogans, but perhaps the best known is "one day at a time." This is simultaneously orienting and humbling, because whether you have been sober twenty years or drank yesterday, today is the only day you can actually choose to abstain or have an attitude conducive to recovery. Mindfulness is very much like this, just the microscopic version: one moment at a time. A day can seem quite long, but it is composed of many moments. Each one is different, and we can see that if we are able to stay with our sensory experience through the body. If we are in our heads, playing old tapes, the uniqueness of each moment is lost. Living through our stories from the past or projecting into the future, we are much more likely to lapse into negativity or a sense of victimhood.

Working with patients in early recovery, we hear a great deal about boredom. Weekends, for example, can be quite long, with no structure and the elimination of the time spent on drug acquisition, use, and sleeping it off. It tends to be lonely, and there is only so much TV you can watch and feel okay about it. So I ask, "What are you interested in; do you like to read?" Often the answers are "nothing" and "no." I might then inquire about what composes a day. You prepare and eat meals, clean up, take a shower, read the paper, do an errand, watch TV, listen to music. Might you take a walk, call someone to get together, go to a meeting? You cannot do all of those things, but you could choose a few. What if you practiced mindfulness, formally or informally?

One of our patients at the day program, Ralph, who was in the habit of waking up very early, began to do mindful walking. He felt the air on his skin and listened to the birds and the traffic. Ralph tends to be very tense and found this walking to be an excellent alternative to drinking five cups of coffee and smoking, which agitated him, created more anxiety, and caused his energy to crash later in the day. With regular practice, he found that the walking relaxed him, and he was seeing his life through different eyes. Once his attention settled into the present moment, there was a whole range of experiences he could be curious about.

Even boredom. Someone recently said to me, "I would rather be in hell than purgatory, because at least something is happening. I would rather be tortured than bored." Wow! Mindfulness practice would allow that person to take an interest in the experience of boredom, a mind state that is unpleasant but has more liveliness than we might think. We might have control over our place in the afterlife or we might not, depending on our religious beliefs. I personally do not know. But I do suspect I might wind up in a nursing home toward the end of this life, with less control than I have now. Wouldn't it be nice to be able to accept whatever happens as opposed to always struggling against it?

This is the spirit of the Serenity Prayer, one of the guiding principles of twelve-step recovery: "Grant me the serenity to accept the things I cannot change, the courage to change the things I can, and the wisdom to know the difference." Mindfulness, as we are defining it— *awareness of the mind-body process with acceptance*—is highly resonant with the Serenity Prayer. And mindfulness practice provides a means of making it real. Recovery and mindfulness are both new languages to the addict and require immersion if they are to be mastered. Ninety meetings in ninety days and noticing one's touch points are both ways of training in different ways to relate to the challenge of overcoming addictive habits and thinking.

I believe the prayer begins with "accept the things I cannot change" because that is a lot of life. Our species, gender, race, sexual orientation, country of origin, economic circumstances; the maturity of our parents, the safety of our surroundings; our genetics, our good or bad luck; the weather, compose a short list of things not in our power to change.

We also cannot control our thoughts and feelings. We can control our attention, our actions, and to some degree, our attitude, which does tend to produce better results, relationships, and even luck. Wisdom comes from clearly seeing life just as it is, choosing to act or not, bringing forth our best energy and efforts, accepting and learning from the outcome.

And if you slip? (Or I should say, "when you slip," because despite our best intentions, old habits die hard.) Just come back as quickly as possible. Slips happen. True, your sobriety date changes, and that is something you cannot control, along with any stories, judgments, or feelings that follow. You *can* control where you next direct your attention and energies.

Recovery is forgiving. The practices from chapters 4 and 5 give us the ability to actualize that forgiveness via the development of concentration, mindfulness, and loving-kindness. Mere abstinence from substances and addictive behaviors is not recovery. However, the willingness to be kind to ourselves with all of our imperfections, honoring our best efforts to heal, most certainly is.

Is Recovery Spiritual?

I hesitated a long time before beginning to address this issue because there are many more questions than answers. For proponents of the recovery systems SMART Recovery and Rational Recovery the answer would be no to the question, Is there a spiritual element to recovery? From these perspectives, recovery is not about a "higher power" but about learning skills to take charge of one's situation. Most would agree that spirituality and religion, or belief in a divine energy, are not the same thing, but the experience of spirit is so personal that it cannot be simply captured.

Spirit can be seen as a life force within each of us. The word derives from the Latin *spiritus,* or breath. The Greek *pneuma* and the Hebrew *ruach* have similar connotations of a vital force of divine origin. Breath is life. Again, we take our first breath upon exiting the womb and our last when we die; in between is our life. But where did it come from? Look around. Where did all of this come from?

I once drove to work and parked my car, as I do almost every weekday. It was late October and there was a chill in the air as I opened the door. The sunlight filtered through the brown and yellow leaves beyond the fence in front of my car. In that moment, I experienced the change of seasons, the coming winter, the ongoing flow of life and time. How is it that this planet is in just the right position in relation to a star to support life? I felt a sense of awe, connection, and joy and walked into my job imbued with the power and privilege of simply being able to walk on this earth.

Is that spiritual? Can we bring this quality of awareness into the mundane as we drive our cars, walk the dog, wash the dishes, eat, speak to our kids or coworkers or the boy at the checkout counter? This is a question for recovery from addiction as well as for mindfulness practice. Are we able to look beyond ourselves and live in a way that honors our existence and its relationship to all of life?

In her poem "Wild Geese," Mary Oliver expresses both the deep yearning to connect to something greater than ourselves and the truth that we are already part of this greater reality if we could only wake up.

You do not have to be good.
You do not have to walk on your knees
for a hundred miles through the desert, repenting.
You only have to let the soft animal of your body
     love what it loves.
Tell me about despair, yours, and I will tell you mine.
Meanwhile the world goes on.
Meanwhile the sun and the clear pebbles of the rain
are moving across the landscapes,
over the prairies and the deep trees,
the mountains and the rivers.
Meanwhile the wild geese, high in the clean blue air,
are heading home again.
Whoever you are, no matter how lonely,
the world offers itself to your imagination,
calls to you like the wild geese, harsh and exciting—
over and over announcing your place
in the family of things.[3]

Recovery from addiction is about so much more than being good. In fact, the attempt to live up to some eternal standard of righteousness ultimately produces its opposite. Often people who present for treatment are exhausted from trying to be responsible for too much and too many. They have lost touch with their essential nature, their life force. You might think that "the soft animal of your body" loves heroin or alcohol, but that is not what Mary Oliver means. She is speaking of our connecting, to this marvelous world we live in, through the body and in so doing experiencing our bond with all bodies. This is the source of healing, of compassion, of recovery.

We will learn more about what causes Robert to hide later on, but from a pure recovery perspective it does not matter. What is critical at this point is that he admit he is an alcoholic, join other addicts, and abide in their simple acceptance of him. You can call the magic that ensues a higher power, God, community, universality, spirituality, or whatever helps you understand it. Essentially, it is about finding a home for the part of us that is defective, dangerous, shameful, or self-destructive. Many people come into treatment and say, "I don't like groups," and once those same people are feeling better, they do not want to leave. Why? Because in this flawed, imperfect, but loving community, they sense their lifeline.

This is the paradox. The very thing that could heal us, that makes us who we uniquely are, is what we hide and hide from. An adolescent girl spends hours in the mirror scrutinizing her face and picking on her skin. Each effort toward perfection creates more problems, leading to more picking. This is then exacerbated by the wasted time, the self-blame, the desperation and shame, fueling a vicious cycle. The results are of course terrible, but once the skin recovers from that episode, more blemishes will appear. And the girl does not realize that the blemishes she really wants to hide are the inner ones. Whether we pick on our face or our fingernails, get lost on the Internet, shoot heroin, or escape from the world as Robert did, we are unconsciously exacerbating our problem by trying to hide it. In the throes of addiction, we deeply want to heal, but we are not thinking clearly.

The addiction is the wound that heals. Recovery is about the acknowledgment of the wound in community and the gifts of empathy and compassion that result. Mindfulness provides a set of skillful means toward seeing how we continually re-create our dilemma so that we can finally accept and come to terms with it. The criminal returns to the scene of the crime. Our conflict is that we play hide-and-seek with ourselves, not realizing that embracing our wound is the greatest gift we could give or receive. The poet David Whyte has compared our perceived failings to the flaws in marble that give it its beauty.[4] In a similar spirit, William Alexander wrote, "In a wonderful, paradoxical way, the gift of addiction is the possibility to walk the path of freedom from addiction. If I were not an addict, I would not be free."[5]

We must understand a problem before we can solve it, and with practice we see how mindfulness can illuminate the processes of both addiction and recovery. Many patients do beautifully in day treatment, only to relapse and return for another round. Invariably, it is because, despite their best efforts, they were unable to see and fully surrender to some aspect of their wound, whether it be fear, shame, or grief. It is a long journey, and recovery is the road, not a destination. There will be victory and defeat, pleasure and pain, gain and loss, praise and blame. The question for both recovery and mindfulness practice is: can we embrace it all?

A Visit to an AA Meeting

It is snowing so hard that I cannot get out of my driveway until the plowman comes at about 10 A.M. He has been up all night, and I walk outside to thank him. Today is the day I had planned to go to an AA meeting at noon not far from my work. Though anyone is welcome, I had not been to a meeting for many years. This is self-help not treatment, and as a professional, I have always found AA meetings to be a very different and inspiring window into the recovery process. Only one patient has shown up to our program, so my schedule is free, but is the meeting going to happen in this weather? I decide to find out; at least I will locate the church and where to park.

The door is open. There are five or six guys sitting at the back of the social hall and an older woman at a table about thirty feet away with some chairs set up in front of her. The coffee is on a side table to our right. It is exactly noon. "I'm Johnny," a man in his late sixties says as he extends his hand to me.

"Larry," I say.

"Welcome, I'm Dick," and we shake hands as well.

"You guys are serious to make it over here; do you live far?" I ask.

"Not too bad," Johnny says, "and I hear the barrooms are open today."

Dick adds, "I drank every day of my life before I came to AA."

Enough said. I later learned that Johnny had arrived early and had shoveled nearly two feet of snow to make a path to the door. And he is almost twenty-seven years sober. Serious indeed.

Anna opens the meeting. They generally get about twenty-five people, and today we number eight. After a prayer, she tells her story. People here know each other well, and they likely have heard much of this, but they listen respectfully. Anna is an old-timer, thirty-four years sober. "We [her family] came over here from South Boston," she told us. "They didn't like us at first, but if they fooled with us," she balled up her fist, "we'd give them one right in the snot locker." Her story is rambling, funny, and full of pain. The raging alcoholic father. The husband who drank and would not admit he had a problem. Five kids, two now dead. Anna went to Al-Anon, finally acknowledged her own problem, and got help. No matter how far she had to walk or bike to a meeting, she was always able to get a ride home. Anna's community got her well. Her husband also stopped drinking, and they are still together.

This is a discussion meeting, so a number of people speak, expressing appreciation for each other, the fellowship, and their sobriety. They also have a lot of heartache. Carl's son is in prison and on a number of psychiatric medicines. "I told him," he says, "if the other guys find out you are on Klonopin and Seroquel, they are going to want some of that, and besides, you don't need all that goddamn medicine. These fuckin' psychiatrists don't know what the fuck they are doing."

Donny is sitting toward the front, by himself. He looks down the whole time he is speaking. About thirty years old, he is married, with kids, and works at a supermarket. He hates his wife and is using drugs, and they are trapped in a cycle of rage and desperation. "Thank God I can come here. This is the only place I can talk like this and people respect me. But I am going to use heroin today. I don't know what else to do."

There is silence for a while, but then people are kind, encouraging Donny that he can get through this without using.

It is now about 12:40, and since only one other person beside me has not spoken, I raise my hand. "I'm Larry. I am not an alcoholic. Actually, I am one of those fucking psychiatrists that Carl was talking about." A few smiles. I told them that I worked right up the hill where the old Choate Hospital used to be, likely the first dual-diagnosis unit in the Boston area. A few of the guys had first gotten sober there and had also attended an AA meeting on the unit called the "Awareness Group" for both the patients and the public, available 365 days a year. Since I worked there just before the hospital closed, it was nice to imagine that some of us had been together at that meeting fifteen years before.

The meeting closed with the Lord's Prayer. We said our goodbyes, and I expressed appreciation for the warm welcome as well as their efforts to keep the fires burning on such a cold day. I told Carl that he was right. Psychiatrists that do not understand addiction *are* overmedicating people in the frantic attempt to treat symptoms, some of which are related to intoxication and withdrawal. And I acknowledged that being a parent is the toughest job.

Just before leaving, I approached Donny and thanked him for his efforts to show up and get some support. He was really low, but I felt some connection and openness. I told him that as good as meetings can be, they probably were not enough for him now. I spoke about our program, and he took a card. "Yeah," he said, "my friend has been there and suggested that I call." I hope he will.

Anna had walked down the hill to the meeting, and I had the privilege of driving her home. She appreciated my coming and adding a perspective they hear infrequently. "Thanks," I said, "the honor was all mine."

9

Mindfulness, Addiction, and Psychotherapy

IMAGINE THE OCEAN with countless waves, each one unique, representing the myriad manifestations of living and nonliving matter on the planet. To our eyes, our individual wave is distinct from the others, as we appear separate from all other beings and formations. This is an illusion but a stubborn one to our concrete, linear minds.

Substance use starts as an attempt to break down these perceived barriers, to connect with something greater than our worldly experience. This may be why alcoholic beverages are called "spirits." We do successfully alter our consciousness, but as we have seen over and over, it does not work for long, and the addict winds up feeling more alone than ever. Recovery is the process of seeing that our little wave, however isolated and in distress, is actually part of the ocean.

Psychotherapy, like recovery, also begins with suffering but emphasizes looking more closely at our single wave: how it is operating in relation to the other waves and how it came to be the way it is right now. We are each born with a distinctive genetic endowment and grow up in a context with our own experiences. Even identical twins may have slightly different talents and tendencies; parental, sibling, and peer connections; good and bad fortune. The overriding task of psychotherapy is to engage in a process with a skilled practitioner that leads to greater awareness of what is not working, how this came about, your strengths and difficulties, your conflicts, your trauma, your grief, and how you are taking responsibility for this state of affairs, or not.

Recovery is mostly about our connection to the ocean, and while psychotherapy emphasizes our own particular wave, they fit together like yin and yang. Each recovery is one of a kind, as the addict seeks his or her own path with its own particular trials. Recovery is also a highly creative process, much like each singer finding his own style or each golfer her own swing. Psychotherapy is also about path, how our individual wave interfaces with the ocean, a wondrous but scary place.

A complete discussion of the range of psychotherapies and their relationship to mindfulness is beyond the scope of this book.[1] Here we will consider just four common forms of treatment encountered by recovering addicts—psychodynamic psychotherapy, cognitive-behavioral therapy, group approaches, and parts work—along with possible applications and associations to mindfulness practice.

Psychodynamic Psychotherapy

One of my early teachers was Norman Zinberg, a psychoanalyst and pioneering addiction psychiatrist. Dr. Zinberg said two things about treatment that I continue to find helpful:

- Psychotherapy is the study of self-deceit and its motivations.
- You meet the patient where he is and take him where he does not want to go.

An early goal of psychodynamic psychotherapy is to learn about how the patient is operating and how his behavior has become problematic or gone awry. What were the childhood antecedents, how did the person adapt to them, and how does the outcome make sense? After the evaluation, the therapist might say something like, "Given your circumstances and constitution, becoming a heroin addict was an understandable course of action for you." Once the patient feels seen and known, it is then possible to explore the territory with more safety.

Let us again return to Robert. He had grown up on an army base, where he recalled feeling happy in his family. However, when he was twelve, his brother, then eighteen, was killed in an auto accident. At that point, "everything broke apart." Robert's parents stopped sleeping in the same room, rarely ate together, and never talked. His mother decided to get a job, and he was often alone after school. Robert was shy by temperament, but he began to experience much anxiety. Within a couple of years, he found that alcohol calmed him down, and he regularly self-medicated, finally acknowledging that he had a problem in his late twenties.

Robert finally left home at twenty-eight and got married at thirty-two, but he was unable to stay sober, and the marriage ended soon after. Robert's introverted tendency was accentuated by his family trauma. Alcohol served both to protect him from his anxiety and grief and to temporarily distract him from his inner sense of lifelessness. Things were not going in the right direction.

The evaluation helped elucidate how Robert had gotten to his current situation, which allowed him to feel understood. He also began to develop a narrative that organized his experience in a new way. Robert was still at sea but now had more of a sense of his coordinates. He saw that through hiding and drinking, he had been getting more lost—ironically, to manage the fear of how lost he already was. This was the addiction. He could still choose to drift as he had been, but now that he was more oriented, he saw that he had other options.

Robert now had a greater appreciation of his life trajectory as well as a certain understanding of the lawfulness of how it had unfolded. True, he and his family were victims of his brother's untimely death, but he also knew that these kinds of things happen, and not only to him. The question now was how to take responsibility for an incident he did not create and the cascade of events that followed. Telling a good story of how we came to be in a certain predicament can help, but it also has limitations. Sometimes it makes our course clear, but often not. Again, what does Robert do now to be response-able to his situation?

Mindfulness training was extremely helpful here as an adjunct to Robert's new understanding. He experienced (only a partial list) anxiety, depression, agitation, restlessness, racing thoughts, lethargy, cravings, urges to drink and to isolate. As these arose, they would spawn stories and judgments about himself and others, leading to greater irritation, more insistent urges, and yet more stories. It was overwhelming and clarifying at the same time. This complex of experience and stories was what fed the addiction, the gasoline on the fire. Alcohol would douse it momentarily only to cause it to roar higher. Mindfulness puts stones around the fire. It will not go out immediately, but it is contained and will eventually subside.

Robert was able to see this in his own experience. He started by noticing his breathing and touch points to ground and distract himself from cravings and racing thoughts. He could observe the urge to isolate as a palpable event in his body but was still free to choose to go to an AA meeting, which he often did. Then he might notice anxiety or dread as he entered the room, self-consciousness as he found his seat, thoughts about other people, and ideas of how they saw him. Whether these moments were unpleasant, pleasant, or neutral, they were all transitory.

Robert's mood began to improve. It is impossible to know how much of that was related to medication, to his newfound connections, and to his greater understanding of himself, but mindfulness was a critical accompaniment. Robert was now able to be *aware of his current mind-body experience with acceptance,* saving him a great deal of the energy he had previously spent fighting with himself. Cravings, sadness, anger, and confusion were not as much of a problem.

Alcohol had been a refuge for him, and he did miss drinking. He did not miss "being in a cave" as much, since he was having so many good experiences, but that tendency was still there. He allowed more light into his apartment and more fear, sadness, and regret to be present without having to run away. Consequently, he was also able to tolerate joy and became more social and even playful.

Some might argue that good psychoanalytically oriented treatment ought to be about the body and the integration of emotions experienced in the present moment with the patient's narrative. This does happen, but often psychodynamic therapy focuses heavily on the story line and fosters dependence on the therapist for support and insight. Mindfulness training is a wonderful accompaniment to this work, giving patients real skills they can use to become more self-reliant.

Therapists who meditate can use their own practices to feel more embodied themselves. They are then better attuned to moment-to-moment changes in the patient's mood states or subtle changes in the linkage between them. Not only does this enliven the interaction but their energetic connection is transferable to the patient's life and relationships outside the therapy.

Cognitive-Behavioral Therapy

Psychodynamic therapy focuses on the deep origins of the patient's problem, often in the past. It is relatively unstructured and open-ended. Behavior therapy has much clearer methods and goals. The debate of whether it is more effective to approach psychological problems via root causes versus concrete behaviors and symptoms has raged since early in the twentieth century.

Aaron Beck was trained as a psychoanalyst in the 1950s. Early on in his career, Dr. Beck set out to prove Freud's theory that depression originated from anger turned against the self, essentially a masochistic impulse. While this idea certainly has some legitimacy, Beck's research uncovered something else. Employing free association, a staple of the psychoanalytic method, he found that the thought streams of depressed patients showed a pattern of negative beliefs about themselves, their capacities, and the future.[2] In other words, mood followed thought.

As you might imagine, this was not well received in psychoanalytic circles. Beck's application to the American Psychoanalytic Institute was rejected on the grounds that his mere desire to conduct scientific studies signaled that he'd been improperly analyzed.[3] He was essentially excommunicated from the psychoanalytic community, many of whom regarded his work as "superficial." However, he continued to test his findings through many studies, continuing to the present day. In response to his critics, Beck later said, "There is more to the surface than meets the eye." He persisted in the face of derision, doubt, and isolation and, in my view, is a hero, as was Freud before him.

This was the beginning of cognitive therapy, which followed on the heels of rational-emotive therapy developed by Albert Ellis. These systems posit that our emotional and behavioral difficulties, such as depression, anxiety, perfectionism, procrastination, and addiction, are largely caused by our self-defeating beliefs.

Depression, for example, is fueled by negative thoughts about the self, the world, and one's prospects. We fear mistakes, failure, rejection, conflict, our emotions. In reaction to those fears, we engage in mind reading, negative prediction, perfectionism, and other methods to protect ourselves from the truth. These strategies, if practiced regularly, can become thinking addictions, which work very much like substances in their ability to shield us from our feelings, which then return with greater force and must then be pushed down repeatedly. As one of my colleagues has said, "We send our feelings down to the basement and they lift weights."[4]

In Robert's case, a catastrophic event *had* befallen his family. He had been a shy but happy boy in a "normal" family with an older brother he looked up to. Then, at the very beginning of his adolescence, he was suddenly an only child, emotionally abandoned by his distraught and overwhelmed parents, shocked, frightened, and alone. The world was no longer a safe place, and Robert received little validation of his experience or support to weather the trauma. So he went inside his own head.

As Robert struggled day-to-day, he fluctuated between feeling like a total victim and thinking he was the cause of his own problems, but since he could not control either what had happened or what his parents did, he blamed himself. This is what traumatized children do. He called himself "gutless . . . letting my parents down . . . ungrateful . . . a loser." He decided he did not "have what it takes" and would not "amount to anything." He asked himself why he didn't die instead of his brother, who had so much more potential. His self-hating thoughts colored his moods, which shifted among sadness, confusion, anger, and despair. This in turn caused him to avoid friendships and activities, further confirming his negative beliefs about himself and limiting his capacity for any constructive action.

The discovery of alcohol solved a number of problems. Most important, drinking was Robert's way to escape his self-hating thoughts, anger, and depression. It allowed him to function, particularly with peers, and have something to look forward to, simultaneously providing some relief, however short-term, and punishing him for his shortcomings. It was a slow suicide and, to his perceptions, about what he deserved; he was renting his life instead of owning it.

Robert's brief marriage totally exposed his fear of connecting with another human being in a relationship, a direct result of his abandoning himself. He had, in fact, been abandoned by his parents and was terrified of reexperiencing the pain of his childhood trauma. The subsequent retreat into his "cave" was simultaneously a means of protection and a manifestation of his deepening process of self-loathing—that's right, an addiction.

The cognitive approach with Robert reviewed his thinking, particularly about himself and how these thoughts were in large part creating his emotional troubles. It drew a direct line between his calling himself "hopeless . . . stupid . . . a loser" and his self-hatred, anger, self-pity, guilt, avoidance, and addiction. These beliefs, in a true cognitive therapy, would then be actively questioned and disputed, to be replaced, one hoped, with more positive or wholesome ones.

The *behavioral* component of cognitive-behavior therapy (CBT) would be to set up experiments in the real world, exposing the patient to the feared outcome—being rejected and abandoned, in Robert's case. The direct experience could then serve to challenge the negative thinking, which in turn might decrease the avoidant behavior, the negative feelings about oneself, and the vicious cycle of self-hatred. Robert was scared to enter the group, but once he did he was accepted and welcomed. When nothing bad happened, he allowed himself to trust and experience a sense of belonging, which began to question the certainty of his expectations of being deserted in his time of greatest need.

Robert's experiences with meditation and mindfulness training demonstrated that his thoughts were not as solid as he had believed. He came to see that the idea that he was "weak" or "worthless" was just an idea, not the truth. These thoughts were challenged by past experiences that demonstrated his strength or worth and by his current efforts to overcome his inertia. Other thoughts, such as "I am afraid of life," had a stronger element of truth. However, regardless of their validity, mindfulness practice sees thoughts as transitory phenomena, like passing cars or clouds moving across the sky. Thoughts can be labeled as "planning . . . worrying . . . mind reading," and so on but do not necessarily need to be confronted directly.

The CBT method of actively questioning and disputing irrational and self-defeating thoughts is now accompanied by another alternative: to just let thoughts simply go by. The mindfulness option has a number of benefits, including:

- Not being as effortful
- Cultivating the modes of allowing/being as opposed to confronting/doing
- Developing the ability to concentrate and stabilize the mind
- Accessing clearer seeing of the relationships between challenging emotions and thought patterns
- Developing an increased capacity to relax into the flow of experience, to accept and be less frightened by our thoughts

Purely cognitive methods can at times feel too much like an intellectual game. The incorporation of mindfulness skills with CBT principles provides the clinician and the patient with a range of tools in approaching problematic thinking without having to attack or dispute every distorted thought.

Group Approaches

Mindfulness-Based Cognitive Therapy

The integration of cognitive-behavior therapy and mindfulness has been achieved in a powerful method for the treatment of depression. Adapted from the mindfulness-based stress reduction (MBSR) program at the University of Massachusetts, mindfulness-based cognitive therapy (MBCT) works with patients in a group setting over an eight-week period. The group is taught formal meditation practices, including the body scan, mindful breathing, stretching, walking, and eating, as well as a range of exercises for the development of mindfulness in daily life. In the context of moment-to-moment awareness, the complex relationships between depressive thinking, the body, and the emotions are increasingly revealed. Mindfulness training cultivates the stability of mind necessary for seeing the self-judgment, worry, and regret that energize the process of depression, thought patterns that have become addictive and destructive.

Major depression, like addiction, is a chronic, relapsing disease, even following effective trials of medication. Clinical research has demonstrated that treatment with MBCT has cut the relapse rate in half for people who have experienced three or more episodes of depression. Psychologists Mark Williams, John Teasdale, and Zindel

Segal, the creators of MBCT, state that every time a person gets depressed, the connections in the brain between mood, thoughts, the body, and behavior get stronger, making it easier for the depression to be triggered again.[5]

Mindfulness training gives participants the tools to observe more closely and reverse this process, disentangling thought from emotion. Through embodied awareness, there is less attachment to the thinking process that promotes sinking into the quicksand of depression.

Mindfulness-Based Relapse Prevention

The points about the relationship between mindfulness and depression could be made about the disease of addiction, which also spirals down in a vicious cycle. Mindfulness-based relapse prevention (MBRP), a group program developed by Sarah Bowen, Neha Chawla, and Alan Marlatt at the University of Washington, is based on both MBSR and MBCT.[6] Participants learn about their tendency to be on "automatic pilot" and how this makes them vulnerable to cravings and urges. In this context, mindfulness practices begin to build some stability of attention, which allows the recognition of triggers in the form of thoughts, emotions, and body sensations.

By developing moment-to-moment awareness and mindfulness in daily life, group members learn to be more fully present to both routine and high-risk situations. They also learn to balance the wish to change problematic habits with an attitude of acceptance and self-care. MBRP explores the relationship between thoughts, images, urges, and feelings. Once participants see that these are all passing phenomena and not facts, they have greater freedom to choose between reacting in the old ways or living in greater balance.

Spiritual Self-schema Therapy

Spiritual self-schema therapy (3-S) is a spiritual strengthening program for drug addicts and HIV patients developed by Kelly Avants, Arthur Margolin, and colleagues at Yale University.[7] Based on Buddhist psychology, 3-S identifies the difference between the *addict self,* a habit pattern of the mind that causes suffering, and the *real self,* your spiritual nature.

The program is structured around a spiritual path consisting of ethical behavior, mastery of the mind, and wisdom. Through lecture, discussion, and meditation exercises, participants develop their "spiritual muscles," which include determination, effort, equanimity, loving-kindness, tolerance, wisdom, renunciation, generosity, and truth.

The intention to develop these qualities gradually strengthens the spiritual self and a sense of interconnectedness. It becomes clear that the addict self is not our true nature.

These mindfulness-based approaches also benefit from what the psychiatrist Irvin Yalom called the "curative factors" of group psychotherapy.[8] These include (not a complete list): instillation of hope, universality, altruism, interpersonal learning, imitative behavior, imparting of information, group cohesiveness, and existential factors. This last category turns out to be critically important in the sense that despite all of our intelligence and cleverness, there are many aspects of life that are ineffable and beyond our understanding. Yalom's existential factors are as follows:[9]

1. Recognizing that life is at times unfair and unjust
2. Recognizing that ultimately there is no escape from life's pain and from death
3. Recognizing that no matter how close I get to other people, I still face life alone
4. Facing the basic issues of life and death, thus living life more honestly, less caught up in trivialities
5. Learning that I must take ultimate responsibility for the way I live my life no matter how much guidance or support I get from others

The nature of addiction is to feel alone in the world and a victim of people, places, and things. Life and relationships are devalued and responsibility disowned. Group psychotherapy is a powerful modality for patients to experience their own value in connection to others. Yes, we are ultimately alone, but recovery is seeing that our little wave is part of the ocean, and group therapy is a laboratory for hanging out with other waves.

If one member has an issue with her mother or son, others also have problematic mothers and sons and are resonating. Still others *are* mothers and sons, and a number are both child and parent. In this mix is a rich potential for interpersonal learning, humor, and experiencing universality and empathy.

Mindfulness practice can provide the necessary distance from all of our story lines and judgments to begin to appreciate that life *is* unfair and the wisest choice is to be accountable for our lives. In group treatment, there are many examples of people taking responsibility or not, with instructive results in both cases. We are particularly interested in the ways people have used or might use mindfulness skills in a given situation. Awareness of breathing or touch points may not seem very impressive initially, but when you have twenty peers practicing and getting results, you might be encouraged to try it. The recovery, spiritual, and community aspects of both addiction treatment and mindfulness training are enhanced by group approaches.

Parts Work

It turns out that there is also a group of subpersonalities within us. In the course of clinical work and in common speech, I hear things like, "A part of me wants to use, and a part of me doesn't" or "I don't really trust him, but I want to." You could see this simply as the nature of conflict, but I find people to be quite comfortable with the idea that we have parts of ourselves. This is normal and not multiple personality disorder (now called dissociative identity disorder), a pathological condition in which the psyche fragments to protect the person from the effects of overwhelming trauma. (Note: I use the words *parts, selves,* and *energies* interchangeably.)

Parts work can be a natural extension of mindfulness practice by bringing psychological meaning to our feelings and experiences. Fear, for example, would be seen not merely as an emotion but as a *part* or *self* that is trying to protect or help us. Once we learn about and appreciate these energies, they tend to relax, much like a person who finally feels understood. And once we hold our parts with wisdom and kindness, the entire system can transform.

Here I will briefly consider two types of treatment, voice dialogue and internal family systems, which utilize parts or selves. These models have followed and been influenced by earlier work, including that of Freudian disciples Roberto Assagioli (psychosynthesis) and Carl Jung (complexes, archetypes), Fritz Perls (gestalt therapy), Helen and Jack Watkins and Claire Frederick (hypnosis and ego-state therapy).

The Voice Dialogue Method

Alison is an eighteen-year-old girl who came to day treatment following an opiate detoxification. She was not excited to come, but in fairly short order she thrived on the group support, took a real interest in mindfulness practice, and was not missing heroin. One Friday afternoon as she was about to leave, she stuck her head into my office and blurted out, "I am going to use!" I invited her in and heard her problem, which essentially was that without the support of the program on the weekend, she was at risk of losing what she had gained.

Alison had a part that wanted to use heroin and one that was trying to stay clean. Being a good girl was not going to work here. We needed to learn about both parts so that she could operate from a more grounded place.

The goal of the voice dialogue method, created by the psychologists Hal and Sidra Stone, is to develop what they call an "aware ego,"[10] which could be seen metaphorically as the captain of the ship, the chairman of the board, or the orchestra conductor. With the help of the facilitator/therapist, the aware ego gets to know each self, appreciating what each one does and has done to help the person to succeed and thrive. Selves carry different energies, and the aware ego's job is to hold the tension between opposite forces, like the ones destabilizing Alison, toward developing a more integrated response.

Once we got a sense of her opposites (use versus not using), Alison moved to another chair and we spoke to the addict self. (The changing of seats helps one perceive the different energies that selves are holding.) Alison is, the addict part indicated, quite tense and highstrung, which has significantly handicapped her socially. Alcohol and then opiates helped her to relax enough to have a peer group and a boyfriend, impossible goals if she were not using. There had been some violence in Alison's childhood, and she was frequently alone and scared. The part, which felt fragile and quite intellectual, had evolved in order to help her get some measure of calm and had a role model in her mother, who had abused Valium. There was some acknowledgment that heroin use was dangerous, but the self expressed the hope that Alison would eventually stop and go to college. I thanked the addict self for her efforts and input and asked Alison to move back to her original seat, which we now call the "place of the aware ego."

Alison moved over and remarked that she felt different, possibly more stable than where she had just been. She was impressed that the addict self was there to keep her safe and functioning. I asked her to switch to yet another chair to speak to the part that wanted to remain drug-free. This one felt much more solid and mature. The part reviewed what Alison had done over the past week and was clear in her determination to build on that work to have the successful life she now knew Alison could have. I asked her to comment on the addict self's point that she was a bundle of nerves who could never succeed without a drug to settle down. This self did acknowledge some concern but stated that she had learned some skills to ground herself, and this would only improve with practice. Besides, using heroin was clearly not a viable solution to the problem of anxiety. I thanked this self, and Alison returned to the aware-ego place.

At this point the voice dialogue subject is asked to notice the shift and the energies of the opposites in order to come to a more integrated view of their situation. However, Alison, immediately upon returning, looked to where the addict self had been sitting and said with some disgust, "Eww, I hate that." She eventually clarified that she did not hate the part—actually, she appreciated what it had done for her at an age when she could not protect herself. What she hated was the energy of the part. She vastly preferred the more solid energy of the one that was choosing sobriety.

This helped her to feel much more confident about the weekend. Over time, Alison's task will be to integrate the protective function of her addict self so that it does not simultaneously jeopardize her well-being. This would likely involve getting to know other selves, including her inner perfectionist, critic, and caretaker, which allowed her to survive her childhood but are now, to use a clinical term, driving her nuts. Heroin (the inner heroine?) provided her some relief from all the internal noise but is now hurting her as well. An aware-ego process that compassionately holds each pair of opposites will save Alison a lot of energy and money and allow her to make better decisions.

Internal Family Systems

Internal family systems (IFS) is another rich and innovative model, developed by Richard Schwartz, a psychologist and family therapist, who discovered, in the context of his clinical work, an internal family of subpersonalities.[11] Similar to voice dialogue, IFS holds the view of human systems as having the potential to be balanced, self-correcting, harmonious, and creative. IFS therapy helps parts to feel understood by what Schwartz calls *Self*, which is our essential nature—wise, intuitive, and loving. Self energy is characterized by the "8 C's"—calm, creativity, courage, compassion, clarity, curiosity, connectivity, and confidence. As frightened, hurt, and neglected parts feel seen and known, often for the first time, they naturally calm down and transform.

Ruth is a trauma survivor with three young sons and a marriage in crisis. She asked to meet with me because she was in a rage and alcohol seemed her only alternative for some relief. Grounding herself allowed Ruth to settle a bit. She was able to see her anger as a part and discovered that it began operating when she was quite young, giving her a sense of control in overwhelming circumstances.

A key question in IFS is: "How do you feel toward the part?" Ruth felt a real sense of appreciation for its role in helping her to feel powerful, safe, and able to move forward in her life. Once it felt heard, the angry part was willing to disengage, revealing a part it had been protecting that was quite anxious. This one helped Ruth understand how drinking had once been an effective strategy, the best she could do at the time. When the anxious energy was able to relax and move aside, we were able to glimpse another part that feels deeply sad and lost.

This one was not ready to speak but was willing to listen to some phrases—"May you be safe, may you be understood as you feel ready, may you be held in care and in compassion." Over the next week, Ruth continued to feel a connection with her parts and was more patient with her husband and kids (whom she noticed also have parts). She began to do regular loving-kindness practice, which further helped her to accept her current experience and circumstances.

10

Mindfulness and Medication

PSYCHIATRIC MEDICATIONS, like most drugs, are for symptom relief. They can be very helpful in the treatment of depression, anxiety, mood swings, racing thoughts, paranoia, hallucinations, and attentional disturbances. Medicines can ameliorate cravings for nicotine and alcohol and block the action of opiates on the brain. They can prevent seizures resulting from alcohol or sedative-hypnotic withdrawal (from Valium, Xanax, barbiturates) and the symptoms of opiate (heroin, Percoset, Oxycontin) withdrawal. That's about it. These medicines do not cure any of the above conditions, but they stabilize the brain chemistry sufficiently for people to feel more in control of their mind-body experience.

Major depression, for example, is a medical condition characterized by depressed mood and poor (or excessive) sleep and appetite and diminished energy, motivation, ability to concentrate, interest in usual activities, pleasure, and sexual interest. Other associated physical symptoms can be lethargy and various aches in muscles or joints directly related to depression or exacerbated by stress or the lack of normal movement.

These emotional and physical experiences (as we saw with Robert) also spawn a range of problematic mind states, including guilt, shame, self-hatred, irritability, hopelessness, and many others. The thoughts associated with this condition do not tend to be positive about oneself, others, or the world. This will worsen mood and well-being, creating a downward spiral. Many patients with depression have been helped with psychotherapy alone, but if they are being repeatedly destabilized by, or stuck in, negative thinking, medicine can help break the cycle. Medication is not the whole story in the treatment of depression or addiction/dual diagnosis, but it can be an important piece of the puzzle.

Medication and Recovery

As late as the mid-1980s, the relationship between psychiatry and the recovery movement was marked by ignorance, distrust, and disrespect from both sides. We have made considerable progress through modalities like dual-diagnosis treatment and the expansion of 12-step recovery to a number of psychiatric disorders. However, the use of psychoactive medicines in the context of early recovery remains a thorny issue.

Some of this tension lies in the relationship between addicts and doctors (I am including advanced practice nurses in this category), a relationship that always begins with an undertone of mutual mistrust. Addicts do not particularly like doctors and have often had experiences where they have felt disrespected or mistreated. The addict mind (or self) is interested in being self-sufficient and ingesting a drug (or performing a behavior) that brings immediate relief. This part of the personality is highly controlling, and outside help is seen as either nonexistent or threatening. The doctor mind has components of both knower and caretaker. Its goal is to keep the patient healthy, that is, sober and symptom-free. The doctor part of the personality means well, but it is a manager and thinks it knows best. What these doctor and addict parts have in common is the need for control and the fear of loss of control.

When the addict is desperate enough, he or she will agree to meet with the doctor. If there is a respectful exchange, the untrusting parts of both can relax enough so that these two human beings can learn about the problem and decide on a course of action. Both want to like the other and do something in the patient's best interest. Since the addict wants relief and the doctor has a prescription pad, it is likely that part of their deal will involve a pill. Whether this is a problem or not is a matter of perspective.

The recovery viewpoint is concerned with the various manipulations on both sides that I just described, resulting in the addict's being medicated. This is particularly worrisome because experienced members of AA know that addicts (themselves included) are predisposed to look for a quick fix to avoid difficult emotions and the hard work ahead. They fear that under stress it will be far too easy to depend upon medicine and move increasingly toward self-medication and relapse. The goal of recovery is self-determination. While taking medicine may serve that end, it also raises fears of the addict's being some combination of weak, lazy, manipulative, or merely compliant— characteristics not resonant with a true recovery.

Doctors and patients with dual disorders might counter that these 12-steppers, however well-meaning, are not clinicians and ought to mind their own business. This perspective would contend that patients with psychiatric illnesses, including schizophrenia, mood and anxiety disorders, and attention-deficit/hyperactivity disorder, require pharmacological intervention as part of their recovery. Without it they are literally "not thinking straight" and are much more vulnerable to destabilization and relapse.

Both have a point. Here is a list of questions to assess for yourself whether it is a good idea to take medicine, regardless of the doctor's evaluation or recommendations:

- Do I believe that I have a dual disorder?
- Are the symptoms (depression, mood swings, anxiety, racing thoughts, paranoia) related to a psychiatric illness or caused by the addiction?
- Does the medicine, desired or prescribed, have any potential for abuse or physical dependence?
- Am I developing skills for well-being not related to medicine, including healthy relationships, diet, adequate rest, exercise, recovery, therapy, and/or mindfulness training?
- Am I taking the medicine as an insurance policy instead of facing my fears and utilizing my resources?

This assessment will require honesty, collaboration, and the willingness to follow the symptoms carefully over time whether or not medicine was initially prescribed. It will involve an ongoing evaluation of the addict's *autonomy,* which comprises the capacities for self-reliance as well as for seeking help when needed. Then there is a foundation for real cooperation, where both doctor and patient respect both their own and the other's agenda and work toward the best possible outcome.

The place of medication, who is in recovery, and who is not is in a continuing evolution, and opinions can still vary from one 12-step meeting to another. There was a time less than thirty years ago when the old-timers felt that drug addicts did not belong at AA meetings. As the baby boomers became more of a presence, this changed, as many of them drank *and* used drugs. Alcoholics and drug addicts clearly were not different species.

Patients on methadone maintenance were not welcome at Narcotics Anonymous meetings, the contention being that they were hooked on a drug and therefore not in recovery. Recovery has always been about the willingness to surrender control to a higher power or to a community of fellow sufferers toward a state of greater well-being. Many methadone patients meet one or both of those criteria and many do not. The same is true of addicts using buprenorphine (a combined opiate agonist-antagonist), tranquilizers, stimulants, antidepressants, or any class of drugs. Whether the drug is "abusable" may or may not be the issue.

Only the addict can really know. As we have seen, recovery is a long, uncertain road, and medication is one potential tool toward greater clarity of thought and stability of mood. Whether a medicine is indicated and necessary should be decided by the patient's best judgment at the time and ought to include conversations with family, friends in recovery, and medical professionals. Then it is all a moving target as the parameters of symptoms, clinical effects of the drug(s), side effects, and capacities to handle life's challenges change over time. The decision whether to maintain or discontinue a drug is no different from any other important decision. And we will see how mindfulness can be an effective tool toward that end.

Medication and Mindfulness

Trudy Goodman, a longtime meditation teacher and therapist, once told me a story from a time when she was working at the Massachusetts Mental Health Center in Boston. Once, in the middle of a day in the 1970s, an announcement came over the public address system that in ten minutes there would be a talk on the subject of psychotherapy and meditation. Trudy was thrilled, dropped everything, and ran over there as fast as she could to hear the presentation—which turned out to be "Psychotherapy and Medication." Oh, well, the PA announcer was a bit ahead of his time.

The two words are close, and their Latin roots are related. *Medicari* and *mederi* mean "to heal or cure." *Meditari* is defined as "keep on measuring" or "to think, to dwell upon, to exercise the mind," but is also related to *mederi*. Meditation is a training ground for mindfulness, the *awareness of present experience with acceptance.* Since each moment is unique, we must continue to "keep on measuring" if we are to stay current as our experience unfolds. And this ongoing measuring or assessing of the distinctive qualities of each moment has great healing potential.

How does that work? The Buddha famously said, "I teach one thing and one thing only—suffering and the end of suffering." By perceiving the true sources of our misery—holding on to, pushing away from, or dissociating from our experience—we have an opportunity to see into its causes, which we are then in a position to uproot. The Buddha was also known as "the great physician" because of his mastery of these toxins of the mind and teaching meditation as a path to emotional and spiritual well-being. Mindfulness training is available to all of us and can play a vital role in the treatment of addiction and dual disorders. However, for many conditions, medicine will be a consideration if troubling symptoms do not improve.

We alluded to this issue earlier in the discussion of medication and recovery: in addiction treatment, there will always be tension between accepting experience versus trying to change it. Let us not forget that our goal is personal authority, and that means an ongoing assessment of whether to be self-reliant or to ask for help. Around the decision of whether to have a psychopharmacology evaluation, psychotherapists can help assess whether the nonmedical modalities are sufficient or if progress would be facilitated by the use of medicine.

The journey of recovery has many uncertain twists and turns. A step is taken that produces a result we like or not. So it is with the use of medicine in dual diagnosis treatment. I will now discuss a variety of conditions where patients and clinicians have seen the synergistic benefits of medication and mindfulness.

Mood Disturbances: A Case of Bipolar Disorder

Consider for a moment the challenges of your own life, including the realms of relationships, work, finances, health, running a home, and so on. You may have noticed that although many of these parameters can go well for even extended periods, there is always some element of flux and an element of instability or low-level anxiety about what is to come. Now, imagine all of this change, pressure, and uncertainty are happening and you are on a perpetual roller coaster and you never quite know what your mood or energy is going to be like from day to day.

Effectively, you are two different people—one who is pumped or jazzed up and another who is depleted and shut down. And this state of affairs seems normal to you and those around you. That is bipolar disorder, or what was known for many years as manic-depression. The diagnosis is made by a history of high and low moods along with other corroborating factors. Patients are often upset to learn that they may have this condition, but mood swings are increasingly well treated with medication.

Unfortunately, it can take years for this problem to come to clinical attention, and by then a lot of damage can be done. I see an impressive number of undiagnosed bipolar patients in addiction treatment because, in many cases, it was ignored or rationalized early on and then self-medicated later. The high, while not always pleasant, is a wave or burst of energy, during which tasks are accomplished (or not) or the person is highly social and impulsive. The lows are miserable, characterized by isolation and irritability; they generally last longer than the highs and are avoided as much as possible, often with substances, which is why the person is talking to me.

Keith came to day treatment following an opiate detox and a stay in residential treatment. He was an extremely bright, appealing guy of thirty, but at this point he needed an enormous amount of structure to stay clean. (The day after he left the residence, his girlfriend caught him with some needles and a bag of heroin, and she was clear he had to stop using or move out.) Keith had experimented with a number of drugs when he was a teenager and particularly liked the euphoria he got from ecstasy. However, he began having panic attacks at the age of twenty, when he first sought treatment. The tranquilizer alprazolam (Xanax) helped somewhat, but antidepressants left him more anxious, nervous, and unstable. This is often a clue to the presence of bipolar disorder, but either it was missed or, more likely, Keith gave up on treatment.

Instead, he began to use opiates and cocaine, depending upon how he was feeling at the time. When his mood was elevated, Keith felt highly energized and "things were clicking." He would get onto organizational or cleaning projects, do massive Internet searches for new job possibilities, or participate in long and vigorous exercise. He could be extremely reckless, particularly driving too fast and having sex impulsively, both of which created enormous havoc in his life. During these periods, Keith slept and ate very little and spent money excessively. These highs lasted a few hours to a day and occurred about once a week. When they ended, he would crash into a low-energy state for several days and sleep, isolate, and watch TV.

Keith was a good example of Khantzian's self-medication hypothesis, which was noted in chapter 1, in that he used stimulants to counteract depression and opiates for anger and irritability. Although he did not know he had bipolar disorder, Keith could feel the crash coming and used cocaine and caffeine to keep his highs going. Eventually, he saw that this was a losing battle and turned to heroin, like a middle-aged man trading his Porsche in for a Mercedes. Then the addiction had a life of its own and to a large extent masked the mood and energy shifts.

Clearly more enthusiastic about mindfulness than he was about the diagnosis of bipolar disorder, Keith initially did not want to take medicine. As he did the grounding and breathing practices, he was more able to focus on one thing at a time. He also began to perceive dramatic energetic shifts, like the August afternoon he felt juiced up and ran fifteen miles and lifted weights, knowing much of the time that he was overdoing it but unable to stop himself.

Once Keith agreed to take medicine, lithium in his case, his moods were less dramatic. Like most big changes, this one had pros and cons. Keith definitely missed the highs but also saw the advantages of a more moderate path. He was more organized and in control and felt more consistently well and rested. Instead of perpetually skiing the double diamonds, he was now on the bunny hill, which was less exhilarating but much more workable in a complex life.

Whether to take medicine is always a choice, also with pluses and minuses on both sides. By taking lithium, Keith had to admit he had an illness that needed treatment, a bitter pill (pun intended) to swallow. He had to give up the excitement of the highs and the experience of being on a roll that he loved. On the other hand, he now actually had a chance to feel a greater sense of stability, a platform off which to act and make decisions, beginning his path to adulthood.

Also, he was much less anxious. You can imagine that if you never know what your mood and energy are going to be, you will frequently be uncertain, get lost, and let people down. All of this uncertainty creates substantial anxiety and tension. Treatment-resistant anxiety, a significant feature of Keith's presentation, can be another pointer to the diagnosis of bipolar disorder.

Mindfulness helped Keith accept his need for medication, which in turn allowed him to see more clearly. He was particularly drawn to grounding and movement practices. If he felt irritable, he was encouraged to leave the group and do walking meditation at a speed that felt right at the time, then return when he felt more able to sit. This fit well with Keith's exercise routine, which is so important in early recovery as a means to become more grounded in the body. Most people have to be encouraged to incorporate exercise into their regimen. Keith needed to listen to his body to learn when enough was enough.

Once he was able to sit still, Keith found both group and AA (which he preferred to Narcotics or Cocaine Anonymous) meetings supportive and inspiring. He used his touch points and breathing to stay present and was, for the first time, able to take an interest in what other people were saying. Of course, he began to hear himself in their stories, which strengthened both his recovery and his interest in doing further psychotherapy after he left the program.

When his girlfriend went on vacation, he experienced some strong cravings to use heroin as well as disappointment that he was not going with her. Keith's new skills made it easier to ride through his urges and feelings and ultimately accept them as part of his recovery process. He appreciated the challenge of working with these experiences, finding them more interesting than merely gratifying the craving or escaping.

While his girlfriend was away, Keith saw how deceived and disappointed by him she must have felt for a long time. This helped him to accept his probationary status, which, upon her return, she found validating and encouraging.

Thought Disorders

When any of us becomes destabilized emotionally, we lose our capacity to be dispassionate about what we think and believe. Far from being able to watch our thoughts, like ripples in a stream, we are more likely to be swept down the stream. This is particularly true for patients who are actively psychotic, not even in the ballpark of reality as most of us know it, let alone the game. People with these symptoms require medicine to limit the racing thoughts, loose associations, paranoia, and hallucinations associated with schizophrenia and other psychotic illnesses.

Some of the newer "atypical" antipsychotic drugs can also treat the so-called negative symptoms of schizophrenia, including apathy, depression, social withdrawal, and poverty of both speech and thought content. These antipsychotic medications or neuroleptics allow patients to think more clearly and reconnect with more conventional modes of communication.

Patients with thought disorders can be highly prone to addiction, particularly to cigarettes, caffeine, food, and alcohol. These substances serve to provide some comfort and respite from the emotional toll of the illness—chronically falling short of life goals, not fitting in, bearing the frustration and grief of having to struggle to understand and to express oneself in the world. One of my patients with schizophrenia would use cocaine with his friends every few weeks. On those evenings, he had the experience of getting away from his troubles and feeling "normal" for a while. He would eventually become more paranoid as a matter of course, but then he could rationalize that his paranoia was related to cocaine and not to schizophrenia.

The cost of substance addiction is clearly high, in the form of chronic lung disease, obesity, anxiety, agitation, and cognitive disturbances. Though we do our best to avoid it, some neuroleptics can create problems with movement disorders and glucose or lipid metabolism and exacerbate issues with weight gain and overall health. It is no surprise then that dual-diagnosis patients with thought disorders also need recovery, psychotherapy, and mindfulness to supplement the benefits of their medicines and keep doses as low as possible.

In the treatment of thought disorders, mindfulness practices can help with

- Grounding in the body and knowing the experience of being ungrounded
- Knowing the difference between thoughts or stories and actual experience in the present moment
- Developing a sense of safety and entitlement to be here and to pursue aspirations like anyone else
- Cultivating the experience of compassion for oneself and for the grief of all human beings who have drawn difficult cards in life

There will be many examples of working with various types of thinking in chapter 16.

Anxiety Disorders

This section is a microcosm of the whole book in addressing the following questions: (1) How are we to bear our nervousness, worry, apprehension, angst, and fear without needing to take a substance or act in a self-defeating way? And (2) what is the difference between "normal" anxiety and an anxiety disorder requiring medication?

Currently in psychiatry, we have many options for treating anxiety, including serotonergic antidepressants, or SSRIs (fluoxetine [Prozac], citalopram [Celexa], venlafaxine [Effexor], duloxetine [Cymbalta]); atypical neuroleptics (risperidone, quetiapine, aripiprazole); anticonvulsants (gabapentin); alpha blockers (clonidine); beta blockers (propranolol); antihistamines (hydroxyzine, diphenhydramine); and benzodiazepines (alprazolam, clonazepam, lorazepam). However, that was not always the case. When there were fewer alternatives to manage anxiety symptoms, primary care doctors and specialists as well as psychiatrists relied heavily on benzodiazepines, and barbiturates before them. These drugs work quickly but have a high abuse and addiction potential. Because of this, I will discuss benzodiazepines as a separate category and then address other medication possibilities in relation to mindfulness practice.

Using Potentially Problematic Medicine: Benzodiazepines

As a grizzled veteran of the pre-Prozac (fluoxetine) era, which began in 1987, this is how I saw it tend to go: The patient comes complaining of anxiety or panic attacks. She or he is put on a tricyclic antidepressant (such as amitriptyline, imipramine, nortriptyline) and often a benzodiazepine, with the understanding that when the antidepressant "kicks in," the benzo will be tapered off. The antidepressant is deemed effective or not, but in either case, the patient rarely if ever comes off the benzo. Most patients are then chronically taking three to five milligrams per day of alprazolam or clonazepam and are terrified of not having it available. Most patients did not abuse the medicine or develop tolerance, but at times they did, and then they had to be detoxed. One woman's plea was: "I am on eight milligrams of Xanax [alprazolam] and nervous now. I will be a basket case if I can't have it." Then she came off the drug and was much better.

How in the world did that happen? Think of a scenario in which you are out in a park on a chilly day and not able to go inside for a while. You have two choices to consider: (1) huddle on a bench in your overcoat to shield yourself from the wind or (2) take a walk. The psychology of choice number 1 is protection. It may work for a period of time; however, if you still feel cold, your only alternatives are to pull the coat longer and tighter or bunch up in it. Each breeze is a new assault creating an element of fear or tension. Choice number 2 is more about using your resources. As you walk, you may be cold, but there are more degrees of freedom. Like a sailboat, you can walk with the wind, against it, or across it. You can quicken your pace to generate more muscular energy and heat. You are more in a position to feel at one with your environment, noting the subtle changes in the weather and in your own body and feelings. You can stop and rest if you choose. You are an actor in your life, not a victim.

Choice number 1 represents my idea of being on benzodiazepines for the treatment of anxiety. They are habit-forming and can cause both sedation and depression. But I believe what is most damaging is the psychological dependence and the shrinking of confidence in one's resources that my patient experienced until she was free of them. Choice number 2 is resonant with the practice of mindfulness, with its components of awareness, continuing assessment, being in the body, making choices, accepting what is, and taking responsibility.

My threshold for using benzodiazepines for anxiety is high, as you might imagine, but there is a place for them. For some patients, it is the best they can do given their circumstances, and the exploration of alternatives can be ongoing. In addiction and dual-diagnosis patients, the threshold is even higher. Our experience is that addicts, despite their best intentions, tend to abuse these medicines or slip into using their drug of choice. Again, there are exceptions, but I always explore a range of medication options, as well as psychotherapy and mindfulness training, before using a medicine that can cause sedation, depression, psychological and physical dependence as well as addiction.

Do I Need Medicine At All?

Elise had been self-medicating symptoms of anxiety and depression for years when she finally decided to come for help. The ideas of psychotherapy and especially psychiatrists and medication had been highly stigmatized in her family—and in the 1950s, when she grew up. Elise learned some simple mindfulness skills in our program, but one morning she reported that she had racing thoughts at night and "that breathing did not work." She had been prescribed sertraline, an SSRI, for her generalized anxiety symptoms and quetiapine, an atypical neuroleptic, for the nighttime agitation and racing thoughts but was not taking them.

The meaning of taking medicine to Elise is that she is "not in control," clearly an unacceptable state of affairs. Prior to acknowledging she had a drinking problem, Elise had routinely used alcohol to get to sleep. She was able to appreciate the irony of this, and she is not alone. Many people use substances to medicate all sorts of conditions, but once they are sitting opposite the doctor, suddenly their body is a temple, not to be polluted by medicine. Elise is able to see that she is definitely not in control now and that the purpose of medicine is, much like alcohol was, to help her to manage her symptoms more effectively. She basically trusts that I do not want her on a drug she does not need, but apparently the sobriety, support, and mindfulness skills have not been enough to help her get to sleep, at least at this stage.

Elise's experience at getting into bed was something like this: Worried about her ability to get to sleep, yet again, she quickly became frustrated, upset about the program, the medicine, herself, not sleeping, having to get up early, being tired the next day. Then her anxiety and anger would build until, guess what? Not very sleepy.

Once she agreed to try the medicine, Elise noticed that the quetiapine, though not strictly a sedative, did slow her thinking and help her to relax. It also cut into the cycle of anxiety, agitation, racing thoughts, frustration, worry, increased anxiety, and so on. The mindful breathing or body scan at bedtime was then easier to do, and as she settled down, it likely helped the medicine to work more effectively. As her antidepressant began to act in a week or so, she had less daytime anxiety. Grounding practices, like mindful walking, encourage being in the body and allow thoughts to settle, moderating their impact at bedtime. It is not unrealistic that with continued practice, Elise will be able to discontinue the quetiapine in four to six weeks and her antidepressant in a year or so.

It is worth repeating: there is always tension in addiction (or any) treatment between accepting experience and trying to change it. Anxiety is part of life, and we all must learn to listen to it, deal with it, and even value it for the information it imparts to us. Certainly, anxiety can be unpleasant and we want it to go away, but controlling it with drugs or alcohol is invariably counterproductive. Once the substance is gone, anxiety and often sleep are problematic, as in Elise's case, and medication may be an option to consider. Medicine and mindfulness can work well together, but their psychologies are different. Medicine is about symptom relief, a control strategy. Mindfulness is more of an acceptance strategy. It is about the cultivation of nonclinging, nonjudgment, and nonreactivity. Relaxation is often the goal of symptom relief with medicine, and with mindfulness training included, it is more likely to happen.

Elise could not accept medicine initially. But her efforts to use mindfulness skills alone, and their "failure" to get her to sleep, demonstrated the place of medication in her early recovery. As she continued to practice and became more quiet inside, she experienced a deep sadness related to how much of her life was spent in the past and the future. Loving-kindness meditation helped Elise to soften her self-judgments and accept her best efforts. She saw that the goal of the practice of mindfulness is to live now and see that when we try to control things we cannot, we suffer.

Elise started to be less obsessional about her housework so that she could see her friends. She had more contact and fun with her peers in the program, began to enjoy coming, and was sad to leave at the end. She admitted that she had not wanted to come, that she had been ashamed, but with the help of her peers, she no longer felt that way. Under her anxiety had been a well of grief from her difficult childhood. Elise asked herself, "What is the point of my life now?" She concluded that maybe it is to be kinder to herself and enjoy each moment as much as possible. By decreasing the load of anxiety symptoms, medication was a vehicle to this understanding. Sobriety, psychotherapy, and mindfulness practice will continue to enhance Elise's recovery process.

Attention Disorders

The ability to be mindful, like any skill, is developed via the repeated practice of the awareness of mind-body experience in the present moment with acceptance. We cannot control our thoughts and feelings. We can control our attention and actions. Unless we can't. Among those who attempt to play baseball, sing, or speak a foreign language, there is a continuum of natural ability from highly talented to nearly hopeless. The latter group can practice and practice, and the results will still be quite limited.

So it is with attention. Many highly intelligent and even gifted kids cannot succeed in school, for example, because they are unable to focus, sit still, or cooperate despite their best intentions. Then they often give up out of shame or frustration. The behavioral manifestations of shutting down or becoming a behavior problem are secondary phenomena and, often, all we see. The good news is that we are now more able to recognize and treat the problem that left so many falling short of their aspirations.

The diagnosis of attention-deficit/hyperactivity disorder (ADHD) is actually a misnomer. People with ADHD can hyperfocus or at times have too much attention on an object, followed by total spacing out.

So it is really more like attention *inconsistency* disorder. There are three subtypes of ADHD—inattentive, hyperactive-impulsive, and combined. The inattentive type is easy to miss early on because a kid in school, for example, will simply perform poorly or seem disinterested. Other manifestations of inattention—poor listening, not following instructions, being disorganized, avoiding work, distractibility, losing things, and forgetfulness—can feel vaguely oppositional or uncaring. Hyperactive-impulsive symptoms are more obvious. A child can seem to be in constant motion, intrusive, and difficult to contain. On the other hand, the same kid can be a whiz at video games requiring prolonged focus.

Attention disorders are now frequently diagnosed, some say overdiagnosed. The current pace of life and technology may cause ADHD to manifest more often, as we (adults as well as kids) are constantly challenged to focus on the rapid unfolding of data, events, and developments—or be left behind. It has been demonstrated that even "normals" will benefit from stimulants such as Ritalin or Adderal, as witnessed by the rampant use of these drugs on college campuses. They are indeed performance-enhancing drugs.

ADHD and Substance Abuse

As we have seen, drugs and alcohol are commonly used to transform or self-medicate or escape intolerable mental and emotional experience. ADHD is an excellent model for this because, untreated, individuals are not able to function to their intellectual capacity. Children cannot focus, are impulsive, procrastinate, and ultimately tend to become demoralized and give up or act out. Adults often appear reckless or irresponsible, with low frustration tolerance. This can manifest in driving too fast, poor time management, and precipitously leaving jobs or relationships.

There is now a great body of work on the interface between ADHD and substance abuse,[1] and the findings are illuminating. They suggest that ADHD leads to attempts to improve attention with substances that, as you might predict, both help in the short run and worsen the situation over time. Conversely, it is impressive to note that of all patients with substance use disorders, 15 to 25 percent have ADHD.[2]

The first substance many kids encounter is nicotine, which has been demonstrated in numerous studies to be a gateway to the use of other drugs.[3] This association has been shown to be stronger in ADHD kids, who are more likely to smoke and to begin earlier and manifest more severe physical dependence on nicotine compared with control subjects.[4] One hypothesis for this link is that nicotine activates dopamine reward pathways in the brain (as do alcohol, cocaine, opiates, and cannabis), which is pleasurable, likely improves the ability to focus, and possibly also enhances the effect of other psychoactive drugs.[5]

ADHD is associated with dysregulated dopamine systems and is therefore treated by agents that increase the availability of the neurotransmitters dopamine and norepinephrine. Stimulant drugs such as methylphenidate (Ritalin) and dexadrine increase the capacity to focus and decrease hyperactivity and impulsivity. In the absence of treatment, this effect is sought through nicotine and its amplifying effect on other substances.[6]

The combination of smoking and ADHD is extremely powerful. In one study, 60 percent of ADHD kids who smoked went on to develop substance use disorders, as compared with 5 percent of nonsmoking ADHD kids. (Among non-ADHD controls, the numbers were 30 percent for smokers and 6 percent for nonsmokers).[7] ADHD patients self-medicate many symptoms, including the sometimes extreme restlessness, impatience, anxiety, and aggression that result from the inability to pay attention effectively.

Pharmacotherapy with stimulants protects against the risks of substance use, despite the fact that these drugs can be misused and sold.[8] Also, subjects treated for ADHD smoked significantly less than those untreated, which could have major public health outcomes over time.[9] Unfortunately, many kids with ADHD never come to clinical attention, even in an era where the problem is well researched and treated.

ADHD, Addiction, and Mindfulness

Gabby is an attractive, energetic woman of forty living with her husband and two boys in an upscale town outside of Boston. She is an artist and very involved with her kids and the school. I know her because she came into our program with an addiction to oxycodone, which had gotten out of control around an episode of severe back pain. Gabby had the social grace of a girl who grew up in the South, but the truth was that she had always struggled, particularly with her ability to focus. Although quite intelligent and creative, she had never done well academically and dropped out of high school at sixteen. Her parents' marriage was unstable at the time, and they had little energy to help Gabby find her way. Consequently, she got involved with an older crowd and was introduced very early to cigarettes, drugs, and sex.

Though she tended to be quite scattered and disorganized, Gabby was able to get her graduate equivalency diploma and a job with a trucking company. To her surprise, she was quite effective working with people and keeping multiple aspects of the work in her head simultaneously. Once promoted to a managerial position, however, Gabby struggled to stay on top of her paperwork, and her desk was always a mess.

She found that a little bit of marijuana helped her to slow down enough to take an interest in staying organized, but it was an ongoing battle. Gabby discovered oxycodone during an episode of back pain following the birth of her second child. Finally, she had found a drug that balanced her mood and energy and allowed her to focus more consistently on her kids, her home, and other responsibilities. It was also effective in blowing away the guilt she felt about a brief (impulsive) affair she had had several years back. Opiates would temporarily turn Gabby into her best, highest-functioning self, overcoming her low self-esteem with perfectionism and hard work. Not surprisingly, Gabby's high performance came at great cost to her body, and she became totally depleted and depressed. She had been started on Adderal (mixed amphetamine salts) by her outpatient psychiatrist but could not experience much benefit while she was still using.

Recovery for Gabby meant that her pusher-perfectionist manager could begin to step aside so she could experience her vulnerability in a safe environment. With sobriety, she was more clearheaded, and medicine was now effective in stabilizing her moods and ADHD symptoms. Gabby was finally able to feel and understand her grief in the context of her sad childhood and misguided attempts to conquer it. Assuming the mantle of star at work, superwife, and mom had clearly not worked, and it was time to face her ordinary life more directly.

Mindfulness practice freed Gabby to do just that. The key was staying in her body and deemphasizing the stories about how great she needed to be to overcome all the mistakes of the past. The present moment was the only one in which she could act (or not), learn, or change. Cravings and urges were *in her body,* experiences she could work with directly.

In the past, cravings had been pleasant when she knew she was going to get some relief. Now they were unpleasant and triggered a sense of deprivation and tension. However, using a combination of simple awareness, urge surfing (discussed in chapter 12), and distraction, Gabby was able to allow these experiences to pass without having to gratify them. This gave her a satisfying sense of efficacy and confidence. Gabby still had back pain but was less afraid of it. She was encouraged to practice mindful walking and stretching and eventually began running again. Pain, like the cravings, would come, but her relationship with it was softer and much less tense.

What was most powerful for Gabby as she became more grounded and aware was seeing her slippery mind in action. She could see the conflict within her of two heavyweight parts, her perfectionist and her addict, and the stories each would tell. Her perfectionist wanted competence; her addict, well-being. Mindfulness practice allowed Gabby to find creative means of reaching these goals without hurting herself. As a businessperson, she commented that mindfulness was a lot like continuous quality improvement (CQI), a management philosophy that contends that most things can be improved: "You hold both sides, make a choice, get an outcome, and then evaluate what happened."

What Gabby was able to accomplish in our program has been studied more formally by the psychiatrist Lydia Zylowska and her group at UCLA. They developed mindful awareness practices for ADHD, informed by existing mindfulness training models such as mindfulness-based stress reduction (MBSR) and mindfulness-based cognitive therapy (MBCT) and adapted to the ADHD population. Their work is founded on the premise that ADHD patients have cognitive deficits, impairments in self-regulation, and comorbid psychiatric disorders that often do not respond to stimulant medication alone. In their sample of twenty-three adults and adolescents who received mindfulness training, 78 percent reported a reduction in ADHD symptoms on a series of measures for attentional flexibility. Adults also showed improvement in depression.[10] This study provides preliminary evidence for what we already know clinically: that mindfulness training and the facilitation of awareness/acceptance of experience, nonreactivity, and self-compassion are likely to enhance emotional regulation in ADHD patients with or without addiction.

In psychiatry and medicine, troubling physical sensations, emotions, or thoughts are often addressed with medication. Part 3 will discuss how mindfulness practices can be helpful for these same symptoms and energies.

PART THREE

Challenges to Recovery

11

Addiction, Recovery, and the Body

BEN CHANGED HIS LIFE by changing his relationship to his body. We have known each other for twelve years, since he first walked into the Bournewood-Caulfield day treatment program, and today he is just visiting. I immediately notice the brightness of his eyes and his energy, that he has lost weight and looks strong. Ben has been sober for twenty years but has had a hard life. Sexually abused from a young age, then discovering he was gay, he drank as a means of numbing himself. Though alcohol did allow him to engage socially and sexually, it also left him increasingly hopeless and suicidal. Ben stopped drinking but then overate, leading to obesity, chronic back pain, and having to leave his job. His road to recovery has been long and complex.

I asked him to reflect on the subjects of addiction, depression, mindfulness, and recovery. He said, "To me, it's all one. My addiction and mental illness can each trigger the other, and then I am in a hole. I need to be present every day; I can only do one day. I tell the people I work with (in AA) that if you are in the past, you get depressed, and if in the future, you are anxious. Only in the present can you be mindful. I ask them, 'Where are your feet?' It sounds simple, but it helped me."

In recent years, Ben did not drink when he became depressed but would go into a trance—basically, dissociating as a form of self-medication. He would just sit alone staring at the wall, move as little as possible, and go into fantasy. He did not shower or sleep on a regular schedule. He would not eat for long periods, then binged on food to subdue his agitation, anger, and sadness. All of this played havoc with his body. He gained weight and became stiff, which was terrible for his back and joints. He was also quite tense, which further aggravated his pain. Then he would become more depressed and withdrawn and would deteriorate so badly that the choices were either to die or to seek help.

Mindfulness practice helped Ben to become more aware of this process. He could feel himself beginning to leave his body and saw that he had a choice to numb out or take a walk to shift his energy. He said, "I stopped just existing and was more aware of what I was doing." He feels anxiety in his body and breathes through it. Changing eating habits was critical. Ben became much more conscious of the experience of hunger, and he stopped using food to escape his feelings "for the most part." "It is what it is," he told me. "It's progress, not perfection."

Embodied awareness gave Ben a new perspective. He became aware of destructive patterns and saw how they worked. Some of what he had to accept in the beginning was how much he wanted to dissociate from his feelings and the pros and cons of doing that. Suicide was always an option, but once he chose life, he could no longer justify avoiding it. He did not want to be mindful of stress, depression, anger, and urges but found that when he did not fight these experiences, they softened and became more tolerable. He could watch the experience directly (the more difficult alternative) or shift his attention to his feet, his breath, the conversation, or the sky. The more he practiced, the more confident he felt to face life as it is. No one had to convince him he was on the right path.

Though he does formal meditation fairly regularly (he is a natural at sitting still), Ben does not expect that newly sober people will, at least in the beginning. Truth be told, many of our patients do not become regular meditators. In early recovery, it is advisable to choose a few simple practices that can be integrated into the day: touch points, mindful breathing, walking with awareness of the body, mindfulness of simple activities.

Even smoking can be an object for mindful attention. Some find it enjoyable, others just do it to reduce stress or out of habit. If you are in early recovery, you may not be ready to give up cigarettes now, but you could notice what is pleasant and what is unpleasant in the experience. Then you are in a position to make a choice to quit (or not) when the time is right. In the meantime, the activity provides another opportunity for embodied awareness. If smoking is just a means of tuning out or giving up on life, that can be seen as well. Everyone knows cigarettes are damaging to one's health; that is not news. But when cigarettes have been a companion for so long, quitting can feel like too much of a loss. Ben still smokes, wants to stop, and has the tools to explore that when he is ready.

The Addicted Brain

Carolyn Knapp calls addiction a "hunger."

> The need is more than physical: it's psychic and visceral and multilayered. There's a dark fear to the feeling of wanting that wine, that vodka, that bourbon: a hungry, abiding fear of being without, being exposed, without your armor. In meetings you often hear people say that, by definition, an addict is someone who seeks physical solutions to emotional or spiritual problems. I suppose that's an intellectual way of describing that brand of fear, and the instinctive response that accompanies it: there's a sense of deep need and the response is a grabbiness, a compulsion to latch on to something outside yourself in order to assuage some deep discomfort.[1]

Brain researchers have demonstrated that the fear, need, and compulsion Knapp refers to have clear biological underpinnings. Although I am not a neuroscientist, I believe it might be useful to unpack the addictive process in order to better understand what is going on in the brain, the body, and the emotions. Drug-taking behavior unfolds in a three-stage cycle progressing from impulsivity to compulsivity.[2]

In the first stage, called *binge-intoxication,* the act of using a drug produces an experience of pleasure or relief, eventually (with excessive use) followed by guilt or regret, increased tension, and further impulsive use, which provides pleasure and relief, more guilt, and so on. Substances such as cocaine, nicotine, alcohol, and opiates recruit a number of neurotransmitter systems, the best known of which is dopamine.

The dopamine network projects from the brain stem (the base of the brain just above the spinal cord), through the limbic system, to the prefrontal cortex. The brain stem receives input from the body and regulates a number of basic systems and processes, including heart rate, respiration, arousal, hunger, and sexual desire as well as our stress response. The limbic areas regulate our emotional and endocrine systems. The prefrontal cortex allows us to think abstractly and symbolically as well as connecting directly to all the other brain regions. It allows us to make the kinds of intelligent choices that distinguish human beings from other species.[3]

The dopamine system effectively uses our desire or wanting sensation to keep us eating and drinking and seeking companionship and sex. It is also at the root of our drive for achievement, for example, to be a great athlete, artist, or entrepreneur. Much of human history—including exploration and discovery, all manner of attainments, war and cruelty—can be understood from the perspective of these neural pathways.

In the addicted brain, drugs (and behavioral addictions like gambling, for that matter) hijack the dopamine system so that the addiction takes priority over anything else. It has been demonstrated that rats, able to press a bar to release cocaine, will continue to use until death, ignoring food and water that are immediately available.

Nicotine is particularly powerful in its ability to keep people smoking despite knowledge of adverse consequences. Researchers in New Zealand studying autonomy over tobacco use administered the Hooked on Nicotine Checklist to a group of adolescents. They found that diminished ability to self-regulate nicotine use was reported by 46 percent of subjects smoking less frequently than once a month and 25 to 30 percent of smokers after one cigarette.[4] Diminished autonomy progressively increased with frequency of use.

In the binge-intoxication stage, the brain is flooded with dopamine, which is initially pleasurable. However, as neurons sense an excess of neurotransmitter, both production and transmission of dopamine will be reduced. Less natural dopamine makes it difficult to enjoy simple pleasures like eating or being outside, and the user now feels unmotivated, joyless, and/or depressed.

This leads to the second, or *withdrawal-negative affect,* stage. This stage is distinguished by drug dependence, which serves the clear pur-

pose of producing enough dopamine to experience any sense of gratification or reward. No longer a vehicle for getting high, the drug
simply allows the user to feel normal. Drug use is now compulsive
despite negative outcomes in the areas of health, relationship, livelihood, and legal issues. The user is now an *addict* with a severe compro-
mise of higher cortical function, clearly not thinking straight. The
prefrontal cortex is also the seat of the "mirror neuron system,"
thought to be the root of empathy. The loss of empathic connection to
other people is why addicts behave like "animals," prioritizing the
next fix over their values and most important relationships. It is also
why recovering addicts need to make amends to those they have hurt.

The third stage, called *preoccupation-anticipation,* is characterized
by craving and persistent physical and psychological problems. This is
the experience that Carolyn Knapp describes, and it captures why addiction is so often a chronic relapsing disorder.

There are two types of craving. The first is stimulated by the presentation of a drug or an environmental cue. I once treated a newly
sober woman who drove to a karaoke bar fully intending to drink
Coke for the evening. However, upon entering the bar, she immediately ordered a beer. How did that happen? Likely the sights, smells,
music, and ambience of the bar created such a powerful association to
drinking that her behavior became automatic.

The second type of craving, which Knapp experienced, is stress
induced, characterized by anxiety and an array of difficult emotions.
In her powerful account of addiction, she reports always feeling an
intense inner agitation, managed by rocking as a child and later with
alcohol. In other addicts, the cycle can be initiated by the use of the
drug (or addictive behavior) itself, setting off the dopamine cascade
and resultant brain changes.

Addiction and Stress

Craving is an occurrence common to all stages of the addictive cycle.
The experience of craving, however, is vastly different depending
upon the intent of the addict. Cocaine addicts, for example, report the
physical release of passing gas or relaxation of muscle tension just
from knowing that they are about to get high. The mere promise
of gratification, whether it be via alcohol, sex, food, gambling, or

shopping, is enough to initiate the reward process. In these cases, craving is a pleasant experience, leading to a predictable outcome. The brain knows this before the drug is introduced. You might say that for active addicts this is a no-brainer.

If you are an addict in early recovery, however, you are conflicted. A part of you is trying hard to stay clean, while another part cares nothing for recovery, being good, or even being healthy. Craving still arrives and is now often unpleasant, an experience you would rather be rid of. There are now two problems: (1) the craving is not going away so fast, and (2) the wanting it to go away makes it stronger. This then intensifies the aversion to the craving, the cascade of difficult emotions and mind states, and the risk of relapse despite your best intent, just to survive the onslaught from your own body and mind.

The resultant relapse, if it occurs, has been induced by what we call "stress," defined by the physiologist Hans Selye as "a non-specific response of the organism to any pressure or demand." A *stressor* is an external or internal event that stimulates a stress reaction. For the addict with mixed feelings about using, a craving is clearly a stressor, since it creates a no-win situation—to be miserable now if I don't use or later if I do.

In conflict-free drug use (that is, no conscious interest in sobriety), craving is not a stressor but an event that heralds the experience of achieving a high or some relief from stress. Regardless of context, a craving is merely a set of physical sensations, emotions, and thoughts that last for a finite period and then fade. It is not solid. The mind, however, gives the craving far more staying power via its aversive reaction. *Stress* is the result of both the craving itself and the attempt to escape it or push it away.

Addiction is slavery to a form of stress reduction that then becomes another stressor. As we discussed in chapter 1, people use drugs in order to get a feeling, get rid of a feeling, or escape. What all of these have in common is a turning away from experience, from our natural stressors, which come in many forms—money, relationships, illness, difficult emotions, aging, confusion, loss, death, failure, success. We run as long as we can deny the fact that we can't hide.

Drugs are a means of establishing a sense of control and predictability. As Ben discovered, the price for this "control" is the atrophy of natural capacities, instincts, and resilience. As the ability to handle life's challenges diminishes, the addict uses his only tool to reestablish that control, which further erodes the ability to function effectively. Fear of change, failure, loss, and death begins to merge with a wish for death to escape all of the pain and struggle.

Joan bought a pint of Grey Goose vodka because she was having a bad day. She was tense and upset from a fight with her husband that morning. She watched the whole process of driving to the liquor store, making the purchase, going home. As Joan was about to open the bottle, she thought about being in treatment and decided to put it aside. After a little while she felt much better and had a nice weekend with her family. She went to the gym twice and felt great.

As I listened to her story, I was wondering what happened to the bottle, and I soon got my answer. On Sunday evening her husband took the kids out, leaving her alone, and she drank. When I asked what caused her to pick up the bottle, Joan didn't know immediately but then wondered if she felt "too good." Indeed, this feeling was unfamiliar to her and unsettling. Though it was good to be sober and her family was pleased, Joan was anxious as she looked at her life—her past mistakes and regrets as well as what was next, including the future of her marriage, in which she had not been happy. Feeling good had been a stressor and drinking a strategy to avoid her fear and uncomfortable feelings. She was also escaping from her responsibility to manage these feelings, from becoming an adult.

Fortunately, Joan was in treatment and able to share and learn from her mistake. It was funny for her to acknowledge her awareness that she was buying a high-quality vodka in a small quantity so that she would enjoy it but not go on a huge bender. Joan felt better but was not sure whether to tell her husband about her slip. He probably knew, and if he didn't, it just proved his lack of interest in her. Thinking about her conflict made Joan feel quite tense and fearful. This felt like a no-win situation, and it was not the time to decide whether to reveal her secret or not. It was time to breathe, walk, notice her touch points, restabilize, and trust that soon she would know what to do. I asked Joan about the blotchy rash on her face. She said, "I'm stressed, I can't hide it."

Stress is about destabilization of our physical and/or emotional systems. Though we do not always feel stressed, the changing nature of our lives makes it a ubiquitous and continuous process. Our routines protect us, as do moments of refuge like reading or turning on the TV after our work is done for the day. A couple of drinks can seem to eliminate all concerns for a while. But stress continues to destabilize us in small and profound ways. Our health and well-being depend upon our ability to bring awareness to this process of destabilization and learn to ride the waves. Much as lifting weights or doing cardio makes us physically fit, mindfulness practice develops an inner steadiness in the face of life's challenges.

Think of the experience of not being able to find something you need, not having the money to pay your monthly bills, or as in Joan's case, feeling pressure to face a frightening issue you have been avoiding. Though these are not life-threatening occurrences, we react with some alarm, and the body goes through a predictable series of events. The core experience is one of hyperarousal, heightened vigilance, tension, and fear. Intimately involved in this process is the *autonomic nervous system* (ANS), which controls the visceral (referring to the internal organs) functions of the body, including arterial pressure, respiratory rate, sweating, body temperature, gastrointestinal motility, and urinary output, among others.

The ANS is activated mainly by centers located in the hypothalamus (a master control gland), the brain stem, and the spinal cord. It also has connections to the limbic system, the center of the emotions, as well as the cerebral cortex in its role of coordinating the stress response. The ANS has two branches, sympathetic and parasympathetic. Activation of the sympathetic branch of the autonomic nervous system releases hormones from the adrenal cortex (cortisol) and adrenal medulla (epinephrine, norepinephrine, dopamine). These increase heart rate and blood pressure; elevate blood sugar; shift blood flow from the gut to the muscles; and increase muscle strength, mental activity, and overall tension.[5]

This is the fight-or-flight reaction, quite useful if we are in actual danger but activated just the same whether we are cut off in traffic or about to miss a plane. In a high-stress situation, the parasympathetic branch, which facilitates relaxation, digestion, reproduction, and growth, is relatively unnecessary and deemphasized. You can see how this can become a problem if high stress is a common occurrence.

In Joan's case, the Grey Goose was an attempt to shift her system from high sympathetic tone to the "rest and digest" mode. This happens every day when people have a couple of drinks after work and seemingly get away with it. But the sympathetic and parasympathetic systems have a natural and finely tuned yin and yang relationship. And it is generally not a good idea to mess with Mother Nature.

If we are chronically stressed by health or life circumstances, this reaction becomes more habitual and more easily triggered, which begins to take a toll on the body. An enormous number of medical problems are stress related, including hypertension, chest pain, arrhythmias, vulnerability to infection, sleep disorders, headaches, back pain, peptic ulcer disease, asthma, inflammatory bowel disease, and irritable bowel syndrome. Arthritis, diabetes, a number of neurological disorders, and many other medical problems are exacerbated by stress. Our minds are beset with restlessness, agitation, worry, anxiety, fear, confusion. We are quick to anger and react. In the UMass Prison Project, I saw that much of the violence and crime committed by the inmates— although clearly this is not an excuse—was stress induced.

Addictions play havoc with the natural stress response and optimal coordination of our neurotransmitters. Serotonin has a role in sleep, mood regulation, anxiety, and setting the body clock (along with melatonin), which regulates cortisol and body temperature. Norepinephrine and corticotropin-releasing factor (a hypothalamic hormone) are involved in energy regulation and the stress cycle. Dopamine is related to mood and reward as well as endorphin release. I do not claim to understand how all of these systems interact, and much is not completely known. However, if all drugs of abuse elevate dopamine levels and then deplete dopamine stores and addicts are chronically stressed, anxious, and dysphoric (feeling unhappy or unwell), we can glimpse a picture of ongoing dysregulation of a number of neurotransmitter systems. This only increases the addict's vulnerability to continued abuse as the sole means to any sense of comfort or stability, however transient.

Mindfulness as a Bridge to Relaxation

Among teachers of mindfulness, relaxation is often underrated. In meditation practice, as I learned it, the crowning achievements are wisdom and compassion. The major means toward these ends are mindfulness, concentration, and metta, or loving-kindness toward others. Many teachers, including me, are careful to point out that relaxation is not the goal of mindfulness practice but a "by-product."

It is true, but let's not kid ourselves. Relaxation is critically important to the well-being of our bodies and minds. One of the seminal contributions to the field of stress reduction was made in the mid-1970s by Dr. Herbert Benson, a cardiologist at Harvard Medical School. In his study of Tibetan monks, Dr. Benson found that they were amazingly adept at slowing their heart and respiratory rates, lowering blood pressure, and producing calming (alpha) brain waves when they meditated. This became known as the "relaxation response," which is essentially a shift in the autonomic nervous system from sympathetic to parasympathetic dominance.

It is probably not an accident that this research was done in Boston, where, as in much of the Northeast, we are extremely hard driving, competitive, and stressed (though no doubt there are a few areas of rural Vermont or Maine where life is not as intense and pressured); generally, the rest of the country is not like us, again with some exceptions (hello, Los Angeles). But truth be told, wherever we live there will be worries about making a living, family, social standing, illness, and death. Things are always going wrong, and our alarm buttons are pushed frequently by stressors large and small.

I have said before that we cannot control the thoughts or feelings that arise in us. We also cannot command our sympathetic nervous system, which controls heart rate, blood flow, respiration, and our stress response. (That we do not have to worry about these functions is quite good until stress makes us sick.) We *can* exercise some control over the parasympathetic nervous system via directing our attention and actions.

For example, deep belly breathing expands the diaphragm, resulting in stimulation of the vagus nerves, which originate in the brain stem and terminate in the abdomen. These nerves contain approximately 75 percent of all parasympathetic nerve fibers, supplying the heart, the lungs, the diaphragm, and much of the gastrointestinal tract and abdominal organs. So deep breathing is an effective means of turning on the parasympathetic nervous system and eliciting the relaxation response.

Deep Belly Breathing

Try this. Inhale through your nose into your belly to a count of five, pause to a count of five, and then exhale completely through your mouth to a count of ten. Do this for four breath cycles.

What do you notice? People often experience a release of tension, a dropping down into the body, or a sense of letting go. This is an exercise that can be done at random times of the day or at regular intervals, anywhere and in any position. It is an excellent way to come back to the body, to the present moment, where our thoughts, agendas, and stressors can be seen more clearly. Then we can choose where to direct our attention and energy.

Ted came to our program extremely stressed and autonomically dysregulated. He is a trauma survivor, terrorized in his childhood by a rageful and highly aggressive father who once threw Ted into the ocean to teach him to swim. He married a woman who was bipolar and extremely disorganized, so life was often frantic and stressful. Ted had used alcohol and benzodiazepines to settle his overactive nervous system for many years. He came to us in benzodiazepine withdrawal, with a heart rate of 104 and blood pressure of 180 over 110. Ted required an antihypertensive initially but also worked intensively with mindful breathing.

By taking deep breaths and exhaling fully, he found that he could lower his pulse by fifteen to twenty beats per minute and decrease his blood pressure as well. Achieving this result had a dramatic effect on both Ted's anxiety and his confidence in his ability to manage internal states that had previously appeared to be totally beyond his control. As he settled down, he reported improved concentration and the ability to read for significant periods of time, which had been a distant memory. Anxiety came but was much less of a problem. Regular mindfulness practice helped Ted reinforce his sense of groundedness and self-reliance, an excellent alternative to self-medication.

There are many ways to elicit the relaxation response. When we meet a friend for lunch, we get a lot more than someone to eat with. As we spend time together talking about our lives, we often have an experience of connection and support that is a neurochemical event akin to a big hug. We go back to work feeling somehow more balanced, optimistic, or rejuvenated. Dancing is another experience of energetic connection with elements of stimulation, movement, and flow that is simultaneously enlivening and relaxing. We can get many of the same benefits from community, music, celebration, sex, and laughter. The phenomenon of laugh yoga leads people in hearty and contagious laughter in a group, with notable benefits to liveliness and well-being. A workplace or home environment with daily laughter is a good place to be. It is true that the best things in life are free.

Addictions often have the goal of disengaging from life as a form of relaxation. Alcohol, for example, is frequently used to modulate the tension associated with the workday and other life stressors. A single drink produces a biphasic effect, with a stimulatory phase resulting from increasing blood ethanol concentration followed by a depressant phase as blood levels fall. This occurs via a complex set of actions involving numerous neurotransmitter systems that excite, reward, and decrease anxiety. This will perk up depleted or tense energy, followed by a sort of numbing out. Relying on alcohol as a form of relaxation is effective but also problematic in several ways:

- Leads to overuse and potential dependence
- Prevents development of other modes of relaxation
- Causes distancing from human connection and support, which is detrimental to relationships
- Creates withdrawal phenomena causing rebound anxiety, agitation, and disturbed sleep
- Contributes to potential medical and psychiatric problems leading to deterioration and breakdown

On a recent August cover of the *New Yorker,* there is a picture of a man alone on the beach operating a TV remote as he looks out over the ocean. The cartoon is captioned "Pause." Certain times of the year capture our need to relax, reflect, and recover, but we also need this on a regular basis. Along with activities like socializing, dancing, and singing, there are many practices that balance our autonomic nervous system. Prayer, chanting, meditation, yoga, exercise, massage, journaling, reading, gardening, and being out in nature all increase parasympathetic tone and help reduce the stress on the mind-body.

However, as powerful as these techniques can be, the experience of alarm (and potential relapse) is just one thought, argument, or phone call away. We need the ability to sustain moment-to-moment awareness in order to right our ship in the face of life's inevitable stressors. The psychologist and meditation teacher Sylvia Boorstein has said that the most serene state of mind can turn to panic by a troubled voice on the other end of the phone saying, "Ma?"

Expansion Imagery

So what is the relationship between relaxation and mindfulness? You can try this brief exercise after you read the instructions: Close your eyes and notice the buzzing of thinking and energy in your head. Now imagine that the bones that make up your skull are infinitely expandable, so that these thoughts and firings can move and dissipate in endless space—like cows in an enormous pasture or the ripples from a stone spreading in a pond. Then bring attention to the rest of your body, allowing a similar flow and expansion of all feelings and sensations. You may find that breathing directly into the energies facilitates this experience. Do this for two or three minutes.

Any number of things may happen in such an experience. Likely there is some thinking, noise, or movement you noticed. It may have gotten quieter or more intense. You may then have had an idea about or a reaction to that. If your mind settled down, it may have happened more quickly or slowly than you anticipated. That could produce another story about how easy or difficult this is, how good a meditator you are, or any number of other possibilities and further brain activity. Physical sensations might also stimulate ideas, concerns, or reactions. On and on it goes, and often the result is not what you would call relaxation. If, on the other hand, you were able to focus on your experience or breathing accepting exactly how chaotic or peaceful your experience was, limiting the commentary, you likely had some measure of calm or centeredness.

Often we think of relaxation as going unconscious with drinking or mindless TV watching. If you look closely (which we don't, that's the idea of being unconscious), unconsciousness is actually a place of tension, where the random bustle of our thoughts actually picks up speed. This is why some people must have the TV on to fall asleep: to use a numbing activity to repress such tension. So there is actually a great deal of stress and increased sympathetic nervous system activity, countered by "relaxing" pursuits that cause more stress. Does this sound familiar? Mindlessness, drug induced or not, is attractive and temporarily relaxing but ultimately causes more problems than it solves.

Mindfulness is a vehicle for allowing the mind and body to be just as they are right now. It is a lens through which we can see the play of wanting, irritation, tension, pleasure, pain, success, and failure. Then all of these states change, in an endless unfolding. If we continue to watch and bring acceptance to this process, we see how little control we have over it and let go of getting a certain outcome.

This is the Serenity Prayer in action. Mindfulness practice provides a technology for this, allowing us to settle into the reality of how things are as opposed to how we want them to be. As we relax, there is greater receptivity, interest, and concentration, further increasing the power of mindfulness. This is a process that balances energy and calm, enhances well-being, and promotes fearlessness in facing the myriad challenges of our lives.

Since our subject is addiction, I will address some common stumbling blocks for addicts: cravings and urges, pain and aversion, and energetic imbalances. Though these obstacles to clarity of mind and open-heartedness are particularly challenging in addiction treatment, they are universal.

12

Working with the Body: Cravings and Urges

IF WE OBSERVE our behavior, a major theme is the body moving toward pleasure and away from pain. On a hot day recently, I got into my car, rolled down the windows to let the heat escape and the breeze in, turned on the climate control, adjusted the temperature and fan level, turned the vents to the right angles, rolled up the windows as the AC began to come on, turned on the radio. Ahhh, now I'm good.

This is a normal response of our quite intelligent bodies moving toward balance. The Chinese system calls it yin and yang. Yin is cool, loose, flowing, relaxed, open, unorganized. Yang is warm, hard, tight, focused, organized. Work tends to be yang. Sweets, sex, drugs, and rock 'n' roll are more yin. The symbol of the black fish with white eye intertwined with the white fish with black eye illustrate that there is yin in every predominantly yang condition and vice versa. Music, for example, is simultaneously both flowing and quite disciplined. Our bodies will naturally gravitate toward a harmonious relationship between these diverse and natural energies.

So, what's the problem? Mainly it is that the body is not entirely running the show. Once our minds discover a way to find comfort that seems to work reliably, it tends to overuse it. As we saw with Jim (in the introduction), who developed a drinking problem, or Ben (in chapter 11), who used dissociation to manage life stressors, we are soon in

the grips of a process that has a life of its own. This process, which we
have called addiction, eventually robs us of our bodily intelligence and
good judgment, but it begins as a means of managing difficult mind-
body energies.

Craving and Urge

Leslie keeps relapsing despite her best efforts and intent. There is a
great deal at stake, as she is a partner at her law firm and her job is in
jeopardy. Leslie's course in day treatment was complicated by both a
mood disorder and a trauma history. However, she was highly motivated, went to AA meetings, worked with a sponsor, was committed
to therapy, took medicine, did regular exercise, and practiced mindfulness. All of this had her feeling much more stable, but she still
slipped with alcohol three times in a month.

These episodes all began with a hot feeling in her sternum, what
she calls "the drinking feeling." Leslie tried to accept the sensation and
breathe through it as she had done before, but before long she was in
the liquor store buying a bottle of wine and then opening it in her
apartment. She intended to have just one or two glasses to quell the
burning but finished the bottle, fell asleep, and was in the store again
at 9 A.M. the next morning buying another. After a brief binge, she was
back in the hospital and then in day treatment again.

What happened to this highly intelligent woman with a huge in-
centive to be sober? Leslie's slips had several characteristic phases:

- Craving—the "hot feeling" was a physical sensation that had
  become associated with wanting (or "needing") alcohol, generally lasting a few minutes.
- Urge—the craving was followed by a feeling of excitement, a
  physiological revving up. This had always been an experience
  Leslie enjoyed: keyed up, with a buoyant mood and a feeling of
  power and anticipation. The urge was like an alarm and akin to
  the stress response.
- Impulse—she felt the unquestioned automatic reaction to gratify the urge.
- Conflict/anxiety—with efforts to be sober, cravings and urges
  began to have some negative aspects, particularly the antici-

pated crash, shame, and fear of losing her job. The good news was that this might slow down the impulse to drink. But the pull toward gratification was strong, and it often won. The rationalization or argument that she would have only one or two to "take the edge off" was part of this phase. Frequently, the conflict created enough inner tension to become another reason to drink.

- Renewed craving/withdrawal—as soon as Leslie had a drink, she could not stop. This was driven by the automatism inherent in the disease of alcoholism. Leslie experienced both cravings and miniwithdrawals as the effect of prior drinks wore off. The combined effect supercharged the ongoing desire for alcohol. This phase could be quite long, with binges that went on for days.
- Guilt—as her binges wore on, Leslie would often be filled with self-hatred and judgment. This could serve to continue the cycle of bingeing and craving or lead to exhaustion and another treatment episode.

Leslie's relapses did not require a craving to get started. Many were stress induced. She could then be triggered by a thought: "I just want a break. It's so nice out; maybe I'll just sit in the sun at that restaurant down the street." Or opportunity. After many awful experiences drinking at lunches and professional gatherings, Leslie's drinking was generally solitary and a means of decompressing. Since she traveled to conferences and to meet with clients, she was often alone in hotel rooms. She would clean out the minibar and then get two bills at checkout to cover her tracks. Airports and planes were other prime drinking sites.

Helplessness and rage were frequent themes. One relapse occurred soon after getting the news that Leslie's siblings were moving her beloved dad out of his house to a nursing home without consulting her. The same afternoon, she was asked to leave a urine sample for a toxicology screen, part of her probationary status at work. She was overcome with feelings of sadness, helplessness, and shame, which quickly turned to anger and defiance.

Leslie could relapse if she felt anxious, fearful, excited, celebratory, downhearted, bored, invincible, angry, cocky, powerless, or rebellious.

She was triggered by situations, thoughts, and emotions in an infinite array, and alcohol was always the answer. And up in her head, painful recollections; rationalizations; and stories of discouragement, vengeance or fear were like rocket fuel toward relapse. Leslie's simple but difficult task was to slow down enough to notice the impact of these events on her body and work with them—not to be a good girl but to navigate through each craving, urge, or impulse to drink. This is an ongoing challenge for Leslie, but she has had success with a few methods.

Wise Reflection

With enough bad outcomes, Leslie began to see the consequences of her drinking and, like many addicts, was able to avoid falling into the hole at times. Alcoholics refer to this as "thinking through the drink," a means of considering probable outcomes and choosing not to go there. Mindfulness training augmented Leslie's ability to stop and look, allowing her to see both the benefit and the downside of having that drink and of not having it. She would then be able to make a choice and consider alternatives to deal with her feelings of wanting, loneliness, disappointment, or anger.

Often Leslie decided not to drink, but not always. If the craving or urge was strong enough, she was often unable to abstain. It was interesting for her to see the difference between choosing to drink versus drinking on impulse. Choosing to drink may not be the ultimate goal, but it was a manifestation of grappling with a conflict. She also no longer justified her slips and was able to recover from them more quickly, minimizing the damage to her health, work, and relationships. It is a work in progress.

Urge Surfing

Urge surfing is the act of riding a craving or urge. The term was coined by Alan Marlatt and Judith Gordon in their work in the 1980s using the cognitive-behavioral method for relapse prevention. Cravings and urges are neurochemical events that then trigger a whole range of physical, emotional, and mental experience—anticipation, dread, anxiety, tension, and stories of hopelessness, discouragement, or victimhood. The stories lead to more tension, confusion, overwhelm, and a vicious cycle with gratification of the urge the only (albeit temporary) escape.

Practice: Urge Surfing

After you read the instructions, you might try this visualization of a craving or urge. Then, when one actually comes, you will be ready.

Bring to mind something you would like to eat, buy, or do that either is not a good idea or causes you to lose control. You will likely be able to notice an experience of wanting that thing, person, or activity. Next, direct your attention to your breath as it rises and falls. See if you can become aware of the craving or urge in your body, noting its quality and location. Now, using your breath as a surfboard, breathe into and along with the sensations as they build. This can be done kinesthetically, just feeling the wave, or it can be visualized and even heard—an ocean swell accompanied by the roaring of the surf. Continue to focus on your breath coming in and going out, pushing the diaphragm upward to squeeze the air out of the lungs, to support your staying present as the wave crests, ebbs, and finally fades.

Leslie's use of urge surfing was an excellent complement to thinking through the drink, combining wise reflection of her situation with a powerful tool for weathering the storm. Merely thinking in these situations can get extremely complicated. Both desire for the drug *and* aversion to the urge are going on simultaneously, creating more anxiety, tension, and conflict. These mental experiences then become intimately associated with the physical ones.

When asked to identify the experience of craving, many addicts speak about their anxiety or anger. They often do not know the difference between an emotion that triggered a craving and the craving itself. Urge surfing allows these experiences to be decoupled and worked with directly, limiting desperation, fear, and storytelling. It also builds a sense of both interest and efficacy in managing a heretofore overwhelming experience.

Keeping Busy

As we know, frustration tolerance is not the long suit of drug addicts. Particularly in early recovery, folks are often looking out over an interminable day with no relief in sight. The requirement to abstain from the usual forms of escape by "being good" may work for a short while. However, soon there is frustration, boredom, and identity confusion that just serve to heighten internal tension. Also, when we cannot have something, we naturally want it more and will experience more cravings and urges.

Structuring experience can be very helpful here and is a critical benefit of day treatment programs, where patients begin to reorient their lives. While keeping busy can be mindless and avoidant, it can also be employed as a mindfulness tool that is distraction oriented. (By contrast, urge surfing is mostly an awareness-oriented strategy.) Leslie is very busy with her career but also needs to pay close attention to transitions and empty time, during which many slips have occurred. Planning activities like AA and sponsor meetings, therapy, exercise, and social and solitary time has been a critical aspect of her recovery.

In her meditation practice, Leslie was able to see herself craving and wanting. She witnessed her busy mind planning the next relapse. She was interested to see that she also had moments of noncraving. Leslie found that loving-kindness practice allowed her to slow down and soften her attitude. She was able to use the phrases in the midst of cravings or difficult emotions as well as to forgive herself for slips and mistakes.

Craving and Desire

Several years ago Arnold Palmer, writing on the subject of golf and life, made the point that the key to success in any endeavor is desire. He is right. What else causes us to move toward what we want, whether it be to turn on the TV, start a business, prepare a nice meal, learn a foreign language, enter a training program, ask someone out on a date, go on a meditation retreat, or spend the evening in a bar. The newspaper is full of people who wanted things, some admirably motivated and some moved solely by self-interest or even causing harm. Many of the latter group then justify what they do with plenty of support from like-minded compatriots. So how do we know which of our desires are healthy and which are not?

We might begin with a simple reflection: is this desire leading toward my goals, to what I really want? If we are moved and inspired, it may be a good idea to act, but it also may not. Are we making a choice or simply reacting?

Steve is a young, married guy who likes to smoke pot, and his wife is upset with how much money he is spending on it. Steve works for a local newspaper and generally gets high in the morning upon awakening. This both quells the anxiety of transitioning into his day and gives him a sense of adventure, enhancing the experience of his assignments.

On further examination, however, Steve just *wants something,* a physical experience in his chest or belly. He feels better just knowing there is marijuana around and is antsy when he doesn't have it. When feeling high wears off, the wanting feeling returns, leading him to smoke again or to look at pornography online, another activity that provides the possibility of a thrill, takes a lot of time, and creates problems with his wife.

Steve has a conflict around growing up. One set of his parts is mature, considerate, and responsible, working toward a serious writing career, a financially solvent household, a happy marriage with a woman he loves, and the opportunity to raise kids. The other group of parts is quite irresponsible—rebellious, pleasure seeking, self-centered, and even exploitative. When reflecting on his adult desires, Steve feels satisfied and connected to loved ones, with a sense of optimism about the future. By contrast, his immature side feels much more restless, chasing after drug highs, sexual excitement, and a sense of power over others.

These two types of wanting feel very different to Steve, and both have their points. The first type of desire, which we might call "aspiration," feels calm and expansive but with tinges of sadness and fear. The sadness is about all the wasted time and pain he has caused his wife. The fear is that it might never happen, that he does not have what it takes to be a man. The second type of desire, characterized by grasping and clinging, has the advantage of bypassing Steve's worries with adrenaline, excitement (dopamine), and the feeling of being on a roll. The eventual downside of this mode is exhaustion, depletion, and a sense of futility. If you play, you pay.

For Steve to make the choice to go down the road of recovery, he will have to negotiate some challenging obstacles. When craving occurs, he will need to

- Feel the craving, tension, anxiety, anger, or other difficult emotion in the body
- Notice the urge, excitement, or wish for release
- Feel the choice—to gratify the urge or impulse or not
- Use wise reflection, urge surfing, or distraction as a means of getting through the storm of desire
- Learn from the result

If successful in averting a slip, Steve can be pleased that he stayed on track with his life goals. However, he now has to bear the loss of getting high as well as face the responsibilities of adulthood. If, on the other hand, he simply reacted or chose the path of gratifying his craving, he got that experience but is now going nowhere in his life and is on the road to losing everything.

Unlike Leslie, Steve was not drawn to a regular meditation practice. He did use urge surfing, mindful walking, and exercise (a form of distraction) to work with his frequent cravings. He is also in psychotherapy (utilizing internal family systems), where he has gotten to know and appreciate both his addictive and mature parts. Steve's challenge to work with craving offers him the choice of whether to face his fears of becoming a man or remain in the old rut. To paraphrase Neil Sedaka, growing up is very hard to do; it is not for everyone. Mindfulness of craving is a critical piece of Steve's path to recovery and adulthood.

Summary

Below is a range of techniques toward embodied awareness and acceptance of cravings and urges.

1. Thinking through the substance or behavior
2. Urge surfing
3. Keeping busy, mindful distraction
4. In sitting meditation:
    - Awareness of grasping, clinging, or lusting
    - Feeling desire in the body and noting your relationship to it. Is this desire moving toward well-being and healthy relationships or not?
    - Awareness of the experience of nonclinging. How does the body feel when it is not grasping or lusting?
5. Walking meditation
6. Loving-kindness meditation
7. Movement in any number of forms, including aerobic exercise, dance, yoga

13

Working with the Body: Pain and Aversion

WE HAVE SEEN that craving is an experience of wanting, grasping, or clinging. Aversion feels more like hating, avoiding, pushing away, or contracting. For teaching purposes, it is important to distinguish these so that we can feel their different energies as they arise. In real life, however, craving and aversion are intimately related. Leslie, for example, appears voracious as she wants and consumes the alcohol provided in her hotel room. But if her drinking episode is triggered by anger or stress, she is simultaneously avoiding her feelings. Steve also has a greedy tendency with drugs and porn, but his aversion is to maturity and responsibility.

The purpose of meditation practice is to develop a balanced awareness of moment-to-moment experience, promoting qualities such as patience, kindness, and wisdom. Craving and aversion are both impediments to this unfolding. They also lead to "suffering," the nonacceptance of unpleasant experience (or "pain.") The good news, however, is that they are also excellent windows into the practice, objects of awareness that are frequently available to addicts and to all of us.

Imagine for a moment the experience of getting out of bed on a cold morning. The alarm goes off and perhaps you are dreaming or simply startled awake. You immediately feel some reluctance (aversion) to the painful reality you are glimpsing. You hit the snooze button. You turn over and luxuriate (craving) in the comfort of the bed. For a moment you fantasize (more craving, plus delusion) about not getting up but realize that's not going to happen, as you feel the cold air on your face. You know it is going to be painful and you cringe (aversion) a bit. Then with a burst or a crawl you make your move out of bed and into the bathroom. Now the shower. Do I have to take one today (aversion)? Yes, your hair needs to be washed. You get in, turn on the water, and adjust the temperature . . . yeah, that's right (craving). Getting out of the shower is the same debate as emerging from bed. You are cold, you dry off, and you are on your journey for the day, a day sure to have more challenges. You may think of these problems as *in your way,* but remember: the obstacle is the path.

Pain, both physical and emotional, is a major player in the process of substance use, stimulating the experiences of both craving and aversion. Our natural tendency is to avoid pain, and with an acute injury or headache, we can often achieve that via the passage of time, changing position, or taking a pill. With chronic pain we employ the same strategies, only they do not work as well. This creates anxiety and triggers a stress response—fight, flee, or freeze—which causes us to worry, get angry, try to escape, and tense our muscles, producing more pain.

By now it is clear that there is nowhere to run, but still we don't surrender but proceed to the last refuge, our heads. There we tell a story or series of stories generated through the lens of victimhood: the pain is terrible, it is never going to go away, I won't be able to earn a living, I will let everyone down, it is going to ruin my life, why me?, if I had not been so (stupid, reckless, unlucky) I would not be in this mess, ad infinitum. We desperately seek relief to get rid of the pain or to escape entirely. And addicts know how to do that.

Unfortunately, what we resist persists, and so instead of eliminating pain, this strategy tends to perpetuate it. Mindfulness practice is a means to become aware of these natural tendencies that are self-defeating. The direct observation of our bodies and minds shows us that pain is not the same as suffering. Understanding our relationship to pain is a critical component in grappling with an addictive process.

The Varieties of Pain

Certain forms of pain require immediate attention—for example, if there is a dull ache in the center of the chest. Once heart disease has been diagnosed, the patient needs to be alert to the onset of discomfort, the conditions that caused it, when to rest and when to move. Back pain, by contrast, is generally not life threatening. However, effective treatment requires patients to develop a similar awareness of symptoms and conditions.

For Ben, my ex-patient who left his job because of back pain, the origin of the problem was some combination of lifting injuries, weight gain, and stress. Ben's functioning gradually diminished as he began to protect his back by becoming more sedentary and gaining even more weight. This created more worry and tension and more pain, which forced him to stop working entirely. Ben then became depressed and withdrew further into drinking, eating, and dissociation in a downward spiral. Though not dead, he believed his life was over.

The major themes in chronic back pain are emotional stress, tight muscles, and guarding against further pain through inactivity. This leads to more fear, desperation, and a deteriorating course, as Ben found out. I personally had the experience of being told to rest with an episode of back pain while I was in medical school. Fortunately, I was poor at following this advice, more anxious about missing class than about worsening my condition. Indeed, state-of-the-art advice in the treatment of back pain is to resume normal activity. And mindfulness practice, as we will see, can help to promote a relationship to pain that promotes healing and limits disability.[1]

Headaches require a different approach, one that emphasizes relaxation. In migraine headaches, the pain comes from the constriction and dilation of blood vessels, producing a sharp, pulsating pain that is often one-sided and associated with nausea and vomiting. Tension headaches come from tight muscles in the forehead or neck. Both can be brought on by stress. Also, since arteries and muscles are intimately associated, one type of headache can lead to the other, producing a mixed picture.[2]

Regardless of whether a headache patient takes medicine, initiating a relaxation response is going to help break the cycle of stress, tension, and pain. Victor, one of the prison inmates I worked with, had extreme pain in the back of his head and neck. One day in his cell, out of total desperation, he focused on his breathing and was amazed that the muscles relaxed within a few minutes. After that he began to notice how his body would accumulate tension in a stressful environment. Victor saw that he could not control what happened in the prison, but he could control where he directed his attention (namely, from his head, that is, his thinking mind, to his body) and his behavior. Using mindful breathing, many people with tension headaches require no medication, and migraine patients often have less severe episodes, reducing their need for drugs.

Marjorie came to day treatment following a three-week binge with oxycodone. She was having severe jaw pain related to temporomandibular joint syndrome (TMJ). Marjorie had just separated from her partner of thirteen years, making it difficult to pay her rent. Along with her drug use, she'd had a recent run of sexual encounters, which did not help her body or her self-esteem. Marjorie was extremely guarded early on and remained in the program only because of severe depression and exhaustion.

Her energy did improve with medication and better rest, but she continued to be irritable, reactive, and intrusive with other group members. Some of this was attributable to her TMJ, for which she received a prescription for Flexeril, a muscle relaxer, from her primary care physician. However, she took six pills the first night without realizing it, and we concluded that she could not take the medicine responsibly.

Having learned some simple mindfulness skills, Marjorie began to pay attention to her pain, which she had always tried to avoid and self-medicate. First she began to notice the act of clenching her jaw and that she had some control of it. Practicing the body scan revealed that she was mostly pain-free, and when she had symptoms, they were neither solid nor endless. She also became aware of the disappointment, fear, and anger that led her to tense as a means of managing her emotions.

When she stopped clenching so much, Marjorie did experience some anxiety and disorientation, but it was not as bad as she anticipated.

Her jaw pain improved dramatically, and she was pleased to no longer be a victim of it. As she relaxed more with other people, they saw that she was quite funny and insightful. Marjorie was able to see her tendency to judge and tell stories about people and was able to apply her newfound awareness practices to improving her communication and relationships.

Kenny was a twenty-five-year-old salesman of medical equipment who also came into treatment with an enormous opiate habit, spending upward of $2,500 a week on Oxycontin to manage chronic abdominal pain. Kenny has Crohn's disease, an autoimmune disorder causing chronic inflammation at multiple locations in the gastrointestinal tract, leading to ulcerations, scarring, and the ongoing risk of bowel obstruction. Kenny has had the problem since age twelve, and part of his small intestine has been removed, but his symptoms of pain, cramping, and diarrhea were only partially responsive to medication.

Opiates, both analgesic and constipating, were the perfect solution—until they stopped working. He also discovered that the drugs helped him to feel energized and that they stabilized what was diagnosed as bipolar disorder. Once Kenny was off opiates, you can imagine the roller coaster he was on prior to coming to treatment.

Medicine helped to stabilize his moods, but there was still the matter of abdominal pain. Kenny realized he was alarmed by any hint of intestinal movement, fearful that another attack of cramps was coming. He had used opiates to manage both the pain and the fear. In treatment, he was drawn to both mindful breathing and walking, initially as a distraction from his abdominal discomfort.

As Kenny looked more closely, he saw how his fear caused him to tense, increasing his pain. He learned a variation of urge surfing to ride the wave of his fear, which made the pain more tolerable. He also used the motion of walking to see his intestinal waves as a natural movement and not something he had to fight against. Once he was struggling less, Kenny was able to experience the sadness and anger related to drawing such a difficult card at such a young age. He was beginning to surrender to his problem instead of fighting it. Now he could choose to respond more creatively, to play the hand he was dealt the best he could.

Working with Pain

Mindfulness practice reduces the suffering associated with pain by changing our relationship to it. We have seen in all of our cases that pain causes fear and contraction, which compounds the problem. So how do we begin to accept unpleasant experience? First we need to come into the body. This can be initiated with a few deep breaths. Often this is enough to start to separate our present experience from worries and judgments. Then we are in a position to develop some stability of mind, enough to see that our physical sensations are separate from our emotions, thoughts, and judgments.

Practice: Making Space

The following meditation uses mindfulness, imagery, and relaxation to investigate the problem of acceptance of pain. It approaches the thorny question: How in the world do I accept something that I wish would go away? It has five phases, each of which touches on the subject of acceptance.[3]

1. *Stabilizing.* Assuming a comfortable, upright posture, take three or four deep, calming breaths. Notice your touch points—feet, butt in the chair, back, hands, arms—and where they are making contact. Experience the natural flow of breath, in and out, and direct your attention to either your nose or your abdomen, wherever your breath feels the most vivid. Continue to notice the sensations of breathing, and when your mind goes off into thinking, fantasizing, or spacing out, simply come back. Do this gently and without judgment. It may distract you from the pain or it may not. This phase can be very brief or longer, if it feels helpful. You might ask yourself, How am I relating to my pain right now?
2. *Noticing.* Shift your primary attention to the area of the pain, moving your breath to the background to support that attention. Notice the nature of the pain sensations—aching, pulsing, boring, piercing, dull, and so on. Simply note the experience to yourself.

3. *Breathing.* Inhale to a count of four directly into the painful area. This may produce a feeling of penetrating, surrounding, or accompanying the sensations. You will be able to notice which of these qualities brings a measure of support or relaxation in the midst of pain—and encourage the one that is most helpful.

4. *Accepting.* Hold your breath to a count of four. Ask yourself, Can I make space for this pain? This is a question, not a command. If the answer is yes, you might use the image of a vast sky, the breeze moving over a meadow, sunlight spreading across a lake. Perhaps you will notice a felt sense of vibration or movement of the energy through or beyond the body. If the answer is no, simply accept that for now.

5. *Allowing.* Exhale to a count of four. See what happens. The sensations of pain may move or not. Notice if you are allowing something to happen or trying to make it happen.

Repeat steps 2 to 5 for as long as your session lasts. You will be able to notice changes in the pain and your relationship to it—the ability to accept and allow—over the course of the exercise.

Pain and Addiction

The experience of pain is vital to our survival. A diabetic with peripheral neuropathy can unknowingly and repeatedly injure a toe, leading to infection, tissue death, and removal of the toe, the foot, or more. Pain signals us to quickly remove our hand from a hot stove and put it under cold water, limiting the damage. We are clearly in trouble without this reflex; however, its link to emotion and stress can become problematic.

Deane Juhan, author of *Job's Body*, points out that pain-specific nerve endings, called nociceptors (from the Latin *nocere*, to harm), herald the oncoming experience of pain. If we interpret this as leading to actual tissue damage (which may not be the case), we will react with fear, triggering a stress reaction. Nociception leads to pain and then suffering—that is, wanting the pain to go away. The case examples illustrate how the combination of pain, fear, and stress can be quelled with alcohol or drugs. This is because these substances are able to separate pain temporarily from suffering—that is, pain is experienced, but we don't care about it so much.

The same thing can happen in a crisis or in a ball game in which an athlete is able to play through a broken arm or foot. The massive release of stress hormones and endorphins facilitates this dissociation of pain from suffering and even reduces pain, as many people who intentionally cut themselves have discovered. However, for the addict, simple pain relief is only one possible goal. Attachments and addictions can develop in relation to any part of the process—the high, the sense of control, the stress, the desperation, or even the pain itself, which the person may feel is deserved.

Nocioception leads to a reflex reaction at the level of the spinal cord, where the sensory pain signal transfers directly to motor neurons. These then stimulate muscles in the area to contract to support the injured tissue, a necessary function to limit tissue damage. However, contraction sustained for too long can become too widespread, creating more pain. Both ischemia, the reduction of blood flow, and the buildup of lactic acid, a metabolic waste product of contracting muscle, can be new sources of pain in this vicious cycle.[4]

Pain, Addiction, and Mindfulness

Drugs can be effective in interrupting this pain/contraction cycle, allowing spasm to subside so that relief is possible. However, in chronic situations, medication use can become a repetitive and addictive mode leading to escalating use, diminishing effectiveness, physical tolerance, rebound pain as doses wear off, disrupted sleep, poor concentration and thinking, and mood instability—as we saw with Ben, Marjorie, and Kenny.

All three of these patients had begun to self-medicate their pain only after being dissatisfied by the results of their medical or surgical treatments. However, it is critical that any patient with chronic pain have a complete medical workup in order to eliminate potential treatable conditions, such as tumors or infections. Reviewing the situation with a physician can help relax patients convinced that they have a serious illness and allow them to receive guidance on the appropriate level of activity for their rehabilitation. Mindfulness training can then be an excellent accompaniment to the other components of their program, including exercise, physical therapy, medication, psychotherapy, chiropractic, acupuncture, and other alternative treatments.

Mindfulness uses the same principle of separating pain from suffering as opiates do, without the side effects. Think of comforting a child who has skinned her knee or bumped her head. The touch and loving words produce competing signals to the fear component of the injury. This elicits a relaxation response that calms the child even as the pain is still present. The pain and tension can now subside gradually as she is supported or distracted.

As we saw with Kenny, the ability to distract can begin to develop a sense of control, which cuts into the cycle of powerlessness and victimhood. With practice, he was more able to turn toward the fear and pain. This natural evolution leads to a number of benefits, including

- More clearly noticing the difference between physical sensations and emotions
- Developing a more neutral, accepting attitude
- Seeing directly that sensations, feelings, and thoughts change and are insubstantial
- Reducing the impact of stories, many of which are untrue
- Feeling more in control and less like a victim
- Enjoying a greater sense of spaciousness and connection to the environment, to other sufferers, and to all beings

As we practice mindfulness, we are creating another cycle, one of relaxation and empowerment. Mindfulness meditation has been shown to produce a wakeful, hypometabolic state, the opposite of the body's reaction to pain and stress.[5] Alert relaxation allows us to focus and learn more easily. It also builds the confidence to approach even feared situations with interest and courage. Pain is no longer the dreaded obstacle that must be avoided but is perceived as part of the greater fabric of life, multifaceted and continually changing.

Working with Aversion

Aversion is the second obstacle to mental clarity, the flip side of craving. What these two have in common is wanting things to be other than what they are, but their energies feel very different. Craving (lust or sensual desire) has been likened to a pond into which many colors have been thrown, causing us to be attracted or drawn to it. Aversion (hatred or anger) has been compared to water that is turbulent or boiling, creating conditions in which we can be swept away or burned. In both cases we are unable to see clearly.[6]

Craving and aversion are intimately related in the pain/stress/addiction pattern. Pain leads to stress, craving for relief, substance use, temporary relief at best, aversion (in the form of frustration and tension), increased pain and stress in an ongoing cycle. Aversion then often devolves into discouragement, self-judgment, despair, and resignation. People can then get stuck in apathy, indifference, depression—essentially giving up on themselves. The good news here is that it is possible to enter the cycle with mindful awareness at any point.

In working with aversion, the key factor is to know the difference between the unpleasant object (pain, in this case) and the experience of avoiding it. This is the whole point of practicing meditation and mindful awareness. As we slow down enough, we are actually able to notice the differences among the experiences of pain, stress, craving, and aversion. Could seeing where pain ends and aversion begins be more interesting than just escaping pain?

Kenny certainly found it to be. He saw that tensing at the first sign of cramping made his situation worse. It gave him a reason to get high, which worked for a while, but he could not earn enough money to support his habit. Marjorie's jaw clenching was an aversion to her anxiety, which worsened her TMJ. This led her to opiates, causing her to withdraw further, creating more social anxiety and paranoia. Ben's aversion to pain took the form of overeating or simply dissociating. These people all came to see that staying present in the body was a more effective strategy than trying to avoid both the experiences of pain and trying to escape from it. And it was also more interesting.

Practice: Pain and Aversion

The following practice is an extension of the making-space meditation. It begins with the sensations of pain, but then brings particular attention to the question, How am I relating to the pain? Here we move from awareness of present experience with acceptance to investigation into our relationship with nonacceptance or suffering.

1. Begin by returning to the making-space meditation, moving through the steps of stabilizing, noticing, breathing, accepting, and allowing the experience of pain. In the succeeding steps, feel free to use the technique of inhaling, holding, and exhaling the breath to a count of four, if that helps the energy to move.
2. Notice if there is any aversion to the pain. Is there tension, fear, expectation, boredom, disappointment, or judgment? See if you can locate the aversion in the body.
3. Breathe into the experience of aversion. This is done with the intention of bringing an element of relaxation or even kindness to your observation.
4. Now ask yourself, Can I make space for this aversion? If yes, simply stay with the sensations using any imagery, visual or kinesthetic, that helps you bring acceptance to your aversion. If you are experiencing a struggle, breathe into that. Then accept and allow for your "bad attitude," feeling overwhelmed, or wanting to give up.
5. Notice how the reaction of anger, fear, or contraction changes over time. How do these observations affect your relationship to the pain and the aversion? As you bring greater acceptance to your reactions without reacting to them as much, is your experience different?

The key question, Can I make space for this pain?, is quite useful and generalizable. Can I make space for this aversion, fear, grief? The answer may be no, and if so, that is what we need to accept. However, the question can also shift us from analysis to observation and acceptance, and from the mind to the body. It also goes to the heart of the difference between unpleasant sensations and suffering in the trajectory of pain. Can we relax into the experiences of "unpleasant" or "not liking"? If so, we are less likely to move into pushing the pain away and fueling the cycle of stress reactivity.

The ability to make space around pain or aversion is largely a matter of attitude. If we can bring a mind-set of openness or interest to these experiences, we are less likely to be lost in them and need to escape. If our attitude is negative or hostile, that too can be a subject for awareness and acceptance. Is it okay to have a bad attitude or a bad day? If the answer is yes, then we can be irritable or in pain but not as miserable.

If you found the exercises difficult or are unimpressed with the results, not to worry. It is the *intention* to make space for any sensation, emotion, or reaction that is important—more important than any concept we have of success or failure. Acceptance of pain and/or aversion is a process that begins with our intention to be happy and well. It is a process of awareness and investigation, not avoidance or control.

That being said, we may have a number of "intentions" operating at any given moment, besides our conscious, healthy one. We may be, for example, invested in our fear, anger, discouragement, victimhood, wish for revenge—and that intention can then drive our attitude and behavior.

Changing our unhealthy patterns is slow, certainly slower than we like. Despite our best efforts, reactivity to these hidden intentions often triggers relapse to addictive patterns and to discouragement that we will never get it right. How different would our lives be if we could accept our pace of change (or make space for our impatience)? As we react less to old habits and behavior, there is a palpable change in our experience, a shift from judgment to kindness. This is an act of generosity toward ourselves that others can feel as well.

Regular mindfulness practice allows us to develop greater stability of mind and see more clearly, less likely to be tumbling forward in a cycle of confusion, powerlessness, overwhelm, and self-defeating behaviors. Beginning to glimpse the true nature of pain and aversion brings a shift in perspective. There is less preoccupation with symptoms, and the ideas of having a life-threatening or disabling illness are called into question. There is less catastrophizing, self-judgment, and victim thinking and greater openness and compassion. We feel more engaged and less alone.

Summary

The following are the approaches and meditations useful in relating to pain and aversion.

1. Deep breaths for relaxation
2. Regular exercise and stretching or yoga
3. Mindful walking
4. Loving-kindness meditation
5. Making-space meditation
6. Pain and aversion meditation
7. Sitting meditation:

   - Careful and repeated noting—seeing the changing nature of the anger, contraction, or bad attitude
   - Seeing the story that is feeding the aversion, for example, feeling "wronged" or needing to be right
   - Noticing how we are relating to our anger or hostility, for example, self-judgment, fear, despair, victimhood, or acceptance

14

Working with the Body:
Energetic States

*Energy is a dynamic force, in constant flux, which circulates throughout
the body. Many people plausibly substitute the word life for the word energy
since the essential difference between the two words is so subtle that it eludes
all but the semanticist.*
    —STEPHEN CHANG[1]

The nation that controls magnetism controls the universe.
    —DICK TRACY

ABOUT FIFTEEN YEARS AGO, I developed an effusion (swelling) in
my knee after playing touch football. After the swelling recurred a few
more times, I went to my doctor, who examined the knee and told me
I almost certainly had torn cartilage and would need arthroscopic surgery. Around that same time, I was told about a guy who practiced *tui
na*, an aspect of the Taoist system of healing that moves energy in the
body. After he examined the knee, he informed me that I was "just not
getting enough chi into that joint."

"You have to forgive me," I said. "I didn't learn about that in medical school." In Chinese medicine, *chi* is the electromagnetic charge

that imbues the body structures and fluids with life force. It is not visible to the naked eye and is most notable when absent. A partial absence of this vital energy leads to weakness and disease; a total absence, to death.[2]

He proceeded to show me five points, four around the knee and one on the heel, and began to press on them. These corresponded with acupuncture points, and some of them hurt so much I was practically singing. I was instructed to work these points myself, as much as I could stand, and after about six visits everything was a lot less sore. I resumed normal activity, including skiing and basketball, and have never had another effusion. Apparently, energy channels, called meridians in the Chinese system, did exist and could be worked with directly. Who knew?

Energy is life, allowing us to breathe, move, speak, think, and maintain all of the metabolic processes of the body. In this book I have made reference to the various forms of energy manifested by human beings. We have instinctual energies (sexual, aggressive, competitive, self-centered), and we also have more socializing energies (cooperative, connecting, altruistic), as well as spiritual energies that yearn to connect with something beyond ordinary reality. Different parts of our personalities carry diverse energies—pressured, pleasing, caretaking, responsible, ambitious, angry, addictive, immature, peaceful, fun loving, vulnerable—in an infinite array that is constantly changing.

In the Western medicine paradigm, our energy system is governed by the autonomic nervous system, which was discussed in chapter 11. The parasympathetic side moves us toward relaxation, rest, and digestion; the sympathetic to adrenalized, stimulated states effective for managing stress and crises. As previously noted, these roughly correspond with yin (spacious, cool, wet) and yang (constricted, warm, dry). We clearly need both, as well as the capacity to find the proper balance for each condition that arises.

This chapter will focus on two energy extremes: too little and too much. They correspond with the next two obstacles or hindrances to concentration and clarity of mind. They are called "sloth and torpor" and "restlessness/worry." Much like craving and aversion, they are two sides of the same coin and major inducers to substance abuse. The ultimate task of mindfulness practice, not unlike tui na or acupuncture, is to allow energy in the mind-body to come into balance. But first we must become more intimately aware of the vast energy play that is our life.

Low Energy States

Henry grew up in a family of strivers and high achievers. He was well endowed also—smart, artistic, personable—but did not get into a top college as his parents and two siblings had. In the spring of his junior year he felt particularly unmotivated, smoking weed every day. Now depressed and unable to focus in class, Henry dropped out. Once home, he got a job at a day camp, but after that ended he made only halfhearted attempts to find other work and again lapsed into an unmotivated state.

Since his life clearly was not working, Henry was willing to come to day treatment, albeit grudgingly. He told me that he had never been a very high-energy type of person, but his friends liked his relaxed approach to life. Smoking marijuana became a habit as Henry got more nervous about falling behind in school. However, the drug could not keep pace with his anxiety, and he spiraled down into depression. Now, his energy system clearly out of whack, Henry agreed to stop using while in the program.

In his mindfulness training, Henry was immediately drawn to the experience of cause and effect. "If A happens, I feel B," he said. "When I can't figure out my major, I feel nervous." He saw that shutting down into a low-energy state was an attempt to manage his anxiety, which worked but at great cost. Henry's habit of avoidance with or without marijuana was very strong.

One physical manifestation of this was the state of his room, which I saw when his dad sent me a text message with a photo. Henry admitted it was a disaster that was spilling into other areas of the house. However, when he began cleaning it, he quickly became anxious and overwhelmed and gave up. I suggested that his anxiety was energy that could be used to accomplish his task. Henry laughed, always a good moment in treatment, and agreed to spend thirty to forty-five minutes a day on his room. Once committed, he was able to use the energy of anxiety as well as accept encouragement and help from his parents, which he had previously been too ashamed to do.

Coming to the program for three weeks helped balance Henry's energy. He did regular walking in nature with his dog, went to the gym, and engaged with his tasks, family, and friends. Henry saw that putting out effort produced energy, and life went better when he stayed grounded in his body. When he went up into his head, worrying about his future or world problems like global warming, he would feel a sense of helplessness and futility and go numb.

The transition out of day treatment was not easy. Looking for work was frustrating, and his parents were clear that Henry had to be actively engaged or out of the house. His urge to shut down was strong. Henry did not know what to do but was guided by the theme of managing his energy. Since he does well when outside, he decided to work on a farm for the spring and apply to schools in Vermont and out West, where he could ski and hike as well as study. Most important, Henry saw that he had considerable strengths, different from his parents' and siblings'. If he focused on taking charge of his own energy system, the comparisons fell away and he could more easily relax into his own life.

Low-energy states can be quite seductive. Though Henry might have been jealous of his high-energy siblings, he was able to enjoy the experiences of being calm, sedated, and drowsy and got quite attached to them. Sleep can be used as a drug and promote a cycle of cocooning that is hard to break, devolving into lethargy, depression, and progressive withdrawal from life. Remember the heroin addict mentioned in chapter 1 who essentially slept through ten years of his life.

In meditation practice, particularly on longer retreats, sloth and torpor are frequent visitors as energy comes and goes. Since meditation requires energy, drowsiness is an impediment, like trying to cut a bagel with a dull knife. It can be unpleasant to be continually fighting sleep or pleasant to be in a twilight state where we can check out and pass the time without doing the work of mindfulness.

If we continually yield to the comfort of sloth and torpor and go to sleep, we will never be able to access the energy that comes from a concentrated mind and a clear purpose. Conversely, we cannot just blast through or avoid our low-energy states. As Henry discovered, working effectively with these conditions requires us to bring acceptance to them and to ourselves.

Energy and Effort

In my work as a mindfulness teacher, I am forever encouraging people to walk. The main excuses for not doing so are invariably about not having enough energy or the weather. I have some fun with the latter, musing about the person's choosing the wrong part of the country to live in or informing her that there is this amazing invention for the rain that she might have heard of. The key to this problem is how to get the motor running in order to discover, as Henry did, that *effort produces energy*. We can see this every day when we accomplish the daunting task of getting out of bed and then, even with inadequate sleep, are able to get through our work or chores. It is also apparent that moderate, regular exercise, which I will discuss later in this section, can significantly enhance energy and well-being.

If these measures do not begin to right someone's ship, we must look further. Barry lost his job doing computer work with a printing company, which he had had for twenty years. His wife worked but also wanted a baby, which Barry did not feel ready for. In our program, he stopped drinking, took medicine, and was encouraged to do regular mindful walking and movement. Barry was frequently stuck at the boundary of not having the energy to make an effort; he would call himself "lazy" and then get more anxious, depressed, and stuck. Often he would choose a nap over walking, when he'd clearly had sufficient sleep the night before. He avoided looking for work, believing his range of skills was too limited to be successful in a new job. Of course, this also increased his anxiety.

When Barry's father came for a visit that summer, Barry was forced to be more active, and his energy did improve. However, during the visit Barry revealed that his father had left the family when Barry was ten, leaving him scared and at a loss to help his mother and younger sister. Since he was not a high-energy person, Barry felt as if he had always been behind and could never catch up. He saw himself as a failure and a fraud, barely able to get through life.

Barry began to watch his tendency to speed up internally, become desperate, and give up, worsening his already low self-esteem. We encouraged him to slow down and notice his anxiety instead of trying to outrun it. This helped Barry to see that his fear was rooted in a conflict about trying and failing, yet again. His lethargy and withdrawal were a way of avoiding the fear of facing the challenges of adulthood—understandable, since he was approaching them with the mind of a ten-year-old. Mindfulness practice had helped point the way to the work he needed to do in psychotherapy.

Working with Sloth and Torpor

To work with low-energy states (drowsiness or dullness of mind), in daily life you can practice:

- Adequate sleep, exercise, and nutrition
- Mindful walking: brisk walking can increase energy; slow walking meditation encourages a fine moment-to-moment awareness that can wake up a sleepy mind.
- Developing a life plan and taking an interest in it every day

In sitting meditation, you can practice:

- Riding the waves of sleepiness
- Working with aversion to drowsiness (as in the pain and aversion meditation)
- Seeing the nature and location of the low-energy state in the body
- Increasing effort to follow the breath or touch points more finely
- Opening the eyes
- Standing up
- Taking a ten- to fifteen-minute nap, allowing the body to let go as much as possible

High-Energy States

Jackie had been revved up for as long as she could remember. She was seen as a troublemaker in her family, where she would rage, destroy things, and get into fights with her siblings. Her parents were of little help, lost in their own problems. Jackie had to leave high school after throwing a chair at a teacher. She smoked pot and drank to blunt her energy and used cocaine to keep it going. At forty years old, she came into treatment depressed, depleted, and "sick of trying to live every day." Jackie's history of mood swings—especially her highs: energetic, active, driving too fast, and having impulsive sex—was not subtle, and she responded to a mood stabilizer. However, she continued to be extremely reactive, particularly to her ex-husband and his wife, and to go into overdrive.

One day she was extremely agitated, stating that she could not breathe. Her daughter had told her that she liked her father's wife, whom Jackie hated. She felt competitive, then panicked about losing her daughter completely. With some help, Jackie was able to ground herself and take a few calming breaths. She was able to see how the story she told herself had frightened her and that it likely was not true. In fact, she appreciated that the woman was nice to her kids. Her revving up was clearly a habit, born of her constitution, mood disorder, and early environment of abuse and neglect. It kept her from eating and sleeping. It was also a means of keeping her moving and safe, though it was now clearly leading to deteriorating physical and mental health.

Jackie began to do regular mindful breathing for grounding and relaxation and mindful walking to balance her energy. As she came more into her body, she was more able to see the relationship between her energy states and inner storytelling. She related numerous instances of restlessness or agitation that triggered stories and vice versa. Jackie also reported that she was paying attention to eating when hungry and sleeping when tired. She still got overwhelmed but now felt that she had brakes to prevent her from going out of control.

Restlessness and worry are so rampant in our culture that they are "normal," the energy that is required to be successful. The drive to succeed in the quest for money, fame, being a good parent, or making a contribution is not the only impetus to restlessness. The tendency to high-energy, agitated, or anxious states can be constitutional, trauma related, or addictive. Jackie had all of these and became an adrenaline junkie in order to manage the enormous vulnerability and grief from her childhood. Then, because the mind and body are connected, she spun out endless fantasies and negative predictions that further agitated her. Only when she began to experience the downside of this way of living did she seek help.

Jackie's relationship with restlessness improved when she began to see it as an energy that arose under certain conditions. This was much more helpful than worrying, trying to fix all of her problems, blaming, or self-medicating. Once she brought greater acceptance to her experience, there was less of a struggle and less energy lost in spinning her wheels. Then she was able to make use of techniques of developing concentration, grounding, movement, and making space.

Balancing Energy with Walking

On a detoxification unit, we are confronted with enormous suffering and limited capacity to alleviate it. In my first such job, the heroin addicts did not receive methadone but clonidine, an antihypertensive that mitigates some of the symptoms of opiate withdrawal—elevated heart rate and blood pressure, aches, and agitation. This was supplemented by "comfort meds," including something for anxiety, pain (nonopiate), diarrhea, and nausea. In the end this was effective if the patient could tolerate one or two days of misery. Since I had little more to offer, I would walk the halls with these people and encourage them to do mindful walking on their own throughout the day.

I noticed that all of the addicts fell into two energetic categories. They were either totally lethargic and shut down or extremely shaky and agitated. It turns out that walking meditation is a good treatment for both conditions, either getting the motor running (effort produces energy) or channeling the excess energy into the walking and allowing the system to idle down, like kicking the accelerator to slow a racing engine. Many benefited, although one morning a patient approached me and said, "Hey, Doc, that walking meditation you showed me doesn't work." I could not have planned my response, but he seemed to get the point: "You know," I said, "I can't sit down and play the piano, because I've never practiced."

Exercise

Until we see that exercise is a habit with clear benefits, we will tend to avoid it. This is particularly true for the addict, whose energy system is out of balance, much like a car that needs a tune-up. Regular aerobic workouts and stretching will allow the pistons to fire in the right sequence and the organism to come into equilibrium. Exercise has a number of benefits around the improvement of cardiovascular health, stress resistance, immune function, and a sense of well-being that has both physiological and psychological aspects. It is not surprising then that people who are fit are less likely to smoke, abuse substances, or overeat.

Exercise has been shown to reduce anxiety through decreasing muscle tension, restlessness, and physical symptoms like cramping, bloating, sweating, and palpitations. Stress reduction is achieved via heightened awareness, release of adrenaline and endorphins, distraction, and a sense of mastery. Improved mood can result from elevated levels of norepinephrine, serotonin, and dopamine and a better neurotransmitter balance. Regular exercise makes the body a more pleasant and powerful place to be.[3]

A recent study done in Denmark addressed the questions of whether exercise treatment can contribute to altering the behavior of drug abusers, their body image, and their self-confidence. Of twenty subjects (out of thirty-eight) who completed the study, which put them through a regimen of both aerobic and socially oriented exercise, fifteen (75 percent) reported either no or reduced drug use. Improvements were noted in fitness level, severity of withdrawal symptoms, urges, and the diminished role of drugs and alcohol in structuring time. Subjects also noted a better sense of their body and energy level and improved sleep and a greater ability to enter social environments.[4] Although it was a small pilot study, there is a clear suggestion that regular exercise is a means for diminished suffering and enhanced well-being in early recovery.

A casual perusal of a typical gym with people watching TV, reading, listening to music, looking in the mirror, and checking each other out suggests that it is quite possible to work out for hours without being in the body at all. Whether you run, walk, stretch, or lift weights, consider being fully present. Then your exercise will be a part of your mindfulness training, leading to fewer injuries and greater embodied awareness and self-confidence.

Sleep

If exercise is avoided in early recovery, sleep is desperately sought. But the addict's efforts to escape his myriad discomforts through sleep are often met with frustration. This is because sleep is a *skill* requiring elements of relaxation and letting go, a skill that has fallen into disuse after months or years of substance abuse. During this period of the addict's life, sleep has been attained via intoxication and passing out, is generally fitful, and ends with a hangover or frank withdrawal symptoms. His sleep-wake cycles are reversed or chaotic. He has lost the natural rhythm of energy depletion through daily activity and a recharging of the battery at night.

Alcohol use, for example, decreases sleep latency (you need less time to fall asleep) but disrupts the second half of the sleep period, likely because of withdrawal symptoms. With alcohol dependence, it takes longer to fall asleep and there are frequent awakenings, poor sleep quality (less slow-wave, or deep, sleep), and daytime fatigue. Abstinent alcoholics can sleep poorly for years, and drinking to transiently improve sleep (which does happen) is a not infrequent cause of relapse.

As we saw in chapter 11, repeated intoxication and withdrawal symptoms produce a chronic stress state and elevated sympathetic tone. If exhausted enough, we will pass out, only to wake one or two hours later, alarmed or wired. The ability to truly let go and rest requires a proper autonomic balance. One study demonstrated that acute stress reduces parasympathetic modulation in all phases of sleep.[5] Another recent paper correlated high adrenal activity in stressed subjects with frequent waking periods.[6]

An addict's sleep will be problematic regardless of the predilection for low- or high-energy states. Both Henry and Barry slept a great deal but woke frequently, never felt rested, and knew they were avoiding life, which created even more anxiety. Jackie could barely rest at all and would keep going until she self-medicated or simply fainted from exhaustion. Only through some training in mindful awareness did these people have any appreciation for when their bodies were asking for sleep.

Sleep is a fine-tuned activity requiring both physiological and emotional balance. Patients are frequently on medicine for mood and/ or anxiety problems as well as sleep. I like to use medicine to treat symptoms as opposed to knocking someone out cold, but at times sedatives (preferably nonaddicting) are needed short-term. Good sleep is also aided by honest living, something addicts are generally not doing when they first come to treatment. A foundation in truth and respect is critical to progress with sleep and well-being.

I encourage my patients to practice regular mindful walking, awareness of simple tasks like brushing their teeth or doing the dishes, and transitions from one activity to another. This tends to damp down the steady flow of thinking and worrying, which often occurs on an unconscious level. It also allows the mind to settle, an excellent investment in the goal of quieting enough to sleep later on.

Likely you have seen articles about sleep hygiene in *O* (Oprah's magazine) or *Ladies' Home Journal,* and they offer very practical suggestions. For example, it is advisable to turn the TV or computer off and have a thirty- to sixty-minute period of quiet transition to bed. Then listen to soothing music or read if you like. Avoid caffeine late in the day, and don't smoke in the middle of the night if your goal is to get back to sleep.

I generally recommend doing two to five minutes of mindful breathing, focusing at the belly to allow the thoughts to settle like sand in a jar of water. You could also do a body scan, which prioritizes concentration and will promote drowsiness when energy is low. If you wake in the middle of the night, just go right to the body or breath. I had to learn the hard way that 3 A.M. is not the time to figure out my life. Yes, there are problems, but your job then is to sleep so you can be sharp and productive in the morning. Once you surrender to this, you will rest more easily, which is rejuvenating and gives the best chance of dozing off.

Since addicts are not long on patience and are often uncomfortable, this is easier said than done. Lori, an alcoholic in our program, told me that when she wakes up at night she says, "Damn it!"

"Does that help you?" I asked, less than seriously.

Clearly not. Lori saw that under her anger was the fear that she would not get back to sleep and would again be tired all day. Could she notice the fear and disappointment, let go of the story line, and return to her contact points or breath? Could she be more compassionate with herself and her best efforts to rest and get back to sleep? Once Lori began to ground herself more regularly during the day as well as at night, she saw how worried she was about her memory, sleep, kids, money, and so on. By the time of discharge, she was less depressed and thinking more clearly, at least in part related to improved sleep. On her exit questionnaire, her final comment was: "Find your ass in the bed. Feel your belly rising and falling. . . . Get your brain back."

Working with Restlessness and Worry

To work with restlessness and worry in daily life, practice the following:

- Regular grounding in the body
- Listening to the body around the need for food, rest, or movement
- Calming breaths to elicit the relaxation response
- Bringing awareness to destabilizations and worry and then regrounding
- Mindful walking to channel and balance energy, feeling for the right pace
- Spending time in nature to connect to something greater than yourself and deemphasize worry

To work with restlessness and worry specifically during sitting meditation, practice the following:

- Repeated noting of the experience of restlessness
- Working with energies that grow out of restlessness—craving (urge surfing, making space meditation) and aversion (pain and aversion meditation)
- Developing concentration with mindful breathing and body scanning
- Bringing awareness to the imbalance between energy and concentration by using one of the following two strategies:

  1. Focus on a small portion of the breath to increase concentration.
  2. Create more space in the mind via opening to the whole body or to sound or by doing a visualization of a vast sky or a natural scene.

- Loving-kindness practice

Energy and Concentration

The two critical faculties of energy and concentration must be in balance for optimal functioning. If energy outstrips concentration, there is agitation, restlessness, and worry. For example, you are in a hurry to find your car in a lot and it is not there. You panic and imagine the worst. Only when you calm down do you realize you are looking in the wrong place. If concentration is much greater than energy, the mind tends to sink or go into a trance. A long drive that requires prolonged concentration can lead to drowsiness as the energy flags. The driver will then require stimulating thoughts or conversation or music or a rest to recharge.

In the throes of addiction, energy and concentration are nearly always out of balance. Too much energy leads to all manner of emotional problems, unskillful speech and actions, and a need to reestablish control through addictive means. Inadequate energy leads to avoiding or spacing out and missing key information. Substance use is initially a means to balance internal processes, establishing a temporary stability, a pseudohomeostasis. Cocaine, for example, can elevate the energy and mood of a depressed person; keep a manic person high; or help a distracted, hyperactive person to focus and calm down. Opiates, alcohol, and tranquilizers have likewise all been employed for either elevating or modulating energy.

People believe they are functioning at peak performance on drugs—relaxed, confident, focused—but there is always something missing. Tony, a highly accomplished editor, believed himself to be extremely effective on opiates. He was energized and efficient, with a feeling of superiority. Eventually, it all fell apart and he went for an inpatient detox. When Tony returned to work, he was surprised to discover the mess in his office. The organizational aspects of his job had been totally neglected during the trance of his drug run. In his illusion of power, Tony had developed a huge blind spot. Opiates allowed him to be *both* energized and concentrated but, unfortunately, not at the same time and with a total loss of the big picture. Tony's addiction had him believing he was smarter than everyone else but ultimately caused him to lose direction and dissipate his energy.

It is the job of mindfulness practice to balance energy and concentration. We have seen that mindfulness seeks an equilibrium between vagal and sympathetic tone and between being and doing. It leads to concentration, clear seeing, and more-skillful choices. And by promoting a greater interest in truth, respect, and ethical behavior, mindfulness training reduces the inner and outer noise. Relationships and recovery move toward greater sanity and wisdom. Our energies and our lives are increasingly more workable.

15

Working with Feelings and Emotions

WE HAVE SEEN that mindfulness practice provides a means to explore the range of energies that are constantly at play in the body. Specifically, we have looked at four of the five hindrances to clarity of mind—craving, aversion, and high- and low-energy states—which are all physical in nature. These hindrances also come in the form of feelings, emotions, and moods, but embodied awareness of these experiences is not our natural tendency. Instead, we will cling to, avoid, space out from, or explain our feelings in our attempt to manage our emotional lives.

We explored this subject in the mindfulness-based stress reduction training at the University of Massachusetts, where I was a participant with regular patients who had not responded to traditional treatments. In the first class, we were taught mindful eating, learned the body scan, and were instructed to practice on our own during the following week. However, beyond concrete practices, there also needed to be training about our tendency to go back on automatic pilot as soon as the practice period was over. In order to begin to capture our moments, we were asked to fill out the "pleasant events calendar." The calendar, which had a line for each day of the week, had several columns:

- What was the experience?
- Were you aware of the pleasant feelings while the event was happening?
- How did your body feel during the experience? Describe the sensations you felt.
- What moods, feelings, or thoughts accompanied the event?
- What thoughts do you have now as you write this down?[1]

People found pleasure in the simple experiences of walking, being outside, seeing the buds forming on the trees, a cup of coffee, a song on the radio, a warm bath, a hug, a joke, or a friendly exchange at the supermarket. Beyond momentary enjoyment, pleasant events could provide a refuge from one's physical and emotional pain—a wonderful insight for patients for whom suffering and desperation were daily companions. So when they filled out the "unpleasant events calendar" the following week, it was with the preliminary awareness that all of life was not misery.

In class our teacher asked for experiences, and Debbie, a woman with treatment-resistant depression, raised her hand. We knew Debbie to be an intelligent and motivated person, and it was a mystery as to why psychotherapy and medicine had not helped her. "I was driving a few days ago," she told us, "and I became aware that this guy was tailgating me. I am thinking he is a jerk and just feel myself getting more and more tense and angry. And then I thought—Oh, this could be an unpleasant event!"

This was Debbie's experience: She was driving just over the speed limit on a one-lane road. Not wanting to speed and get a ticket, Debbie continued on, with no seeming escape from the other driver. As she checked in with her body, Debbie felt herself gripping the wheel tighter, the tension moving up into her shoulders and neck. This led her to feel increasingly trapped, agitated, and angry. "What an asshole," she thought; "doesn't he have anything better to do?" She also began to doubt herself. "How long have you lived in Massachusetts? This is how people drive. I am more of an idiot than he is to get so upset." She considered turning off to let the guy by but also felt vengeful and wanted to irritate him as well. Afterward, she felt exhausted and depleted.

Debbie had a moment of insight. "This is why I am so depressed," she said. "I am really nice on the surface, but if something gets me angry, I tense up on the inside, feel alone and terrible, then wind up blaming myself." Psychotherapy may have explained the roots of her anger but had never uncovered this particular tendency of mind. Once she saw the connections between her mind, body, and emotions, Debbie felt encouraged. Her victim tendency, which had fueled her depression, was something she could work with and take responsibility for.

Another way of looking at Debbie's experience is that she had a multiple-hindrance attack. Her initial experience of anger and aversion was followed by wanting to get away or get revenge (desire/lust), agitated and desperate thoughts (restlessness/worry), self-doubt ("I'm the idiot"), and finally exhaustion (sloth/torpor). Debbie's particular constellation of hindrances fueled her victim tendency, both her blind spot and her addiction. She was able to feel justified as the injured party (the benefit) but had also become increasingly depressed (the downside).

This is a general truth that you can check out in your own experience: often when we destabilize or freak out, we are having a multiple-hindrance attack. When addicts relapse, for example, we can invariably find elements of desire, aversion, agitation, exhaustion, and doubt. Before, during, and after all of the emotion and storytelling, there are many moments to work with.

Feelings Link Mind and Body

Our working definition of mindfulness is "awareness of the mind-body process in the present moment with acceptance." As discussed in chapter 2, information enters our mind-body through six sense doors (seeing, hearing, smelling, tasting, touching, and thinking), after which there are three possible reactions or "feelings"—pleasant, unpleasant, or neutral. In meditation practice, we see that feelings emerge from the body and then condition the mind, giving rise to emotions and thoughts.

Our purpose here is not to become Buddhist psychologists but to slow experience down enough to see how the body, feelings, emotions, and thoughts are connected. This is what Debbie was able to glimpse. It is also a means for those caught in an addictive cycle to feel more interested and proactive in understanding their experience and options.

Practice: Awareness of Feelings

The following exercise can be done in five to ten minutes. Begin by noticing your touch points and posture and allow your body to feel well supported on your chair or cushion. Bring a soft focus to your breathing, at either your nose or your belly. Thoughts will occur, and when they do, just return your attention to your breath.

Once you begin to feel a bit more settled, open up your field of awareness, which might now include your breath, body sensations, sounds, emotions, and thoughts. As your experience unfolds, make note of the feelings of pleasant, unpleasant, or neutral. This is not analyzing but simply noting. For example, is the awareness of the breath pleasant? Is it unpleasant or neutral? Just notice. If you get caught up in thinking, just return to your awareness of the breath or touch points. You can use those as your objects of focus to settle once more. They will also vary in feeling tone.

When you open your eyes to stop formally meditating, spend a few moments continuing to notice the ongoing changes in feeling tone of your experience.

What did you notice? Was it all gray and neutral, or were there shifts from one moment to another? Did you experience sensations or sounds with different feeling qualities? Was there any connection between physical sensations and feelings? Did you have a thought of, say, something nice to look forward to or a worried thought or painful emotion? Do feelings come out of those as well?

Viktor Frankl, the Austrian psychiatrist and author of *Man's Search for Meaning*,[2] spoke in his book of the numbing and horrifying conditions of the Nazi death camps. Even there, amid the inner torment and daily terror around losing one's life, there were pleasant moments: a bowl of soup, a warm fire, a beautiful sunset, a small kindness. Frankl's astonishing achievement was to stay open to such experiences and not totally succumb to his baser nature or totally give up in a setting of such cruelty and hopelessness.

Conversely, in the context of the most pleasant and sought-after experiences—the seemingly perfect house, relationship, vacation, job—there will be unpleasant moments. And then styles, technology, the economy, and we ourselves keep changing, often in unpredictable ways. Feelings are like the weather or the ocean. We cannot control them, but we can learn to accept them, putting on a raincoat or riding the waves.

Addictions are attempts to control our feelings and emotions, attempts that are ultimately ineffective. Let us now look at a range of common emotions and how they become problematic in the context of addiction.

"Pleasant" Emotions: Happiness, Joy, and Success

I have been a psychiatrist in the Boston area since 1985, and professional sports are hugely popular here. During my time, the Celtics, the Patriots, the Bruins, and the Red Sox have all won championships. The playoffs can be very compelling, and patients would be understandably excited about the games. But I have noticed that the day after the title was won, no one was cured. In fact, patients were no happier than the day before and were much more interested in talking about their life concerns than celebrating.

Now, this is not to say that winning is not fun and even a thrill to be enjoyed. It is. But victory brings no lasting happiness, and to get attached to victory is a poor strategy, since it cannot exist without defeat. In a similar way, trying to separate gain from loss or pleasure from pain is like trying to separate hot from cold. It can't be done. But the addictive process carries the insane belief that pleasure can exist without pain and that the pursuit of pleasure (or escape) provides the best hope for happiness, however momentary.

Addicts in recovery can relapse when happy for a number of reasons. The most common is that the use of alcohol and drugs goes as well with a good day as with a bad or a neutral one. Alcoholics drink. It is just what they do. An addict may use as a reward, to celebrate a success, or to amplify a positive mood or sustain one. Some of this behavior is illness driven, as the full consequences of the binge cannot be known while in the throes of the addiction, whether it be to drugs, sex, food, gambling, or anything else.

A more subtle problem is that addicts, whether born into dysfunctional families or not, eventually have lives distinguished by much pain and loss. Joy, when experienced, is not to be trusted and can even feel frightening. Success is feared. Life has shown, again and again, that the other shoe is about to drop, and the disappointment can be crushing. Fool me once, shame on you, fool me twice, shame on me. As naïveté and openness to life are worn away, the addict protects herself with cynicism, callousness, and apathy. Now the best she can do is control the flow of joy, which is no joy at all.

Mindfulness training provides no quick fix here. However, it does give the addict a means to open the aperture of the lens to reveal a slightly bigger picture. Take lust or craving, for example. The young man who knows he is about to have sex with the object of his desire tends to be in a good mood. Similarly, for the addict about to get high, a craving is a pleasant event. For the addict in early recovery, however, a craving is likely to be more mixed. The possibility of gratification is pleasant, the fear of relapse unpleasant. There might also be a component of shame for considering using or anger for having this predicament. Then a lot of stories or judgments.

As we practice embodied awareness, we begin to develop the capacity to see all of this operating. Winning and losing, joy and sadness, happen under certain conditions, only to fade or yield to the opposite. If we pay attention, we may have more winning or joy, but there are no guarantees. What is likely is that we will develop a greater capacity to accept and flow with our experience.

With less internal and external struggle, we are less stressed and more likely happier. Mindfulness practice initially builds concentration and stability, which allows us to take an interest in the flow of experience. Greater interest leads to greater courage to look further, a hedge against the addict's desperate tendency to grasp after pleasure and avoid pain.

"Unpleasant" Emotions

The quotations around *pleasant* and *unpleasant* are there because, while emotions can be driven by simple feeling tones, we quickly sense both the impermanence of an experience such as joy or pain. Our complex minds are always looking for trouble, and our emotions provide plenty of opportunity. *Emotion* has been defined as "agitation of the passions often involving physiological changes." It derives from the Latin *emovere,* meaning "to move out, stir up, or excite." Emotional experience is inseparable from our bodies, thoughts, and behavior.

Sadness and Depression

What is the difference between depression and sadness? Since most of our patients in early recovery have experienced both, the conversation generally uncovers the commonalities and differences. Both can be brief or long, and clinical (or major) depression often requires medicine. Both can have a cause or not. Ultimately, we discover that sadness is an emotion that feels enlivening, with a quality of connection to others or to our own experience. Sadness can be unpleasant, often because we are thinking about what caused it or because we are ashamed to express it openly. But most people agree that crying or communicating sadness to someone who cares allows us some release or relaxation.

Depression, on the other hand, is almost exclusively unpleasant. Although we can "feel depressed," the experience is largely one of feeling deadened or shut down. It is possible to be sad *and* depressed, but the crying spells often do not bring relief and just fuel the depression. This is likely because the depressed state is generally accompanied by thoughts of hopelessness, worthlessness, and victimhood run amok. The head rules, and instinctual life is severely restricted in an emotional state characterized by low energy and vitality and dysregulated sleep, appetite, and sexuality.

Depression can also be like a drug. Its main positive (if not exactly pleasant) aspect is that it can be a form of anesthesia, blunting the experiences of anxiety, sadness, grief, anger, desperation, and feeling overwhelmed. Depression can also be a means, partly unconscious, of eliciting caretaking. As with most drugs, the benefits are short-lived or limited and the costs are high.

Mindfulness practice in the treatment of sadness and depression is a matter of gradual exposure to the experience that is being avoided. The first step is often the simple awareness of touch points—the feet, hands, or sitting bones and the breath. This often brings a mild set-tling of tension, even relaxation related to shifting awareness to the body. Repeated practice of mindful breathing and walking begins to develop some stability and groundedness. From there, some of the feared emotion is glimpsed without dire consequences. Once it is obvi-ous from direct experience that turning toward emotions brings bet-ter outcomes than avoiding them, it is only natural to pursue that course of action.

Zarita came into treatment around the one-year anniversary of her husband's death. She had worsening anxiety and depression, despite medicine and therapy, and was now totally incapable of focusing on daily responsibilities. Zarita was not sleeping well and believed that she was seeing her husband and hearing his voice at night.

Grief is a state of sorrow related to a loss. It can contain any num-ber of emotions, including sadness, anger, fear, shame, and guilt. Peo-ple who are grieving are not necessarily depressed—it is a natural process of being human and loving—but those who present clinically generally are. And grief can be enormously addictive, a place of suffer-ing that often feels deserved, which simultaneously punishes, pro-tects, and reassures the griever that she is a loyal and good person.

Zarita revealed eventually that her husband had committed sui-cide via drug overdose. He required a penile implant secondary to dia-betes and "did not want to live that way." Despite understanding this, she felt guilty about being an inadequate wife (clearly not true) and keeping the cause of their father's death from her children. Zarita had a strong tendency to isolate and indulge negative thinking, inevitably leading to the conclusion that she should be with her husband.

She was with us from the late summer to midfall. We encouraged her to do mindful walking outside every day and to check her attitude and energy level. At different times, she was drawn to focusing on her body or on her surroundings. Zarita's first observation was how much she lives in her head, and she saw by contrast the benefits of noticing the changes in her body and feelings. She was moved by the brilliant foliage and an expanded view of her own life. Zarita felt less agitated and confused but began to notice swells of grief containing sadness, anger, and guilt. For these she was able to do urge surfing to ride out the waves of pain. She also used the making-space meditation to allow the energy of her emotions to move.

As Zarita felt more stable, she was more open to group support, began to experience compassion for others, and felt much less alone. She began to connect with her family, had fun with her grandson, and told her kids the truth, which was a huge relief. As she glimpsed the end of the program, Zarita experienced more anxiety, along with bouts of grief, but was relating to them differently. She began doing loving-kindness practice for herself, her husband, her family, and her fellow patients. Life was still hard but felt more workable. Zarita felt some guilt about finally clearing out and organizing her husband's belongings, but she also felt some satisfaction in making space for herself.

Fear and Anxiety

We are fortunate to have been born human, but beneath the veneer of any health, peace, or pleasure we might enjoy, we sense our fragility. We fear death, failure, illness, abandonment, feeling unloved, and any number of tragedies that could destabilize our lives. Have you noticed that when you travel, something always goes wrong? That is how life is, but since we want to be happy and not dominated by fear, we set up routines that keep it at bay. If we can go to work, pay the bills, and keep our families healthy, maybe everything will be okay. But also maybe not.

Fear triggers the stress reaction (fight, flight, or freeze) that we discussed in chapters 11 and 13. We can fear dogs, heights, or tight spaces. If we are cut off on the highway or walk into a dangerous part of a city, we need to mobilize the physiological arousal, muscular readiness, and mental acuity to keep ourselves safe. Fortunately, for most of us facing danger is not routine. Unfortunately, however, we do routinely activate these same reactions around time pressure, traffic jams, perceived slights, relationship problems, and any number of unpleasant events that befall us. Things' not going well tends to make us afraid.

Like fear, anxiety can also trigger a stress reaction, with physical symptoms including dry mouth, sweating, shakiness, and increased heart rate. With anxiety, there is often a sense of dread or unease but no clear object. Psychopharmacologists routinely treat anxiety; cognitive therapists attempt to turn anxiety into fear to develop more adaptive responses. In real time, however, they can be hard to distinguish, since fear can create anxiety and vice versa. This is likely what Franklin Roosevelt meant when he said, "The only thing we have to fear is fear itself."

The mental expression of anxiety is our tendency to worry. If we wake up in the middle of the night with anxiety, we might attribute a cause to it such as our health, our finances, an important meeting, or a problem with one of our kids. We engage in obsessing, mind reading, and negative prediction, and guess what? We generate more fear, more anxiety, and a multitude of potential catastrophes. The physical and mental aspects of anxiety are like the chicken and the egg.

Now, if we could surrender to this conundrum, our anxiety and worry would gradually recede and we could get back to sleep, trusting that we will see the problems more clearly in the light of day. If only. Instead, our unfortunate tendency is to react to the stressor of anxiety via fighting, fleeing, or freezing. And like any habit or drug, these reactions all have benefits and liabilities.

Substances and other addictive processes quell some of this noise via getting high, self-medication, and escape. Addiction is both a metaphor (relief seeking but self defeating) and a vehicle for experiential avoidance. Alcohol allows a young woman to put aside her fears and enjoy sex. Overwork brings money, success, self-esteem, and social standing to a man in the midst of a midlife crisis. There are benefits, but if these modes become habitual ways of handling anxiety, the downsides can be problematic, even disastrous. Mindfulness training helps us to hold our fear and anxiety more lightly, without so much reactivity. Accepting these energies is far more workable than fighting or escaping them.

Sylvia came to treatment following an incident of losing her temper and berating a coworker. She was coordinating a project and became impatient with the woman's poor cooperation. This was not the first time this sort of thing had happened, and when we explored the pattern, it appeared that Sylvia tended to feel pressured, become anxious, try to suppress these feelings by being nice, then become overwhelmed and eventually nasty. This had also been a problem with her daughter, from whom she was currently estranged.

I learned that Sylvia had a long history of anxiety problems, had been dependent upon Valium, and had recently detoxed. Her current medication regimen did not eradicate her anxiety, which was fueled by her constant worry about her job, finances, and family. Sylvia immediately recognized her tendency to live in her head and used touch points and mindful walking to feel more grounded. One day a cousin reported to Sylvia that her daughter said she did not miss her, which caused her to worry anew about never reconciling with her daughter or seeing her grandson again.

Since she had been feeling more solid on her feet, Sylvia was impressed by this destabilization. She saw how unpleasant news and events led to worry, anxiety, and an experience of helplessness. The next day she was still upset but not feeling it as intensely. This experience gave her a broader perspective on her own suffering tendency. She knew that her daughter loved her and had a moment of faith that they would eventually work things out. There would be more anxiety and upset to come, but she was in a better position to handle it.

Sylvia had another bout of anxiety when she was about to return to work, since the same difficult people would still be there. She was able to use the making-space technique and felt she could do the same with her impatience and irritability once back in the office.

Toward the end of her time in day treatment, Sylvia had a dream of a tornado blowing through the city and taking down some buildings. This appeared to be about the energies inside her that she had been suppressing in the attempt to be nice. She then had a second dream of approaching her daughter and receiving a warm hug— clearly related to her own growing self-acceptance. Courage is about accepting fear and assuming authority for our actions. Sylvia saw the new task of owning her power and all of her emotions. Making more space for anxiety had already made it a lot less threatening.

Anger

So, does Sylvia have an anxiety problem or an anger problem? Though she self-medicated her anxiety with Valium and needed detox, her benzodiazepine dependence was temporary and really a sideshow. Her real addiction was to anger as a protector of her vulnerability, signaled by anxiety. It worked, of course, and then created huge problems for her.

Anger, whether overt or hidden, is a frequent theme in the addictive process and generates stress, disrespect, and loss of control. Anger carries the energy of aversion or wanting to push away, which we discussed in chapter 13. It manifests along a continuum from mild annoyance to rage. Explosive anger in the form of threats, blaming, or striking out provides a release but has serious potential consequences to physical well-being, relationships, and financial and legal status. Anger that implodes is also extremely destructive, resulting in depression, anxiety, and even psychotic symptoms. It has been demonstrated that anger in the form of inner hostility is a risk factor for heart disease. The stress reaction generated by internalized anger can exacerbate any number of physiological and metabolic processes.

Anger is considered one of the basic emotions: mad, sad, glad, and afraid. And yet, in my own experience, anger generally does not arise out of nowhere. It tends to be preceded by something else that lights the fuse of anger. I learned this not in my psychiatric training but one August day in the late 1980s when my son was a baby. I owned a windsurfer at that time, and after putting my boy down for a nap, I told my wife I was going over to a lake not far from our house. It took a while to load the board on the car, arrive, unload, and rig it all up. After a brief chat with some friends, I got down to the lake, and just as I was putting the board in the water, the sky darkened, the wind died, and it started to rain. I felt the wind go out of my own sails as well, in an experience I would call disappointment. Then I felt just a hint of anger.

"Look at that," I thought, "I get disappointed first." I had never actually seen that. My particular tendency if something didn't go my way, if I felt thwarted or unduly pressured, was always to get angry. You might call it my default position. Other possible reactions to the same frustrations might be to become irritable, tense, depressed, confused, or hopeless. I was genuinely surprised to see that my anger had an antecedent.

As you might imagine, I have had plenty of opportunity to explore this as a parent. The big three precipitants to anger for me were

- Anxiety ("We have to get out the door, he's refusing to put on his clothes")
- Disappointment ("She did not pick up her room as I asked")
- Confusion ("What is it going to take to get these kids to cooperate?")

A fourth trigger, shame, was one I saw frequently in prison work, as a cause of impulsive or violent behavior. Remember Ricky, the inmate who beat a man so severely he wound up back in prison for eight years? What he called "disrespect" was likely an attempt to humiliate him that resulted in his losing his mind. Another common example were guys who drank or used drugs to blunt their fear or sense of powerlessness and then, once disinhibited, did something that landed them behind the walls.

In the UMass Prison Project, we taught mindfulness as a means for inmates to begin to recognize the physical, emotional, and mental signals indicating they were shifting into the red zone. We were a companion program to a larger course about addiction and criminogenic behavior, and I was pleased one day to hear our work valued by the coordinator of the entire program from the Department of Correction. "That's a solid curriculum," he told me, referring to the addiction course, "but without what you guys are teaching, the first time they get angry, it is all out the window."

He was right, but why is that? Daniel Siegel, author of *Mindsight: The New Science of Personal Transformation*, explains this phenomenon in terms of the three major areas of the brain I referenced in relation to the stress response.

> The middle prefrontal area—the region that calms the emotionally reactive lower limbic and brainstem layers—stops being able to regulate all the energy stirred up, and the coordination balance of the brain is disrupted. That's my understanding of what happens when we go down the "low road," moving directly from limbic impulse to speech and action, and detouring away from the prefrontal "high road," where we are flexible and receptive rather than inflexible and reactive. We "flip our lids."[3]

Sylvia's success in treatment was in making the connection between flipping her lid, which threatened her job and relationships, and her anxiety, fear, and disappointment. Her mindfulness training allowed her to slow down the action enough to contain her automatic reaction and make the choice of her next move. She might then simply do something to calm herself or speak, now or later, honestly and with respect for both herself and the other.

Just a small postscript to my almost-windsurfing experience. I took a brief swim to cool off, derigged the boat, and loaded it on the car. As I was driving home in the rain, I realized that I never got angry about the dying wind. "You mean that's it," I thought, "something doesn't work out and I'm just disappointed?" Somehow I missed the drama and the big victim story. This was a new experience, and I was slightly disoriented. I could see that this was a better response—less reactive and more mature. However, I also understood my attachment to anger as a means of protection from pain.

For men anger is often a means of feeling powerful. All of the emotions—fear, sadness, disappointment, jealousy, shame, guilt—become converted into anger. Sylvia's story shows that this can happen to women as well; it is just less common. Clearly, it is healthier to transform anger, feeling our underlying emotions and vulnerability. But as with any drug or addictive process, anger has pros and cons, and we let go of it when we are ready.

Shame and Guilt

Maurice had been drinking since the age of sixteen and said that alcohol helped him to "feel alive." His wife of twenty years had died a few months earlier, and he had relapsed after fifteen years of sobriety to escape from the pain and grief. In day treatment, Maurice learned some simple grounding practices, mindful breathing and walking, and discovered his strong tendency to go up into his head. He also noticed a torrent of negative thinking, particularly worrying about the health of his elderly parents and that he had not been a good son. The good news was that group support, medicine, and mindfulness practice had kept him from relapsing yet again.

Eventually, Maurice began to settle down and see some of the feelings under all of his thinking. He began to feel the grief around losing his wife and then anxiety and a stream of racing thoughts about his father, who was slipping into Alzheimer's disease. Maurice revealed that many years ago, when he was using heroin, he had stolen a lot of money from his father. Although he had been forgiven long ago, Maurice was still pained by the recollection.

Underneath his anxiety and worry, Maurice was experiencing both shame and guilt. *Shame* carries a sense of being flawed or defective. Our actual functioning falls short of our *ego ideal,* that is, what we could be. Maurice carried the belief that he was an awful son, with corresponding feelings of unworthiness and self-hatred. Alcohol both numbed these feelings and was the only means Maurice had to an experience of vitality.

Guilt comes from an inconsistency between our behavior and our *superego,* the internalized sense of right and wrong we get from family, society, and the Ten Commandments. Maurice had lied, stolen, and not honored his parents. In his guilty state he blamed himself for any number of things, including his disability from a back injury and his father's deterioration. He was lost but finally acknowledging how lost.

We introduced Maurice to the difference between *guilt* and *remorse.* Guilt is harsh: "I'm a total idiot screw up; I don't deserve to live." Remorse has a softer, less judgmental feel: "I made a big mistake. I wasn't thinking clearly and I regret my actions. I want to make amends to anyone I hurt, learn from this, and move on the best I can." Maurice was able to feel the difference between guilt and remorse in his body and thoughts. He saw that his guilty ruminations were not helping him and learned not to indulge them so much. He could not control what happened in the past, but he could control where he directed his attention and his current actions.

Maurice also did metta practice. He repeated phrases like: May I be peaceful, may I be protected from harsh judgments, may I feel joy, may I be kind to myself. He also sent wishes to his parents for health, happiness, and ease of mind and heart. Not surprisingly, this brought up feelings of unworthiness, shame, and guilt. At those times, Maurice was encouraged to shift to his breath or even do mindful walking if these feelings became too painful, and then return to the metta practice when he felt more balanced. Maurice felt a strong connection to friends in the program and was able to extend his desire for their happiness to all beings. He experienced this practice as a prayer of the heart and the beginning of compassion for himself and for fellow sufferers.

Addictions are time-honored methods of escaping shame and guilt, simultaneously inflicting self-punishment in an endless loop. When I think about the therapeutic action of day treatment, it seems that the main factor may be the experience of kindness and camaraderie in the face of our defectiveness and past misdeeds. The staff gets some of this benefit as well, one of our little secrets. That is recovery—we are flawed and still lovable. As Maurice discovered, mindfulness practices are means to accepting our faults and developing our hearts.

Neutral Feelings and Boredom

Early recovery from addiction comes in many shapes and styles, but they all fall into two basic groups. One is characterized by agitation, anger, drama, and feeling overwhelmed. The other is more depressed, discouraged, and shut down. However, regardless of the presentation, recovering addicts are vulnerable to boredom. Consider the life of a drug addict and the activities, external and internal, that make up a typical day or week:

- Planning to get the necessary money and then getting it
- Acquiring the drug
- Dealing with danger and risk
- Using, including the necessary equipment and mechanics
- Evaluating the drug(s) in terms of price, quality, safety, experience
- Complaining about the lifestyle, the exhaustion, the risk, and so on
- Lying and covering up the lies
- Having an identity, a function or usefulness, and a raison d'etre or life purpose

The lifestyle brings the addict in contact with myriad personalities, places, and scenarios. Moreover, it requires the development of a skill set that is necessary to negotiate the obstacles of the life, whether the addiction is to heroin, gambling, or sex. It requires competence, savvy, strategy, and creativity. It also involves a lot of deception and a good memory for the lies, cheating, and alliances. Eventually people burn out, but for a while, this can be quite compelling. And when it all goes away, when all of this is lost, it is understandable that life, though not as crazy, is also not as interesting.

Boredom is defined as "a state of irritability or fatigue due to exposure to something uninteresting or because of having nothing to do." Nothing to do. This is not only about addicts. We are always doing— work, chores, calls, e-mails. Then it's television to "relax" and watch actors, athletes, or game-show contestants do their thing, not to mention TV programmers manipulating us to keep watching and advertisers getting us to buy products we don't need. Finally, we turn it off, but we often watch longer than planned because we do not want to face the quiet, the uncertainty of who we are, what to do next, or what we really ought to do, like go to bed.

Clearly, we are addicted to being entertained by things new and "special." The flip side of this, what we call "ordinariness," causes us to lose interest but is also unnerving to the part of us that wants novelty—"Is that all there is to life?" Drugs, food, sex, and gambling provide a temporary respite. Boredom serves a similar function as a cover for emptiness, doubt, helplessness, confusion, discouragement, fear, or desperation. I have heard boredom defined as "hostility without enthusiasm." It is similar to depression in its quality of numbing out to emotions feared to be too painful. When we lapse into boredom, we kill the present moment, both deadening our inner life and protecting ourselves from it.

Boredom and Meditation

Meditation practice is not about entertainment or diversion. It is about learning to be where we are, whether it is pleasant, unpleasant, or neutral. Boredom is an unpleasant experience arising out of ordinariness or not enough happening. The initial task in meditation is to note it and return to the breathing. This brings two important results: (1) the building of concentration and (2) a partial distraction, allowing us to feel less imprisoned by boredom. This is particularly important for addicts who escape from pain as a reflex.

As the mind and body settle, we experience more moments of calm and peace. Boredom may still be present at times, but it is not so solid or frightening. It is just another emotional state that comes and goes or turns into something else: possibly what the boredom is covering, such as loneliness or anger. Then you are really on to something, namely, facing feelings and emotions without fear. It requires practice, but the simple acceptance of boredom, shame, or grief opens that door.

Mickey was in his early twenties and had been smoking marijuana daily since the end of high school. When asked why he was coming for help, he said, "My regular life is not good enough." Mickey had been with us about a year earlier but did not succeed in abstaining from marijuana. He missed smoking weed, which enhanced the simple acts of eating or watching TV, gave him a social life, and numbed him out. Otherwise, he was just a guy with a retail job and no friends. Mickey felt better clean but was lonely and bored. He only came to treatment because marijuana no longer gave him a sense of purpose and left him with even lower self-esteem and an empty bank account.

When he tried to meditate, Mickey could not sit still. I encouraged him to walk mindfully as a means of channeling this energy and to use his touch points to ground himself in his body. He was interested in the possibility that his boredom and agitation were related in some way. I learned that Mickey had played hockey and though not very big, was the type of kid who was "not afraid of anything," who would never back down in a physical encounter.

He was also no dumb jock, having completed a program in information technology, but somehow he could not move toward a more challenging career. His strong tendency to isolate himself left him lonely and caused him to see AA meetings as a place he could not belong. Mickey began to see that he *was afraid of something*, namely of growing up and developing both vocationally and socially. The experience of boredom was a screen for those fears, which had previously been kept at bay by smoking marijuana.

Mickey used the making-space technique for bringing greater acceptance to his fear. In doing so, he encountered his edginess, irritability, and impatience. Could he now accept those feelings without escaping? In the program, Mickey had developed a foundation of group support, psychological insight, medication, and mindfulness practice. He walked, skated, grounded himself, and made space for a range of energetic and emotional experiences. He went to a baseball game and was pleasantly surprised at his ability to just sit there and enjoy himself. Mickey saw that if he did not cover his feelings with drugs or boredom, he could face them one at a time. And when he dropped some of his worries, he began to get some fresh ideas about moving forward in the career and social arenas. If Mickey could make friends with his own fears, he could belong in the world as well.

Feelings—pleasant, unpleasant, and neutral—are mind moments that link the body, emotions, and thoughts. A victory, a hopeful thought, an ice-cream cone, a hug, a disappointment, a headache, a sudden fear, walking to the car, and brushing teeth compose our experience, fuel our stories, and land in our bodies.

Addiction represents a futile means to control experience, fostering the belief that we can maximize pleasure, avoid pain, and ignore the neutral or ordinary. It creates an illusion of authority and simultaneously begets an internal struggle. Why health is chosen over disease is a great mystery, as many addicts just give up on themselves. But once that choice for recovery is made, mindfulness is a tool for stabilizing attention, seeing into the nature of the addict's emotional conflict, and replacing self-judgment with kindness and self-acceptance.

16

Working with Mind States

MARGARET HAD AN ORGANIZED, mental approach to life. She devoted herself to managing her household and caring for her husband and two teenage daughters. By all accounts, Margaret did an excellent job, but she was highly self-critical and reactive if the slightest thing went wrong. She would often become overwhelmed and drink in a binge pattern. At times Margaret barely ate or slept for days and would require hospitalization.

In treatment Margaret learned some grounding practices. Once, when she was particularly up in her head with worry, I asked her if she could direct her attention to her body. She said, "Yes, when I'm here" (at the program). Apparently, at home Margaret was totally identified with her inner manager, who ran an efficient household but cared nothing for Margaret's own well-being. While in this part, Margaret often did not even experience hunger or fatigue. Hard work and worry kept her emotional life at bay, and if all else failed, she drank.

Living from the neck up, Margaret was stuck in the reality she constructed with her thinking. One night when her kids were out, she made a nice dinner, expecting her husband at his usual 6:30. He finally called at 7:30 saying he was out with coworkers. I asked Margaret how she felt hearing that. "Pissed off," she said, "but then I blamed myself." As a husband who was trained early on to call if I was going to be late, I was interested in her reaction, so I asked, "Why would you do that?"

"Well," she told me, "he works hard and deserves to go out with his friends. Besides, I probably should have called him. That would have avoided the whole problem." I asked Margaret if she had another feeling prior to anger. Eventually she was able to identify disappointment, but she had not been aware of it as she ate by herself.

Margaret revealed that she hated conflict. She grew up as the oldest of three girls whose father had left when they were very young. Margaret's job was to help her mother, period. If she complained or asserted her own needs, her mother would withdraw emotionally, likely overwhelmed or feeling bad about herself. So Margaret did the next best thing: quelled her own desires, both physical and emotional, which eliminated both her complaints and her conflict in one fell swoop.

Then she constructed a series of stories justifying that behavior, stories with themes of her own incompetence, selfishness, unworthiness, and lack of consideration for others. Her compliant attitude got her mother's approval and avoided the experience of abandonment. Her husband, the stand-in for her mother, was an upgrade in the sense that he made a good living, freeing Margaret to do what she did best, selflessly care for others. But the bargain included the ongoing denial of her own needs.

In the program, Margaret had learned about assertive (or effective) communication. Here is the simple model for this:

I feel _____ when you _____.

I asked her if she could say something to her husband like, "When you don't come home and don't call, I feel very disappointed and angry."

"I don't think I can do that," she said. Not yet. She will need a stronger foundation in recovery and greater inner stability before she can risk that her emotions might either be disregarded, throwing her back into her childhood trauma, or might totally upset the apple cart. In this chapter, I will use Margaret's example as well as others to illustrate the nature and function of thought in meditation and daily life. The discussion of a number of mind states, including doubt, storytelling, judgment, and comparison, will probably feel familiar.

Thought and Security

Margaret constructed a reality that included the danger of expressing emotional need and how she ought to behave in order to circumvent that danger. Her rules for herself were designed to protect her from rejection and abandonment or, more accurately, from her fear of those outcomes. Even a hint of that fear would cause her to self-medicate with alcohol. Much of our thinking is about the past, which we know, or future, which we don't know. By predicting the future based on the past, we gain a sense of what might happen, but at great cost.

Think of a circle divided into three sections: what you know (K), what you don't know (DK), and what you don't know you don't know (DKDK). By thinking we know when we don't (the future will be the same as the past), we avoid the anxiety of not knowing (DK) but are exposed to the vulnerability of our blind spot (DKDK). Addiction (to drugs or beliefs) provides just enough denial to facilitate this pattern, leading to problematic physical, emotional, financial, and legal outcomes. I have said to patients (a bit glibly, I'll admit): "I make a living because I'm better at not knowing than you are." A key element of the mindfulness training is to build the muscles of not knowing.

Patients in early recovery tend to be some combination of disoriented, confused, and worried. Once in treatment, the task is to develop a new plan, since the drug of choice is no longer working. But what is the difference between planning and worrying? Both are thinking about the future, but they feel very different.

Worry is born of anxiety and has a feeling of pressure or desperation. It often involves conflict, and there is a sense of no-win. This leads to more anxiety, more worries, and a tendency either to make poor decisions or to suffer in silence. *Planning* has more of a stabilizing feel. We think about the future from a grounded place in the present, looking at priorities, values, goals, and possible courses of action. Inevitably, these alternatives will have uncertain outcomes, but we are then in a position to consider the possible contingencies or next moves.

Remember: we cannot control our thoughts and feelings. We certainly cannot control what other people are thinking or doing, though this can be a huge source of worry. We *can* control where we direct our attention and our actions. The practices of mindfulness and meditation help us to develop enough stability of mind to see how we are trying to control what we cannot and how this causes us to suffer. Grant us the serenity. . . .

Meditation and Thought

Meditation practice is not about thinking or figuring things out. My practice began with the instruction to follow the breath at the nose or belly and be willing to come back when the mind drifted away. Not only was I not very good at this, but in the quiet of the meditation hall, my mind was going ninety miles per hour down the freeway telling one story after another. That, of course, led to many explanations, possibilities, theories, hopes, worries, and fantasies.

For my mind it was a field day, but it was not meditation. Before I could meditate, I needed to surrender to the fact that there was no way to defeat, suppress, or control my thinking.[1] Even more difficult was accepting the fact that thinking could not provide all of the answers.

Once I allowed my thoughts just to be there and looked directly at them, I saw that they often just disappeared or drifted in and out of my awareness. As I made space for this to occur on its own, I was freer to focus on my breathing, body, feelings, or thoughts as they arose and passed away. Only then could I see how attached I was to my thoughts, and like Margaret, I had many rules for what it meant to be a good person. My particular variation was on developing the new and improved version of myself, with the ultimate goal of feeling worthy and lovable. Naturally, I turned meditation into a project or competition with myself. Poor performance led to a lot of self-judgment, despite the fact that there is no scorecard in meditation.

Over time, as I learned to allow the experience to unfold, I saw that having a worried (or pleasant) thought is no different from having a pain in the back or an itch. They are all just passing phenomena with no real substance. There is still a part of my mind that believes the answer to the puzzle is in my thinking, but that is just another mind state. The true benefit of meditation is not in the content of our thoughts but in the silence under the entire passing show. As we develop the capacity to see the insubstantiality and impermanence of our thinking and beliefs, we are less identified with them. And we suffer less.

If you believe that you are already not identified with your thoughts, just turn on FOX or MSNBC and listen to a conservative or liberal commentator. You will likely see that politics is like any sporting event, with villains and heroes, right and wrong. This mind-set is why the world is as it is, why we don't listen to each other and can't settle differences peacefully. As individuals, we cannot control all of that, but we may be able to learn about our own minds. As Gandhi encouraged us: "Be the change you want to see in the world."

Doubt

We have discussed four of the five hindrances or obstacles to a clear mind and open heart. Here is a brief review of these four, which are energies observable in the body:

- Craving: the energy of desire or grasping
- Aversion: the energy of anger, resentment, or pushing away
- Restlessness and worry: agitation, anxiety, racing mind, or excessive energy
- Sloth and torpor: lethargy, exhaustion, boredom, dullness of mind, or low energy

Doubt, the fifth hindrance, is a predominantly mental energy. For that reason it can have seductive power, often masquerading as wisdom. Doubt is a major player in constructing a reality that keeps us safe and in line. However, it also maintains the integrity of our blind spot, keeping us a slave to our thoughts and fears. To illustrate this, let's look at the role of doubt in Margaret's multiple hindrance attack the night her husband did not communicate with her.

As she waited for her husband, Margaret experienced both *desire* for him to arrive and then *restlessness and worry* when he did not. His calling late brought up significant *aversion* in the form of anger initially directed at him. Then came the *doubt,* which questioned the legitimacy of her anger and turned the blame toward herself. It all made sense. He does work hard and deserve time with friends, and she might have called. But the doubting thought ultimately served the function of shifting the aversion and responsibility to the only place that felt safe to the vulnerable child inside her. Her *exhaustion* and sense of defeat naturally followed. This pattern had occurred many times before, often resulting in drinking.

In fact, many slips and relapses are ignited by doubt. "I can't get sober . . . it's not worth it . . . I'm not worth it . . . my life isn't worth anything" is the kind of self-talk that keeps the cash registers ringing at the Bournewood-Caulfield Partial Hospitalization program and others like it. If we can turn those declarative statements into questions—"Can I get sober?" or "Is there anything worth living for?"—we then have subjects for inquiry or investigation. We are aiming at moving these questions into the *don't know* (DK) segment and shrinking the size of the blind spot (DKDK). It is also very good information to *know* that we have a blind spot, so that we do not, for example, get sideswiped when we change lanes on the highway.

Margaret may not be quite ready to change how she lives. However, the awareness of self-doubt provides her with a new opportunity. She admits she is afraid to validate her own feelings, and she is not alone. One young man in our program realized he worried continuously as a means of not experiencing his emotions. He was pleased as his worry diminished but also noted that "it is scary not to worry. When it gets too quiet, I'm nervous and I don't know exactly what to do or even who I am." Margaret's similar task is to be afraid and to open, at her own pace, to her self-doubts and to not knowing. With recovery, psychotherapy, and mindfulness practice she has a chance.

Storytelling

The ultimate addiction of the human mind is to describe itself and track our progress so that we can survive and propagate our species. I learned from the meditation teacher Joseph Goldstein the Buddha's discovery that what we habitually reflect on becomes our inclination of mind. The practice of mindfulness provides insight into our tendencies to be lost in these habit patterns that cause us to suffer. This could be about the acquisition and use of heroin or equally about our tendency to tell stories about ourselves, others, how everybody is doing, and what it all means.

Mark Twain once said, "I'm an old man and I've known many troubles, but most of them never happened." Indeed, our stories are often not true, but when we tell them constantly, they seem to be. The Federal Communications Commission has rules as to what is permissible on the radio, but there are no such rules for our own minds, and this can be disastrous.

Russ wanted to die. He tried to hang himself with a rope, which fortunately broke. The suicide attempt was the culmination of many years of depression managed by alcohol, marijuana, and a string of girlfriends. Now in his early sixties, Russ felt at the end of the road with overpowering loneliness and a sense that he had "nothing to offer." This conclusion came out of the facts that his last real relationship had been twelve years ago despite his being sober for longer than a year on more than one occasion. He had begun to substitute pornography for live women but had recently lost interest in that.

In the program, everyone liked Russ. He had rugged good looks, an impressive moustache, and a gregarious energy that both women and men were drawn to. We learned, however, that despite having many friends over the years, he had always felt alone and ashamed.

Russ grew up in an environment of chaos and neglect. He left school in the seventh grade and, after a brief career in crime, worked successfully as a carpenter for many years. He married very young but was unable to handle the responsibility of having a wife and a young son. It was clear that Russ's lack of any guidance and of male role model were major factors in his inability to sustain a relationship with a woman or, more important, with himself. As he turned increasingly to addictive modes—drugs, sex, self-cutting, and pornography—his loneliness intensified.

Coping: Top Hits

Early on in treatment, Russ acknowledged how sad he was and how much he was fighting with his thoughts. He was introduced to the idea of numbering the "top hits of the week." These were recurring examples of self-talk that replayed over and over, much like songs on top 40 radio. Here are some of them:

- "What a worthless piece of crap you are."
- "You did it to yourself."
- "You're a lousy father."
- "You'll be banging nails your whole life."
- "People know you're a loser."
- "You don't deserve to live."

Russ was interested to see that he *was* doing it to himself and that he might do something else. He became increasingly adept at catching these thoughts as they arose and just letting them go by like ripples on a lake. He tried not to fight with the thoughts (we almost always lose that one) but began substituting others he knew to be true that were more wholesome: "I trust people here . . . people love me . . . I want to feel like a decent person." He used loving-kindness practice to amplify the experience of feeling gentler inside. Mostly, Russ saw that if he believed his negative self-talk, he suffered, and if he did not, he was happier.

"The Work" of Byron Katie

Now a famous author and teacher, Byron Katie was once an ordinary woman who was so depressed she slept on the floor of her halfway house because she believed she did not deserve to sleep in a bed. One day she had an insight very similar to Russ's, that believing our thoughts creates emotional pain. She elaborated this into a radical reality method that she calls "the work."[2] Katie has people reveal a simple story or judgment about themselves or someone else and subjects it to four questions and a "turnaround," which is essentially the opposite of the statement. The goal is to get closer to the truth while limiting suffering—the exact same goal as the mindfulness training. These are the four questions:

- Is it true?
- Can you be absolutely sure it's true?
- How do you feel when you hold that thought?
- Who would you be (or how would you be different) without that thought?

Russ had enormous pain around having abandoned his son at three years old, and one of his long-running hits was "You should have been a better father." When we did "the work," the answer to the first two questions was yes. There was no doubt about it. How did he feel holding that thought? "Terrible, wracked with guilt, self-loathing, and regret. Like a total failure." Before asking the fourth question, it was important to acknowledge that Russ might not be ready to drop the thought, "I should have been a better father" (particularly if he was sure it was true), but if he could, how might he be different? Russ felt a deep sadness but was quite calm as he said, "I would accept that I did as well as I could at the time."

Now the turnaround: "I should *not* have been a better father." Is that true? "Yes," he said, "I should not have been a better father because I wasn't, but I want to be now." Russ contacted his son, now nearly forty, who was willing to meet. They had a wonderful exchange, and his son accepted Russ's apology. Now, did he deserve to be forgiven? Clearly yes, since he had been. Could he accept being pardoned? Not right away. But Russ *was* able to accept *that he was not ready to fully accept* his son's forgiveness, and that felt workable for now.

Relating to Stories

As Russ began to question and drop some of his thoughts, he was more able to feel the emotion underneath. He saw that the *story* ("I am a lousy father") explained his *experience* (guilt, grief) but was not the same thing. Repeatedly seeing his thoughts come and go diminished their power over him. On one occasion, he was outside feeling confused. He just noticed his feet on the ground and felt the cold air, which helped him return to his body and the present moment. With practice, Russ calmed down, had fewer negative thoughts, and was more easily able to catch the ones that came. With less inner noise and self-criticism, he had more energy for his recovery, his relationships, and his emotional life.

For better and for worse, energy and action follow thought. The major challenge in dealing with our thinking is not getting swept up in its content. In discussing the approach to strong emotion, Joseph Goldstein suggests being aware of three aspects of our experience.[3]

This method is equally applicable to working with troubling thoughts or judgments. Here are the three factors:

A. The external event and/or the inner story
B. The emotional reaction
C. How we are relating to the story and the emotion

Our natural tendency is to loop between items A and B. That is, something occurs that upsets us and we tell a story about it or we have an ongoing thought pattern based on the past or future (A). This causes an emotional reaction (B). If we feel wronged by another person, we tend to feel outraged, judgmental, or victimized. We can also blame ourselves, fueling a cycle of self-hatred. In either case, both the story and the emotion elaborate into an inner or outer vendetta.

What makes the situation more workable is directing attention to item C—to our relationship to the thought/emotion complex. This is the path to assuming authority for what arises in our own minds. Russ had avoided responsibility for much of his life. Once he saw there was no one to blame but himself, his self-judgment turned deadly.

When Russ shifted his attention to how he was relating to his thoughts, he saw his tendency to identify with them—that is, simply believing that he was a loser or hopeless because he had the thought. This awareness allowed Russ to reflect on the truth (or not) of these ideas or just allow them to pass on. This weakened the identification and self-judgment and promoted a softer, kinder attitude toward others as well.

Judgment

Indeed, Russ was quite judgmental—of himself, the program, the guys living at his sober house. He would think, "What a bunch of losers," gossip, and mind everyone's business but his own. He eventually saw that his judgments were a type of story where he was highly invested in his opinion. He knew that his self-judgments had almost killed him. Gradually becoming less attached to them gave him a greater freedom to move on with his life.

Judgment is not an entirely bad thing. Artists, athletes, editors, doctors, housepainters, and housewives can all have excellent (or poor) judgment. Even judges. Hearing the stories of patients who have been in court, I have witnessed some horribly unfair and narrow-minded decisions as well as many thoughtful ones. Adults tend to have better judgment than adolescents because of greater experience and maturity and fuller development of the prefrontal cortex. Here, judgment is about discernment or having good sense. The addict has notoriously poor judgment, since he is lost in his head with a limited agenda and is often operating a few sandwiches short of a picnic.

In the context of mindfulness practice, judgment is often about finding fault with self and others but can also take the form of a positive opinion or conclusion. As beginning meditators we see our relentless tendency to track how we are doing, giving ourselves a running report card. Our job here is simply to notice each instance of that and return to our breathing. It may be helpful to count the judgments—and we can rack up quite an impressive total.

We can become quite harsh with ourselves when we see how judgmental we actually are. If this becomes a problem for you, you can turn to the method of putting your hand on your cheek and softly saying "judging." Techniques such as loving-kindness meditation or concentration-oriented practices such as the body scan or mindful walking can also help with a storm of judgment.

When judgment arises, I have found the A-B-C method to be very helpful in relating to the experience differently. Someone does something to make us angry and we judge him or her, then tell a story and loop between the story and our anger. Simply seeing the act of judgment changes our relationship to what has happened, inviting us to learn about our own reactions.

This is also the gateway to the psychological meaning of judgment. In our lives we encounter many people and behaviors that just go by without much notice. At times, however, we have strong negative reactions. This is not just by chance. We tend to judge harshly the parts of ourselves that we don't like. When Russ called the guys in the sober house "losers," he was, for the moment, disowning the part of himself that feels like a loser. Margaret judged her husband for being inconsiderate, which she, of course, would never be. In fact, this energy of "inconsideration" was so deeply disowned that as soon as she got angry at him, she reflexively considered his point of view and turned the anger on herself.

The ability to see our judgments and reclaim our disowned parts is one of the best ways I know of to expand our consciousness and humanity. Difficult people can actually help us to grow up and assume authority for all of who we are. We can ask ourselves what it is we cannot stand about the other person and then ask: "Do I have a part like that?" We often do.

We disown our selfishness, meanness, stinginess, narrow-mindedness, laziness, and lack of trust and criticize others for having these qualities. The ironic result of this is that the more we disown an energy, the more we seem to draw it into our lives. If we hate being needy, for example, we will encounter it in our partners, children, dogs, or coworkers. Hyperresponsible women seem to get boyfriends who smoke pot and can't seem to find a job. Then they judge these guys, who become even more irresponsible. The key principle here is that judgment (particularly the silent variety) drives people further into the opposite of who we want them to be.[4]

The way through is to become aware of our judgments. The overresponsible (and exhausted) woman judges her boyfriend as "irresponsible . . . lazy . . . a slacker." Does she have an energy like that? Almost always, she can identify a part that would like to relax and do less. Her task is not to become exactly like her boyfriend but to speak to him from a place of understanding her own capacity for laziness and her wish to be less responsible. She has shifted from simply judging to taking responsibility for her thoughts and actions.

Often this leads to a softening of positions. The boyfriend feels less blamed and less defensive. Likely, he wants to do better but has been stuck in fear, avoidance, and opposition. He has also been judging her for being a controlling pain in the butt. However, as her awareness and tone changes, the woman might remember that she initially loved his relaxed approached to life, the perfect accompaniment to her take-charge but at times uptight style. As this is communicated, her boyfriend may recall how much he had appreciated her encouragement and interest in helping him pursue his goals even when he struggled. By owning her own judgment and coming more into her body, our woman has quietly inducted her boyfriend into a more cooperative and creative place. Now they might be able to do business and love each other as well.

The flip side of judgment is idealization. "I could never be as beautiful and brilliant as she is" may be partly true but can also be a denial of our own potential for beauty or brilliance. One of the most destructive aspects of the addiction process is the progressive disowning of our inner richness, our difficulties, and our latent strengths. The practice of mindfulness holds the promise of learning about and being free to be more fully who we are.

Comparison

If we watch our own minds, we see that, indeed, we are slaves to relentless judging and idealizing of others. Comparing is a type of judgment and so rampant in our consciousness that it deserves special mention. This is particularly true in early recovery, when the self-concept of the addict is in great transition and turmoil. The addictive substance or behavior of choice is often a vehicle to increased self-esteem, a sense of belonging, a source of meaning and purpose, or all of the above. Once in treatment, one can go from "the man" to a "loser" very quickly. The comparing mind isolates, judges, and creates a sense of tension and stress that is often out of our awareness.

From a young age we all learned to compare as a means of tracking our status, acceptability, and prospects for success in any number of arenas. Remember those polls from high school? Brainiest, most athletic, best looking, best personality, most likely to succeed, best listener, best all-around. If those are not winnable, you might go for class clown, most outrageous, biggest flirt, biggest outcast, most tattoos, drugs, sex, or fights. As young adults and in midlife, we continue to compare around money, possessions, career and marital success, attractiveness, cleverness, or how our kids are doing. As we age, it may be more about health, who planned better for retirement, or who has longer to live. Our parameters keep changing, but whatever our designated troop, competing and comparing can remain strongly linked to our self-esteem and self worth.

Ian was twenty-two and had a ten-year history of enormous social anxiety. He was a very handsome guy and a talented athlete, artist, and musician with a large social circle for most of high school. However, in his senior year he began to withdraw from peers, and he left college after two months, unable to handle the social environment. Ian used alcohol to elevate his mood and marijuana to calm down. He eventually crashed into a severe depression for which he was hospitalized and then discharged to a residential treatment community. There he was unable to relate to peers because of constant fears of not fitting in, not being cool, being an outcast, hurting and offending people.

In day treatment, Ian was quite shut down. He acknowledged feeling trapped in his head, making constant comparisons—with other people in the program, with friends who were more successful, with himself at an earlier stage in his life. He particularly feared saying something stupid. Ian received a crash course in grounding. He was encouraged to notice his touch points, breathing, walking, peeing, and anything else that might lessen or distract him from the steady mental barrage. As he became more communicative, Ian was able to identify a cycle of shame, social withdrawal, and addiction that had brought him to this point.

He admitted that he had never really had a solid group of friends and believed that much of his social success had been about his status. As this became less important to his peers later in high school and certainly in college, Ian got more anxious. His repeated monitoring of himself and others further impeded his ability to be present. As his self-perceived ranking plummeted, he became increasingly stressed, bleak, and hopeless. Ian could now see that the process of social comparison was a major source of his loneliness and desperation.

As he observed his own mind, Ian saw that he had a part that insisted he be the best at everything and cared only for money, sex, and recognition. Another part wanted "peace and love," everyone to like him, never to disappoint anyone, and to live on a higher spiritual plane than everyone else. That he had an adolescent brain that produced grandiose thoughts was not necessarily a problem. Ian's dilemma was in trying to reconcile all of this intellectually while simultaneously tracking his place on several pecking orders and having the most sex and the most inner peace. That will drive you nuts.

What eventually helped Ian was learning to come into his body and connect with his actual experience. He learned to step back from the process of cycling between his comparative and competitive stories and his fear of not measuring up. He had developed some stability from mindful breathing and walking and was more able to see that the stories and emotions were all impermanent and insubstantial. Further, he began to see two more inevitable results of comparing: (1) everything is about "me," and (2) it causes separation from others and loneliness.

When his younger brother came home from college, Ian saw the disparity in their accomplishments, felt bad, and wanted to withdraw. Fortunately, he was able to notice his disappointment and put it aside enough to enjoy the time with his brother, who he recognized had a different life from his own. Ian also began painting again after many years. This is an activity with many choices and possibilities, hard to do if he is stuck in his head and much more fun when he could stay present for the next color or line. This was also a nice metaphor for his life going forward.

Years ago I was on a retreat at the Insight Meditation Society in Barre, Massachusetts. I was doing walking meditation in a large room with a number of other people and right next to a monk who was also practicing. This may have triggered my concern about how I was being perceived, but I became aware of how others were walking and a question about how I stacked up against them. Then one person left the room. I thought, "This is *walking,* for god's sake, and you are turning it into the freaking Olympics."

I saw in that moment that everyone has his or her own path, life, and agenda. These change based on any number of factors that have nothing to do with me! People left the walking room to speak to teachers, go to their rooms, go to the bathroom, or have a cup of tea. Some were inside, some were outside on the grounds of the meditation center, on the road, or in the woods, walking (or running) at different speeds. The vast majority of human beings were not on retreat, just doing what they had to do. Somehow, I was fortunate to be born into circumstances where I was exposed to this practice and was able to be here. I was walking with awareness, that was all, and comparing myself to anyone else was not helping me to do that. I felt happy and connected to the people in that room and beyond. It was a nice moment.

PART FOUR

Authority amid the Full Catastrophe

17

Compassion

YOU MIGHT WONDER what compassion has to do with mindfulness and with assuming authority for ourselves amid a continuous stream of sensation, feeling, emotion, and thought. If you think about an authority figure you admire—a parent, teacher, mentor, sponsor, boss, coach, to name a few possibilities—you will likely see that person as thoughtful, fair, considerate, and having a strong sense of him- or herself.

The person is also likely to be kind. You catch more flies with honey than with vinegar, and effective leadership depends more on connecting than on commanding. So as we marshal our own energies toward any goal, the same principle applies. In the context of early recovery, where inner instability is a daily fact of life, the cultivation of kindness, patience, compassion, and self-acceptance is particularly important.

To Suffer With

The prefix *com-*, from the Latin, means "with, or together." Among the many common (from *communis*) examples in any dictionary of the use of this prefix are *companion* (one who eats bread with another), *community, compete* (to strive with), and even *combat*. *Pati* means "to suffer." To have *compassion* is to feel the willingness to share the suffering of another. It is related to *sympathy*, which also means to feel together or to feel for, and *empathy*, to feel into or to identify. *Pity* suggests sorrow related to another's misfortune as well but has a feeling of distance or superiority. Pity is thought of as the near enemy of compassion, looking like it but not feeling like it.

If you will indulge my etymologic pursuits a bit longer, you will recall that addiction comes from the Latin *addicere*, to be given over as a slave. Addicts might be the objects of pity but are more often objects of contempt, both in our culture and within themselves. The essence of the addict's experience is to suffer alone, with the only reliable companion being the drug or addictive behavior. At the core of recovery is the acceptance of being flawed *and* not being so alone in a state of defectiveness and misery and in the need to escape. Mindfulness is a means toward truth, respect, clear seeing, and wisdom. Compassion allows us to be kind to ourselves as we learn.

Golf as Metaphor

Many of you have no interest in playing golf, and many others, like me, could write a short book on our relationship with this devilish game. The act of hitting a golf ball requires concentration. It involves assessing a number of parameters, including distance from the hole, the way the ball lies, the terrain we are standing on, the weather—particularly wind and humidity—any hazards or obstacles, and where we want the ball to land, among others. Then we have to choose the best tool for the job and establish a stable foundation. We briefly allow all of these factors to settle in, then focus on the target and swing the club. Finally, we accept the result and walk to the next shot.

Does this sound at all familiar? Golf is a challenging mindfulness practice, since it entails the ongoing application of awareness of current experience, concentration, and acceptance. In a sport like basketball, there are also errors, in the form of missed shots and bad passes, but these quickly go by in the continuous action and the ability to recover on the next play. And you have teammates who also make mistakes. In golf, regardless of support from other players, the results of your own actions wind up on *your* scorecard, not theirs. It is possible to cheat, but we know when we do it, and in the end there is nowhere to hide.

I am not a very good player, but that is not a problem. If we are not playing for our family to eat, there are few things less important than a golf score. My problem was accepting the results of my efforts: somehow, I should be better than I am. If you are looking for a new way to suffer, I recommend this highly. You might think that someone who has meditated for twenty-five years and teaches mindfulness would be further along in the area of self-acceptance of poor golf shots. But it turns out that we are where we are and we teach what we need to learn.

Probably everyone who plays golf shares this tension around self-acceptance to some degree, but some have more perspective and humor than others. One day I went to the course on my own and joined three guys who were friends to play a round. On the first tee, one of them, who was relatively new to the game, was up first. He took a big swing and barely hit the top half of the ball, which rolled about twelve feet down the fairway. Definitely embarrassing, but here is what happened next: after a moment of silence, with club still in hand, he dropped down into a low crouch and held his hand up as if to shade his eyes from the sun as he looked far off into the distance. This was hilarious and we all cracked up laughing, but I was thinking, "That's how I want to be."

We cannot really know his experience. It is possible that he was so evolved that the shot had nothing to do with him personally. That is, he did not see it as "my" shot, having no attachment to it at all. More likely is that he was briefly disappointed or embarrassed but quickly shifted to making fun of himself in a brilliant moment of spontaneity, a moment with equal parts of awareness and kindness. The laughter of his playing partners was born of empathy, since all of us had no doubt done the same thing ourselves—and had not been nearly as lighthearted or creative. Our duffer had shown us our own potential for self-compassion.

Kindness and Compassion

Golf is, after all, just a game, but suffering is suffering. My personal experience with golf, for example, has given me a better understanding of suicide. I have seen my mind go from disappointment to anger to discouragement, despair, and wanting to quit the game. The person who relapses goes through a similar sequence of repeated frustration, disgust, and giving up on sobriety and him- or herself.

In addiction treatment, our patients have made countless "poor swings" and hit many shots out of bounds. They then often rage against themselves and get lost in the woods of numbing or escaping emotional pain, and life problems multiply. In early recovery, they begin to glimpse the despair and self-hatred they have been avoiding. Communal experience and psychotherapy clearly help the loneliness and self-judgment, mainly because peers and professionals offer kind attention to one's difficulties. But what about when day treatment ends or when the therapist is not available? Can we do this for ourselves?

Practice: Sending Kindness

1. Assume a position of stability and support and take three calming breaths. Continue to breathe, fully centering in the body.
2. Bring to mind a current difficulty and feel the emotion, pain, or tension it brings up in the body. Locate the sensations and allow them to be there.
3. Evoke the feeling of loving-kindness within yourself. You might repeat phrases like "May I be happy . . . may I be patient . . . may I be openhearted." Or you might bring to mind a divine being, a spiritual teacher, a caring authority, or a loyal or devoted animal who is aware of your particular suffering. Then have that being send kindness directly to the place in your body where you are in pain.
4. Accept this kindness as best you can on the in-breath and release the hurt, pain, or tension on the out-breath.
5. If there is a sense of struggle or resistance, settle back into the breath to come to equilibrium.

In chapter 5 we discussed metta practice, which sends the energy of loving-kindness to ourselves and to others. When we evoke the experience of loving-kindness and turn it toward pain, that is compassion. It is a wonderful and powerful practice that blurs the distinction between "my pain" and pain in others and has the capacity to open our hearts to the problems of being human. The development of this attitude is beautifully captured in the poem "Kindness" by Naomi Shihab Nye.

Before you know what kindness really is
you must lose things,
feel the future dissolve in a moment
like salt in a weakened broth.
What you held in your hand,
What you counted and carefully saved,
all this must go so you know
how desolate the landscape can be
between the regions of kindness.
How you ride and ride
thinking the bus will never stop,
the passengers eating maize and chicken
will stare out the window forever.
Before you learn the tender gravity of kindness
you must travel where the Indian in the white poncho
lies dead by the side of the road.
You must see how this could be you,
how he too was someone
who journeyed through the night with plans
and the simple breath that kept him alive.
Before you know kindness as the deepest thing inside,
you must know sorrow as the other deepest thing.
You must wake up with sorrow.
You must speak to it till your voice catches the thread of all sorrows
and you see the size of the cloth.
Then there is only kindness that makes sense anymore,
only kindness that ties your shoes
and sends you out into the day to mail letters and purchase bread,
only kindness that raises its head
from the crowd of the world to say
It is I you have been looking for,
and then goes with you everywhere
like a shadow or a friend.[1]

Often this experience of communal pain is the one addicts most want to avoid. When patients tell me, "I don't like groups," it is generally about shame of being seen and is often expressed as not wanting to hear other people's problems. Either the lives of others are of no interest or their troubles are too painful to bear. Ironically, it is the group that allows them to carry their own troubles more lightly.

Something magical happens as a patient surrenders to this crucible of suffering. She is suddenly not alone, is free to speak or not, is not judged when she does, is able to identify with others and learn about herself. He often sees that his pain is less than that of others, that his support actually means something, that he can sit there and feel connected to his life and his pain in a new way.

The Practice of Tonglen

Tonglen meditation is a powerful method for working with the difficult emotions that arise in early recovery and beyond. My own introduction was by the Tibetan Buddhist teacher Pema Chödrön on her tape entitled "Good Medicine." The medicine she refers to is confronting the poisons of fear, anger, selfishness, and confusion, which are then transformed to the healing energy of compassion.

Tonglen literally means "giving and receiving." The practice is the reverse of the "sending kindness" meditation in that it asks us to breathe *in* the pain that we and others are experiencing right now. We then breathe out what would help us and all people that are suffering in the same way. This is not for the faint of heart and should be approached gradually. It is clearly going against the grain for addicts who have spent years or even decades seeking pleasure, escaping pain, and avoiding the truth about themselves, particularly in relation to their emotions.

Addiction is a problem of selfishness and small-mindedness. It is a prison but also a form of protective custody. Pema Chödrön speaks directly to the problem, her understanding highly resonant with the course of addiction and recovery.

> When we protect ourselves so we won't feel pain, that protection becomes like armor . . . that imprisons the softness of the heart. We do everything we can think of not to feel any-

thing threatening. We try to prolong feeling good about ourselves. . . . When we breathe in pain, somehow it penetrates that armor. A kindness and tenderness begin to emerge. . . . When we breathe out relief and spaciousness, we are also encouraging the armor to dissolve. The out-breath is a metaphor for opening our whole being. When something is precious, instead of holding it tightly, we can open our hands and share it. . . . We can share the wealth of this unfathomable human experience.[2]

Recovery is about this very process. Group treatment and 12-step meetings gradually wear away the shame, loneliness, and sense of defectiveness inherent in the experience of addiction. The addict encounters suffering in himself and others, builds his muscles for turning toward it, and has a healing experience of common humanity.

Informal Tonglen Practice

Tonglen is going in exactly the same direction. It is a means for confronting the tendency to isolation and self-pity, taking charge of one's emotional life, and joining the human race. The practice is very powerful when used informally, or as Pema Chödrön says, "on the spot." When a difficult emotion arises, the simplest version is to say to yourself, "Others feel this way." If you are deeply sad, frightened, or confused, it is true that right in this moment there are many people on the planet that are having the same feelings.

The next step would be to get closer to the experience. If you became impatient, for example, you would feel the energy of tension, agitation, or judgment and would breathe it into the body. Then you would breathe out what would help you and all of the other impatient people—patience, kindness, self-acceptance. If you then felt guilty for your impatience, you would breathe that in and then possibly send forgiveness, a fresh start, or a broader perspective to yourself and all of the many other people who are currently feeling guilty. This is the heart of compassion, turning your attention to the common suffering with the intention to join and heal.

Remember Maurice (from chapter 15), who stole money from his father to buy heroin? He was also introduced to tonglen practice to

work with the shame and guilt that came up frequently and was causing him to drink. Getting close to these emotions did hurt, but as Maurice made space for them, they were less frightening. He was able to
see firsthand that accepting his experience (pain) was a superior alternative to pushing them away (suffering).

Maurice was also able to feel the pain of other addicts who had let
their families down. He used his own experience to be creative in
sending healing to all of those who had been thoughtless and regretted
hurting others. He breathed out remorse (instead of guilt); a forgiving
parent (outer or inner), which he had; a caring community; and self-
compassion. At times it felt like too much to bear, and Maurice could
shift to simple grounding practices or metta. But tonglen was in his
toolbox.

Formal Tonglen Practice

Along with doing tonglen as feelings arise, it may also be useful to
practice more formally with current themes or issues in your life.

Formal Tonglen Practice

After an initial brief period of mindful breathing in order to
ground and stabilize your attention, follow these four steps:

1. In the spirit of recovery, imagine your little wave as part of the
   great ocean. As you drop down into that image, experience a
   flash of openness, spaciousness, or connection.
2. Focus on the texture of your experience. Breathe in troubled,
   racing, closed in, heavy, dark, tense, or lost. Then breathe out
   cool, light, airy, refreshing, confident. Breathe these qualities
   in through all the pores of your body. Your exhalation then
   radiates outward in all directions.
3. Bring a personal situation to mind. You have the choice of focusing on the suffering of a family member, a friend, or yourself. Now inhale getting close to the pain and exhale its opposite
   or what would help or relieve the problem. For example, if you
   breathe *in* fear, frozen, tension, you might breathe *out* spacious,

loose, relaxed. If you breathe *in* agitated, fragmented, disorganized, you might breathe *out* contained, calm, centered.

4. Now universalize, breathing in the pain of all people in the same situation—grieving, angry, craving, in physical pain, lonely, hopeless, or stuck. Then breathe out healing in all directions—patience, generosity, forgiveness, connection, kindness, wisdom. Be creative and extend your circle as far as your comfort level. You might include all recovering people, their families, all who are affected by the problem of addiction, all beings who are suffering in this particular way right now. If you are holding resentment, it is possible to include the person you are upset with, who may be having a similar experience. This can be a means to get beyond the story line and soften some of your hard feelings.

5. Finally, end your tonglen meditation and return to the breath, allowing the experience to settle.

Erika is a young single mother who had a cocaine problem. Her daily habit had begun as a treat after a long day. Her son, now five, was intense and demanding and fought sleep until Erika was at her wits' end. She also worked in customer service, frequently had to field angry calls, and once broke down in tears after getting off the phone. Because she was feeling assaulted from all sides, her drug use escalated.

When Erika was introduced to formal tonglen practice, she breathed in her anxiety and had a surprising insight. In that moment she saw both how sensitive she is to the energies of other people and how much she has to fight against those energies to protect herself. At work Erika had to fend off verbal attacks as she tried to keep her composure. She had to suppress her rising anxiety and anger at the customers, which created more tension, and would proceed to judge them as idiots and herself for being so sensitive. At home she would respond to her son the best she could until finally losing her temper in total frustration. Then she experienced more judgment about her limited patience and adequacy as a mother.

Erika was frequently awake at night with fearful thoughts about her son's problems, their future, her job and finances. She felt guilty about her boy's not having a father and wishing at times that he hadn't been born. As if being a single parent were not hard enough, Erika felt tormented by her own thoughts and frequent fatigue. More cocaine helped at first but then became unmanageable.

Erika began to use tonglen when she put her son to bed. She would feel his restlessness and breathe it in, breathing out peace and calm. She inhaled her own impatience and exhaled patience and forgiveness to herself and all of the parents wishing at this very moment that their kids would go to sleep. If she was disappointed in herself as a parent or employee, she sent self-acceptance to all disappointed, self-judging people.

While this was not a miracle makeover for either her son or her customers, things clearly went better. Erika was also not so tense, not fighting within herself and having to recover from all of her blow-ups and guilt. As she slowed down, she was able to see how she judged her son and customers as "selfish, demanding, and inconsiderate." Was she like that at all? Absolutely, but she had largely disowned these qualities in her heroic attempt to hold everything together at home and at work. That is, until she became a cocaine addict.

Once she saw that she needed to be more "selfish" around her own well-being, Erika's judgments of others softened. Though her son was still small, she began to glimpse a future of better self-care and more fun for herself. Because of her tendency to absorb the energy of others, relationships with men had always been problematic for Erika. The practice of tonglen showed her that if she was able to manage her own energy field, having a successful partnership would be a possibility.

18

Addiction, Trauma, Mindfulness, and Recovery

MY GOAL IN writing this book has been to convey the power of mindfulness, both formally practiced and in daily life, in addiction and dual-diagnosis treatment. Over the past thirty years or so, training patients in moment-to-moment awareness has been effectively utilized in addressing a vast array of medical and psychological problems. So many have benefited from learning these simple practices, compatible with any belief system. I have repeatedly seen that the cultivation of mindfulness skills can help us, in all of our complexity, to know the difference between pain and suffering, what we can control and what we cannot. Making these distinctions is what I believe allows us to assume authority for our lives, grow up, help others do the same, and become more loving, compassionate beings.

Mindfulness is currently a hot subject. Two excellent recent books are entitled *The Mindful Way through Depression* and *The Mindful Path to Self-Compassion*. Have I written "The Mindful Way through Addiction"? I would say yes, but not exactly. The patients I see, for starters, have not come to learn meditation. There are some exceptions, as our program has become better known and mindfulness is increasingly seen as a viable treatment modality. But even so, mindfulness, in all of its brilliance and power, is often not enough.

I suppose this is because of the nature of addiction, a mysterious, multifaceted, and shape-shifting problem. Maps and metaphors can be helpful as long as we remain flexible and don't get too attached to any one. There are four descriptors that I find capture the essence of addiction: *disease, powerlessness, clinging* (or craving/aversion), and *trance* (or dissociation). We also saw, in chapter 1, that "addiction" is on a continuum. We all have bad or self-defeating habits; have felt helpless; have craved, raged, and escaped into fantasy. Many have been drawn to meditation practice to learn about how to suffer less and be happier. This is true for me and for the vast majority of practitioners— including those teaching these skills to their clients and patients.

For deeper, more-entrenched problems, however, addiction was the "treatment" and only later became the illness, an illness that requires the integrated approach that this book has outlined. Mark is a musician with bipolar disorder and alcoholism. He remarked at the end of his time in the program that "the four pillars [recovery, psychotherapy, medicine, and mindfulness] are like a jazz band. Each has its own voice and role, and the trick is to orchestrate them so that they come in or blend at the right time and with the right intensity." Billy has ADHD and was cocaine dependent. He loves basketball and was able to utilize mindfulness in his play with excellent results. He described how the game "slowed down" with moment-to-moment awareness, and he was able to integrate this understanding into other areas, such as disagreements with his girlfriend. Billy was a little disappointed that there were only four components to treatment, not five, as on a basketball team, but then realized that he could be the point guard of this team. We had a fun exchange about a point guard's role of seeing the whole floor and finding the open man. He is also a leader in facilitating the other "players" in an evolving process of communication, effectiveness, and creativity.

Finding Truth in a Moving Jigsaw

Since you have read this far, you are aware of many pieces of the puzzle. One set of pieces, which we might call "the problem," includes addiction, psychiatric diagnosis, genetics, constitution, and issues around early development, family, relationship, health, livelihood, spirituality, and legal matters. We all also have unique tendencies toward craving or aversion, high- or low-energy states, dissociation, particular emotional and mind states, disrespect, and lying. Another set of pieces is what we might call "the solution." This includes recovery, psychotherapy, medicine, mindfulness, truth, respect, and authority.

Mindfulness is not the entire answer. However, it assumes a central place in the healing process in its ability to see the field (outer and inner), assess what is happening right now and make a choice to speak to it, and take action or not. In early recovery there are any number of challenging experiences: Physical discomfort often goes on longer than we like. Medicine does not work quickly enough or there is confusion about symptoms and/or side effects. Life is just plain difficult. The rate of progress is not impressive. Is there any progress at all? Then there are emotions, thoughts, and impulses related to a given situation—or unrelated. Our life puzzle is in constant motion. Addictions are an attempt to control or freeze the action. Mindfulness helps us to become aware of this tendency and to choose to surrender to life just as it is.

Possibly the most important benefit of holding the intention to live one moment at a time is seeing that we are often not doing that. We are lost in regret, pessimism, unrealistic expectations, or the cloud of our negative attitude. Mindfulness allows us to see all of this operating, notice our reactions, and change course. We begin to operate our vehicle with greater skill and the confidence to enter more challenging territory . . . which brings us to two more puzzle pieces that are critical to acknowledge in the context of addiction treatment.

Trauma and Codependence

Trauma and codependence are huge subjects, included here because Mark, Billy, and many of the patients presented have had some element of physical, emotional, or sexual abuse and/or severe neglect in their histories. A full discussion of the impact of traumatic experience on the mind, body, and relationships is far beyond the scope of this book. However, these topics deserve special mention in order to help connect the dots between trauma, addiction, stress, mindfulness, and recovery.

Trauma is about the exposure to an overwhelming single event or to ongoing events during which one felt victimized without protection or social support. It can be at the hand of the supposed protector, as in the case of abuse by a parent, or in the face of rape, bullying, war, or natural disaster where help was either not available or not provided. However, regardless of the scenario, the common experience of victims is to feel alone with their terror and overwhelm, powerless and thrown back on their own resources to manage.

Addiction, whether to a substance, behavior, or thought pattern, is a behavioral metaphor for the process of avoiding intolerable experience, often the feeling of helplessness or desperation. It is not surprising then that addiction and trauma often go hand in glove.

This is partly explained by one of the huge challenges for trauma survivors: to assume response-ability for something that was clearly not their fault. While the experience of victimhood (to disown authority) is alive and well in all human beings, for the trauma victim, it is not simply a matter of psychology or character.

In post-traumatic stress disorder (PTSD), the trauma is and continues to be a living presence in the psyche and the body. Here you have a problem in which people are hyperaroused at baseline, autonomically dysregulated, tense, and continually scanning for signs of danger. Reminders of the traumatic event(s) can and will suddenly trigger the stress cycle and the unleashing of body memories, flashbacks, and nightmares. Understandably, trauma survivors are very much in their heads, ungrounded, with strong tendencies toward paranoia and dissociating from reality—means of protecting the psyche from being flooded or overwhelmed.

Dissociation is highly resonant with the process of addiction, which is also about turning away from or avoiding intolerable experience. Both have short-term benefits and long-term payback. Dissociation in PTSD can also be an addiction. The traumatized psyche becomes attached to any number of behaviors and internal experiences that make life and emotions manageable. Remember Ben (in chapter 11), who, after getting sober, sought refuge in food or by going into a trance for hours?

The joke in my generation—"reality is for people who cannot face drugs"—can be extended to "reality is for people who have not been traumatized." It is quite simply difficult to be a person with a body and mind when you have been a victim of significant abuse or neglect—let alone safely inhabit that body or mind.

Relationships are also not safe, particularly in the aftermath of shaming, abusive, and neglectful parenting. *Codependence* can be defined as "a psychological condition or a relationship in which a person is controlled or manipulated by another who is affected with a pathological condition." And the flip side: "a situation in which one person feels a need to be needed by another person." Codependence (like any addiction) seeks stability but reinforces harmful behavior patterns. It is a relationship addiction with the goal of stabilizing the inner turmoil of the addict in the same way a drug does. The term was originally associated with a family disease of unwittingly "enabling" an alcoholic. However, it turned out that regardless of whether drinking behavior changed, family dynamics continued to be mired in shame, anger, and mistrust.[1] It is now understood that codependence is about trauma much more than alcoholism.

Abused children tend to have trouble with both self-esteem and personal boundaries, making it difficult for them to feel good about themselves and to belong. Codependents additionally have problems recognizing their adult needs and wants as well as owning and expressing their reality appropriately.[2] They have a strong tendency to disconnect from their body as well as from their natural instincts for aggression, sexuality, and self-care.

Margaret (in chapter 16) got angry at her husband for not coming home, then suddenly turned it on herself. This was the best she could do at the time to maintain a life she felt she could manage. Like any addiction, codependence is a trance state with elements of protection, disorientation, and loneliness. It limits the addict's experience of who she is, what she wants, and what is real—for better and for worse.

Mindfulness and Trauma

Kelly had a horrific trauma history and came to treatment after a suicide attempt. She had been avoiding her pain and fear with drugs, sex, and constant motion. Now in her late fifties, Kelly was smart enough to recognize a losing strategy. Since she had known recovery in the past, she easily recommitted and thrived with group support. Kelly's peers looked up to her as a woman of kindness, maturity, and wisdom, which helped rebuild her self-respect.

The psychotherapy aspect of treatment focused on how substances both helped and compounded her problems with mood, anger, and anxiety. Kelly's conflict was whether to actually feel her feelings—and not feeling them was clearly leading toward death. This was a nice segue into her mindfulness training, where she began to open to the range of her experience: sadness, fear, anger, shame, physical pain, and craving as well as support, connection, calm, confidence, self-esteem, laughter, and joy. There were also the stories: "I can't do it . . . I'm not worth it . . . it's too hard . . . I can use one time . . . fuck it . . . fuck everyone!"

As she returned again and again to her breathing or walking, Kelly began to develop more inner stability and saw that all of these experiences showed up and then passed on. She had good days and bad, hope and discouragement, pain and respite. Her rageful part wanted to give up or take the whole house down, but then she felt better later in the day. Seeing the same process in others helped her feel less alone and compassionate for their suffering and inspired her to keep practicing one moment at a time. At the time of her discharge, Kelly's note to the staff said, "I want to thank you all for teaching me to be grateful for the good days and graceful for those not so good. . . . And seeing that my feelings will not kill me but not feeling them may."

This sounds like a great ending, but life goes on, and everything has pluses and minuses—including addiction, dissociation, and mindfulness. Many trauma patients have seen their flashbacks recede with simple grounding practices. Then some of them leave treatment. Why? People can become attached to the arousal (physical or sexual), the terror, the shame, or simply the mode of dissociation. But mostly they are afraid to change.

Mindfulness practice is about grounding; focusing; appreciating our endlessly changing physical sensations, feelings, and thoughts; and being kind to ourselves and others. We can see how this would be difficult for trauma victims who dissociate as a means of managing uncertainty and a turbulent inner experience. It is not safe to be still, not safe to allow natural feelings or energy to flow. Even kindness can be suspect, particularly if it was ever used as a manipulation.

Trauma is characterized by physiological dysregulation. If the brain identifies any scenario as dangerous, the system will go into either hyperarousal (fight or flight) or hypoarousal (freeze or submit). The treatment of PTSD seeks steadiness and balance, but quiet and relaxation can be threatening. Despite the patient's conscious intentions, the pull toward dissociation is highly unpredictable. Some trauma victims have even been triggered by the meditation instructions, which contain an element of hypnotic suggestion. Mindfulness training has helped stabilize many trauma survivors but must proceed at a measured pace.

Coping: What to Do?

Recovery from trauma, like recovery from addiction, requires a complete physical, emotional, and spiritual commitment. Victimization took place, and it wasn't fair or right. The first contemplation is how to take responsibility for something that was not your fault. This bears some analogy to alcoholism, a disease you cannot control, and drinking, a behavior you can. Also, the addict and the person with PTSD both tend to live in their heads, are not thinking clearly, and do not trust easily when they enter treatment. They both are also going to deteriorate and die young if they keep going down the same path.

It is critical for the trauma survivor to improve self-care. Daily exercise, even if it begins with just a walk down the block and back, is important for embodiment and releasing stress. Healthy and regular eating provides energy, pleasure, and self-kindness. Sleep is often difficult and fraught with fear and impatience, but it is important to rest and accept slow progress. Keeping oneself and one's home clean is a source of self-esteem. All of these are also opportunities for mindfulness practice, taking interest, and experiencing pleasure in simple moments.

Recovery is essential, in the sense of not being alone. Trauma survivors are drawn to isolation as much as addicts, and it does not work. At one time or another, all are stuck at the fear, shame, or grief barriers—which will require the help of a skilled professional. Psychotherapy, both individual and group, can provide a safe place for support and stabilization. Over time, exploration and working through the trauma may be pursued, but sometimes that is not indicated or even possible. Medicine is usually of value for mood, anxiety, and psychotic and/or attentional symptoms but is not always necessary.

Mindfulness is initially about grounding, a goal that is often approached with some ambivalence and a strong tendency to forget.

Repeated reminders and seeing results in the form of stability or relaxation are helpful. Practices are oriented to concentration and returning to the present moment through the touch points or breath, with kindness. The body scan is helpful for grounding, concentration, and awareness of sensory experience. We encourage people to do mindful walking and notice subtle changes in pressure, motion, temperature, sound, and smell. They can focus very narrowly or open the lens very wide. Being in nature in all kinds of weather is a wonderful practice for connecting beyond ourselves.

Finally, some people do beautifully with the loving-kindness or tonglen practices, either alone or in combination with prayer. Trauma is so deeply lonely, frightening, and shaming. The spirit of recovery is in feeling the connection to all survivors and all beings.

How Much Truth Can We Handle?

Jordan is at a crossroads. A successful sales rep for a pharmaceutical company, he lost his job because of too many positive drug tests. This is Jordan's second time in therapy. Several years earlier he'd had an affair, which nearly ended his marriage. This time his concern is whether to tell his father the full story of his being fired. Jordan is unclear how his dad, a recovering alcoholic, would receive the news. He both cares about his father's opinion of him and wants to protect him from disappointment and worry. He also wants to be seen and known.

Jordan's childhood was quite dark. It was often tense at home, and there were frequent and violent blowups. His older sister detached from the drama, so Jordan felt it was his job to track his parents. He recalled going out to play and making them promise that they would be okay while he was gone. Jordan felt aware of the angry, sad, and desperate energy around him as well as the constant need to put out fires.

This is how codependents are made. Jordan had developed a part that was highly skilled in monitoring the emotional tone and well-being of others. The dark side of this was his ability to spin the truth or simply lie if it served him. But now he was exhausted from covering his tracks, and his deceptions had nearly gotten him a divorce. We discovered that Jordan also had a part that was very interested in truth and integrity. When he holds things back, he feels guilty and longs for the ease of being more direct. Jordan was interested in the benefits and liabilities of lying and telling the truth as a means of learning about the problem:

1. Lying, omitting, avoiding

   Pluses:
   - Maintain an image
   - Maintain a sense of normalcy and control
   - Regulate self-esteem
   - Limit his father's disappointment and worry
   - Avoid confrontation

   Minuses:
   - Loss of connection
   - Eventual loss of trust
   - Feelings of sadness, guilt, shame, conflict, and fear of discovery
   - Not facing the problem
   - Not being seen for who he is
   - Turning to alcohol and drugs
   - Having to remember and perpetuate the lie
   - Exhaustion

2. Telling the truth

   Pluses:
   - A chance to be seen and known by his father
   - Opportunities for support and deepening of connection
   - Opportunity for wisdom and insight into the problem
   - A chance to be seen and known to himself
   - Gaining trust
   - Having the ease and freedom to be who he is

   Minuses:
   - Having to admit a problem and be accountable
   - Confronting his father's disappointment and worry
   - Risking his father's disapproval
   - Having to change how he operates

As Jordan explored the parts holding these different points of view, he was able to appreciate both sides, but it was really no contest.

Telling his father the truth was clearly the better alternative. The only problem was that he was not ready. He felt close to his dad and had forgiven him for not showing up in his childhood. However, Jordan still felt compelled to protect his father (and himself) from the painful truth. That is what codependents do despite all of the effort and exhaustion.

The habits of deception and duplicity were clear obstacles to the happiness and peace of mind that Jordan longed for. He had spent much of his life feeling like an impostor. His deep wish was to be genuinely loved for who he is, not just his successes. Would his dad still love him? Yes—but it was more about respect. Men are supposed to hold it together. Also, his father's well-being centered, in Jordan's mind, around his adequacy as a parent, and telling the truth might jeopardize that.

How much truth could Jordan tolerate? Lying had been a means of survival but a tiring one that entailed doing other people's business. What would it be like to stop protecting his father? How would it feel to take charge of his own life, to be accepting of himself, not just to survive?

When I introduced Jordan to mindful breathing, this was his reaction to a brief exercise: "My mind quieted and concentrated, and I felt some relief. Then I had an urge to rush through it, to manage or fix things. On the third breath, I slowed down and surrendered to concentrating again. There was a certain immediacy."

In a second exercise, I asked him to focus on his energy. He could feel the difference between the relaxed, body-centered energy and the agitation associated with "my brain trying to take over, pulling me back to the usual reality." Then I had Jordan direct his attention to his heart area and recite the metta phrases: "May I be safe and protected from inner and outer harm, may I be healthy and strong, may I be happy, may I have ease of well-being."

This was his account of his experience: "When it was quiet, I said to myself: 'Be kind . . . do you deserve a peaceful place . . . why not?' I didn't know the answer, but I didn't feel stuck. I felt light, and my mind felt free of control. I had an image of people around me—my wife, my father, and others too. They were smiling, like I might be well."

Beginner's luck or just beginner's mind? Jordan still did not know exactly what to say to his father, but there was so much more space around the experience. He began to see his current dilemma as part of a greater process of his own growth, maturity, and self-acceptance. How much truth he could handle today is different from his capacities both yesterday and tomorrow. Jordan saw that if he could stay open to his experience, it would naturally unfold. He could do his best to love himself and others, learn the difference between his business and theirs, and remain aware of what he could control and what he couldn't. He was beginning to see the possibilities for claiming his life in a new way.

Freedom and Responsibility

In his book *Seven Habits of Highly Effective People,* Stephen Covey makes a distinction between the words *liberty* and *freedom,* which in America are used interchangeably. *Liberty* is a condition of the *environment,* essentially having a number of options, such as whether to go to a gathering where people are drinking, hang out with sober friends, go to a meeting, or stay home and do any number of things. *Freedom* is seen as a condition of the *person,* the inner power to exercise those options. Freedom implies *responsibility,* the ability to respond thoughtfully and flexibly, depending on the circumstances.[3] Viktor Frankl, when he spoke to American audiences, was fond of saying, "I recommend that the Statue of Liberty on the East Coast is supplemented by a Statue of Responsibility on the West Coast."[4]

Political discourse in democratic societies is often about balancing liberty with responsibility, both personal and for the country as a whole. During times of great fear or difficult financial times, there is a strong tendency for people to hold on to what they have and disown responsibility to the more vulnerable members of the society. On a personal level we do the same thing under stress when we choose a quick fix over our own health. We are, in the words of the psychologist and addiction expert Anne Wilson Schaef, a "nation of addicts" with an endless appetite for substances, food, sex, work, and material consumption, leading to a pervasive malaise that deadens the senses, precluding effective change.[5] When a country comprising 5 percent of the world's population uses 25 percent of the energy, something is clearly out of balance. This is likely what Viktor Frankl meant.

Mindfulness practices are tools toward the cultivation of freedom,

responsibility, and personal authority. Becoming grounded and embodied helps the mind to become more concentrated and flexible. We
are less easily destabilized, more confident and able to handle uncertainty and ambiguity. Our blind spots begin to shrink, and we are less
afraid to ask for help. This gives us a surer hand in our own direction
and allows us to be a greater resource to our family, friends, work, and
community.

Recovery and mindfulness both explore the questions of what
leads to suffering and what leads to freedom. Joseph Goldstein has said
that "if we understand the causes of happiness, then, when we cultivate those causes, happiness follows." On the flip side:

> If our lives unfolded randomly, with no physical or moral laws
> operating, then we could not influence the direction of our
> lives at all; we would be subject to the winds of chaos. . . . We
> establish some stability and focus in our mind and see which
> elements in it lead to greater peace, which to greater suffering.
> All of it—both the peace and the suffering—happens lawfully.
> Freedom lies in the wisdom to choose.[6]

The initial motivation for substance use is usually about exploration and doing what feels good. It can also provide some structure in
the form of a peer group or symptom reduction (particularly anxiety),
but the liberty-stability quotient is generally quite high. The presence
of substance dependence and addiction signals that the fun is waning
and use of the drug is much more about structure and stabilization.

We all eventually make commitments to relationship, career,
and/or lifestyle. Generally speaking, devoting our energy to choices
that provide both predictability and flexibility goes a long way toward
determining our chance to be happy. The freedom to determine our
direction depends on values, balance, perceptiveness, and creativity—
not just falling in the old rut, following the next desire or impulse.
Dogs that learn to come when called get more freedom than ones that
don't. The same is true for people who are trustworthy and reliable.

Jordan was highly identified with looking good. He had succeeded
at that goal at the cost of feeling like a fraud. Now, if he is to grow, if he
is to allow himself to be truly seen and known, he will have to let go

of that identification and risk looking bad. The good news is that he does not have to do it all alone and without a net. In his brief experience with mindfulness, Jordan saw that his task is to be honest about how much fear, risk, and truth he can handle at a given time. Once he has done the best he can right now, his next job is to bring acceptance to his efforts. There will likely be some discouragement along the way, causing him to retreat into contraction or avoidance of the truth.

If, however, he continues to practice mindfulness in the context of his recovery, none of this has to be a problem. The desire, the aversion, the fear, the identifications, can all be observed, investigated, and let go. Let the addiction or impulse have its say, then choose.

We Are Not Here Forever

We know we won't live forever, and still we forget to stay present in our lives. Addiction can be a disease as well as a behavioral metaphor for the way we all suffer through our cravings and attachments. Recovery is a process of letting go of these in the service of being free. I have noticed that aging often brings a certain mellowing but not necessarily wisdom. That is because the fear of letting go can win out over our wish to be more fully who we are. When this fear is faced and overcome, the results can be brilliant. The New Zealand poet Fleur Adcock is able to convey this in a poem called "Weathering," written during a personal retreat to the lake district in England.

> My face catches the wind from the snowline and flushes with a
> flush that will never wholly settle.
> Well, that was a metropolitan vanity, to look young forever, to
> pass.
> I was never a pre-Raphaelite beauty, and only pretty enough for
> men who wanted to be seen with passable women.
> But now that I am in love with a place that doesn't care how I look
> or if I am happy, happy is how I look and that is all.
> My hair will grow gray in any case, my nails chip and flake, my
> waist thicken and the years work all of their usual changes.
> If my face is to get weather-beaten as well, it's little enough lost for
> a year among lakes and fells,

where merely to look out of my window at the high pass makes
   me indifferent to mirrors
or to what my soul may wear over its new complexion.[7]

We do not know if the poet meditated, but we do know that she
left behind confining identities and faced herself during a critical period in midlife. She was also living fully, powerfully, and very much in
the body. Mindfulness practice can help us to bring this same spirit to
our own lives as we age, even with its attendant fears of illness, pain,
and death. Aging is in no small part about loss, and our happiness depends upon how we relate to it. Can we recognize what is inevitable,
direct our attention to what we can control or enjoy, act or not, accept
the results gracefully, and move on?

We all fear some aspect of the aging process—the loss of attractiveness, capacity, or health, or death itself. As we have seen, learning
to relate differently to the experiences of storytelling, doubt, judgment, and comparison can make our fears and shortcomings less solid.
Also, if we look closely, these phenomena and our relationship to them
continue to change.

When I was a psychiatry resident, I rang the bell of my therapist
one spring afternoon, and when she came to the door, I commented
on the beauty of her yard. But I suddenly felt very sad as I noted yellow
forsythia blossoms on the ground and green beginning to appear. She
smiled in a way that both accepted and joined my experience and said,
"There's a lot more to come." I was sad and it was okay. We never quite
know how much or how little time we have. We may have goals,
plans, or regrets, but we can only live today.

You can find excellent discussions of mindfulness practice and
aging in *Living in the Light of Death* by Larry Rosenberg and *The Mindfulness Solution* by Ronald Siegel.[8]

Living Well: The Habit of Effective Time Management

I want to return to Stephen Covey, whose *Seven Habits of Highly Effective People* provides a map for personal authority. His seven habits
begin with the development of a foundation in character and values
leading to effective communication and optimal well-being.

Habit 3 is called "Put First Things First," a means of organizing life around one's priorities. Think of a simple four quadrant matrix comprising the parameters of *importance* (in line with your deeply held values) and *urgency* (pressing or critical).

Quadrant 1 is urgent and important. This consists of things that must happen or serious problems will ensue—crises, emergencies, critical events in relationship, business, or any field of endeavor.

Quadrant 2 is not urgent and important. This includes activities that are not imperative but are highly valued and generally contribute to health, well-being, and success. Examples of this are adequate sleep, good nutrition, reflection and planning, exercise, spirituality, meditation, important reading or research, valued relationships, rich artistic or cultural experiences, and fun.

Quadrant 3 is urgent and not important. Examples of this are the phone ringing during dinner from a number that is "not available" or the unanswered e-mail. The essence of quadrant 3 is that the urgency comes from the priorities of other people.

Quadrant 4 is not urgent and not important. These activities are often pleasant but not in line with your values. In retrospect, they often seem like a waste of time. Excessive or mindless TV watching, intoxication, procrastinating, and gossiping belong here.

Covey's point is that our energy belongs in quadrant 2. This is obvious on its face, since these are wholesome activities, but choosing them will also minimize crises, our time spent in quadrant 1. Prioritizing the health of the mind, body, relationships, and business allows us to head off problems before they get out of hand. There will always be pressing matters, but we can now handle them against a background of stability, predictability, and well-being.

Since quadrant 2 activities take time, it is natural to wonder where all of that time comes from. The answer is that it comes from quadrants 3 and 4—limiting interactions that pleasantly waste our time but are not in line with our personal goals. Selfish? Absolutely. But also necessary in order to use our energy in the most effective way possible. The codependent in us wants to be nice, which is fine unless it comes at the cost of what we need or what is most important to us. Habit 3 (the management habit) flows directly out of habit 1, being proactive or responsible, and habit 2, taking leadership for one's life around a set of values or principles.

But what do we really value? You may have noticed that I put "fun" in quadrant 2. Most people would agree with that. But TV and intoxication can be fun too. Why are they in quadrant 4? What about *Masterpiece Theater*? Can going to fifty baseball games or movies in a year be a quadrant 2 (not urgent but important) activity? For some people, it certainly could be. What sort or amount of socializing belongs in quadrant 2 versus 4? There is also the issue of pursuing excellence, which takes time. When do the benefits of our achievements in work or skill development begin to get out of balance with our health or relationships and become a problem?[9]

Living effectively is a moment-to-moment business, and mindfulness practices can help both to plot and to direct our course. We are all unique packets of energy that are changing as we sit here. We may be excited, bored, comfortable, or antsy, and none of it lasts. In different seasons of our lives, we may prioritize work, relaxation, friends, travel, family, or learning a new skill. You may have had drug or alcohol use as a central focus for a number of years. That may not seem like a great use of time, but some lessons could only have been learned through that experience.

In any case, it's over. Can you now take your new understanding into the next moment and do the best you can? This is the most powerful means I know of to focus energy productively, bring acceptance to the outcome, and continually reevaluate priorities.

The Place of Meditation Practice

Once while I was on a meditation retreat with Sylvia Boorstein, she told the group: "Mindfulness practice is what we do in order to be fully present in our lives. This," she said, assuming her meditation posture, "is remedial mindfulness."

As we have seen, there are both formal and informal practices, and both are important for training us in developing new habits of directing attention and returning to the present moment. I recently asked a woman who was leaving our program what she would take with her from the mindfulness instruction. She had done quite well, so I was surprised when she simply replied, "The breathing." Mildly disappointed, I asked what she meant.

"The breath brings me into my body," she said, "and I'm not so caught up in my thinking. It's a moment of freshness. I am beginning to see my thoughts as not so solid and not necessarily even true. I am not a victim of my opinions anymore. And I feel freer to decide what to do next." Well . . . I felt humbled but also pleased. She had gotten a great deal, but I wondered if she would sustain her gains.

Regular formal sitting meditation is a way to remember to apply the practice consistently in daily life. When you begin, the main principles are to keep it simple and be kind to yourself. You might start with short sittings in the morning and evening. Here and there, you might be moved to sit longer and find a rhythm that works best. If you miss or stop for a while, you are in good company. It is easy to rationalize not sitting. Just come back to meditating in much the same way you return to the breath when the mind drifts off.

I encourage you to sit regularly in the same way that your dentist recommends that you floss and brush your teeth. Meditating literally rewires your brain. Research has demonstrated thickening of the cerebral cortex and greater preservation of cortical neurons with regular practice.[10]

Recovering addicts who go to ninety meetings in ninety days may be resistant, irritable, or bored. However, they stabilize because they are showing up again and again to a community where most people are wanting to get well and choosing responsibility over the liberty to get high or avoid feelings. The results don't lie. Addicts who slip often say they stopped going to meetings, isolated, and lapsed into negativity. Reconnecting with recovery, their wave becoming part of the ocean, helps promote a sense of optimism and of not being so alone. Mindfulness practices empower recovery by improving the odds of keeping the mind on track, seeing more quickly when it is moving into dangerous territory, and promoting kindness and compassion.

If you are not near a meditation center, you can use books, tapes, or CDs for support. It is also extremely encouraging to join a group that sits together and discusses the practice. This could be based on Buddhist teachings or recovery principles or be through your place of worship. It is all going in the same direction.

Kindness and Resolve

As a beginning psychotherapist, I was encouraged by one of my mentors at the Boston University School of Medicine, Dr. Bill Malamud, to "put money in the bank of self-esteem." When a person feels bad enough about himself, he sees everything through that lens. Then his thoughts, feelings, and actions spring from that dark place, leading to problematic relationships, depression, and despair. It's true, successful psychotherapy begins with kindness.

The Dalai Lama has said, "My religion is kindness." When baited by journalists to express his anger at the Chinese, he replied, "They have already taken my country. Shall I allow them to take my mind as well?" His practice has been the unconditional acceptance of all beings and particularly the valuing of one's enemies. They are the ones that challenge our patience and our stability by evoking the internal enemies anger and hatred.[11] The more we can overcome these emotions, the more we can care for the happiness of others and ourselves.

As human beings, we cannot survive alone; a sense of belonging is critical to our emotional well-being. Some children have been fortunate enough to grow up in families where they learned kindness the way others learn more than one language. However, many come from backgrounds of pervasive unhappiness, chaos, abuse, and neglect. The relationship of these children to simple kindness is skewed, leading them not to feel entitled to it, not to trust the experience, or simply not to see it at all. Codependence is a desperate attempt to feel stable via caring for others that does not lead to happiness. We have seen that addictions lead to greater confusion and isolation, further distancing us from the source of well-being.

Recovery is the beginning of kindness and compassion. Initially, it simply provides an experience of not being alone and adrift with one's suffering. Living one day at a time is a hedge against becoming overwhelmed by the prospect of interminable and unbearable pain. Mindfulness training makes the project of recovery even more workable by breaking experience down into smaller bites. Then cravings, anger, agitation, and afflictive emotions can be accepted and let go. With increasing stability of attention, it becomes possible to see more clearly which mind states lead to happiness and which to greater suffering, emphasizing the former and discouraging the latter.

Once we know what kindness feels like, it becomes easier to direct it toward ourselves. When we have been wounded, this does not come naturally, but when cultivated, it can save a huge amount of energy. When describing the benefits of mindfulness in our lives, Larry Rosenberg said: "The terrain is rough to walk on and this is your choice for getting around: You can drive a big truck that carries long strips of leather and roll them out wherever you go. Or you can get a pair of shoes."[12]

The skill of mindfulness does give us the capacity to approach what we have previously avoided and provides a certain sure-footedness in the realm of difficult mind and body states. As an accompaniment to recovery and psychotherapy, mindfulness practices help us to feel more connected to and comfortable with our own experience and closer to all of humanity. And learning to balance self-care with caring for others, particularly challenging in the addictions, seems much more doable.

It does take practice and the willingness to show up every day, but the potential rewards are great. The Talmud says that if you save one life, you save the world. If you are healthier and happier, wiser and more compassionate, everyone who comes in contact with you benefits. Just imagine if everyone made this commitment.

The Scottish mountaineer, W. H. Murray, wrote:

Until one is committed there is hesitancy, the chance to draw back; ineffectiveness. Concerning all acts of initiative and creation, there is one elementary truth, the ignorance of which kills countless ideas and splendid plans: The moment one definitely commits oneself, then Providence moves too. All sorts of things occur to help one that would never otherwise have occurred. A whole stream of events issue from the decision, raising in one's favor all manner of unforeseen incidents and assistance,which no one could have dreamt would come their way, Whatever you can do, or dream you can, begin it. Boldness has genius, power and magic in it.[13]

This is the grand project of your recovery, your happiness, and the ability to truly author your own life. It is the greatest contribution any of us can make. It happens one moment at a time and, if you have not already begun, it is my deep wish that you begin now.

Notes

Introduction

1. Ellen Bouchery et al., "Economic Costs of Excessive Alcohol Consumption in the U.S.," *American Journal of Preventative Medicine* 41, no. 5 (2011): 516–24.

CHAPTER 1: Addiction

1. Lance Dodes, *The Heart of Addiction* (New York: HarperCollins, 2003), 5–6.
2. Richard Sandor, *Thinking Simply about Addiction* (New York: Penguin, 2009), 2–3

CHAPTER 2: Mindfulness

1. Alcoholics Anonymous, *The Big Book*, 4th ed. (New York: Alcoholics Anonymous World Services, 2001), 417.
2. Hal Stone and Sidra L. Stone, *Embracing Our Selves: The Voice Dialogue Manual* (Novato, Calif.: New World Library, 1989), 19.
3. Reinhold Niebuhr, *The Essential Reinhold Niebuhr* (New Haven: Yale University Press, 1986), 251.
4. Wu-men, "Ten Thousand Flowers in Spring, the Moon in Autumn," from *The Enlightened Heart: An Anthology of Sacred Poetry*, ed. Stephen Mitchell (New York: HarperCollins, 1989), 47.
5. Saki Santorelli, current executive director of the Center for Mindfulness in Worcester, Mass., is credited with naming these steps; personal communication with author.

CHAPTER 5: Going Further with Meditation Practice

1. Kristin Neff, *Self-Compassion* (New York: HarperCollins, 2011), 119.

CHAPTER 6: Chaos and Exhaustion: What's Bringing You?

1. Epictetus, *The Art of Living*, ed. Sharon LeBell (San Francisco: Harper-SanFrancisco, 1995), xii.

CHAPTER 8: The Path of Mindful Recovery

1. Joseph Campbell, *The Hero with a Thousand Faces* (Cleveland: Meridian Books, 1969).
2. William Alexander, *Cool Water* (Boston: Shambhala, 1997), 19.
3. Mary Oliver, "Wild Geese," in *New and Selected Poems* (Boston: Beacon Press, 1992), 110.
4. David Whyte, *Poetry of Self-Compassion*, audio CD (Langley, Wash.: Many Rivers Press, 1991).
5. Alexander, *Cool Water*, 14.

CHAPTER 9: Mindfulness, Addiction, and Psychotherapy

1. For a fuller exploration of the interface between psychotherapy and mindfulness, see Christopher Germer, Ronald Siegel, and Paul Fulton, *Mindfulness and Psychotherapy* (New York: Guilford Press, 2005) and Christopher Germer and Ronald Siegel, *Wisdom and Compassion in Psychotherapy* (New York: Guilford Press, 2012).
2. Gratitude goes to Louise Beck and John Longo for our discussion of this subject.
3. Daniel Smith, "The Doctor Is In," *American Scholar* (Autumn 2009).
4. Quote from the psychologist Anthony Martignetti.
5. Mark Williams et al., *The Mindful Way through Depression* (New York: Guilford Press, 2007).
6. Sarah Bowen, Neha Chawla, and G. Alan Marlatt, *Mindfulness-Based Relapse Prevention for Addictive Behaviors* (New York: Guilford Press, 2011).
7. D. Marcotte, S. K. Avants, and A. Margolin, "Making a Shift from the 'Addict Self' to 'Spiritual Self': Results from a Page 1 Study of Spiritual Self Schema Therapy (3–5) for the Treatment of Addiction and HIV Risk Behavior," *Mental Health, Religion, and Culture* 8, no. 3: 167–77. The entire 3-S program can be downloaded at www.3-s.us.
8. Irvin D. Yalom, *The Theory and Practice of Group Psychotherapy*, 2nd ed. (New York: Basic Books, 1975), 3–4.
9. Ibid., 84–85.
10. Hal Stone and Sidra L. Stone, *Embracing Our Selves: The Voice Dialogue Manual* (Novato, Calif.: New World Library, 1989). This is an introduction to the theory and practice of voice dialogue. Many other books, CDs, tapes, and trainings are available at www.delos-inc.com.

11. Richard C. Schwartz, *Internal Family Systems Therapy* (New York: Guilford Press, 1995). See also Richard Schwartz, "Is Meditation Enough?" *Psychotherapy Networker* (Sept./Oct. 2011): 34–56. Further resources may be found at www.selfleadership.org.

CHAPTER 10: Mindfulness and Medication

1. Many studies have been done by the psychiatrists Timothy Wilens, Joseph Biederman, and colleagues at the Massachusetts General Hospital.
2. Timothy E. Wilens and Steven Fusillo, "When ADHD and Substance Use Disorders Intersect: Relationship and Treatment Implications," *Current Psychiatry Reports* 9: 408–14.
3. Joseph Biederman et al., "Is Cigarette Smoking a Gateway to Alcohol and Illicit Drug Use Disorders? A Study of Youths with and without Attention Deficit Hyperactivity Disorder," *Biological Psychiatry* 59 (2006): 258–64.
4. Timothy Wilens et al., "Cigarette Smoking Associated with ADHD," *Journal of Pediatrics* 153, no. 3 (2008): 414–19.
5. Biederman et al., "Is Cigarette Smoking a Gateway," 261.
6. Ibid., 262.
7. Wilens and Fusillo, "When ADHD and Substance Use Disorders Intersect," 409.
8. Timothy Wilens et al., "Does Stimulant Therapy of Attention-Deficit/Hyperactivity Disorder Beget Later Substance Abuse? A Meta-analytic Review of the Literature," *Pediatrics* 111, no. 1 (2003): 179–85; and H. Upadhyaya et al., "Attention Deficit/Hyperactivity Disorder, Medication Treatment, and Substance Abuse Patterns among Adolescents and Young Adults," *Journal of Child and Adolescent Psychopharmacology* 15, no. 5: 799–809.
9. Biederman et al., "Is Cigarette Smoking a Gateway," 261.
10. Linda Zilowska et al., "Mindfulness Meditation Training in Adults and Adolescents with ADHD: A Feasability Study," *Journal of Attention Disorders* 11 (2008): 737.

CHAPTER 11: Addiction, Recovery, and the Body

1. Carolyn Knapp, *Drinking: A Love Story* (New York: Bantam Dell, 1996), 58.
2. George Koob, "Neurobiology of Addiction," in *Textbook of Substance Abuse Treatment,* ed. Marc Galanter and Herbert Kleber, 4th ed. (Arlington, Va.: American Psychiatric Publishing, 2008).
3. For a more detailed and excellent discussion of brain anatomy and

physiology, please see Daniel Siegel's book *Mindsight: The New Science of Personal Transformation* (New York: Bantam Books, 2010).

4. Robert Scragg et al., "Diminished Autonomy over Tobacco Can Appear with the First Cigarette," *Addictive Behavior* 33, no. 5 (2008): 689–98.

5. Arthur C. Guyton, *Textbook of Medical Physiology*, 5th ed. (Philadelphia: M.B. Saunders Co., 1976), 768–69.

CHAPTER 13: Working with the Body: Pain and Aversion

1. An excellent discussion of the chronic-back-pain cycle and its treatment can be found in Ronald Siegel's book *The Mindfulness Solution: Everyday Practices for Everyday Problems* (New York: Guilford Press, 2010). More complete treatments of the subject of mindfulness and chronic back pain can be found in Ronald Siegel, Michael Urdang, and Douglas Johnson, *Back Sense: A Revolutionary Approach to Halting the Cycle of Chronic Back Pain* (New York: Broadway Books, 2001); and Jon Kabat-Zinn, *Full Catastrophe Living: Using the Wisdom of Your Body and Mind to Face Stress, Pain, and Illness* (New York: Dell Publishing, 1990).

2. Dennis Turk and Justin Nash, "Chronic Pain: New Ways to Cope," in *Mind Body Medicine,* ed. Daniel Goleman and Joel Gurin (Yonkers, N.Y.: Consumer Reports Books, 1993), 126.

3. The exercise is a variant of one that has been used in Acceptance and Commitment Therapy called "Expansion"; Russ Harris, *The Happiness Trap* (Boston: Trumpeter, 2008), 101–3.

4. Deane Juhan, *Job's Body* (Barrytown, N.Y.: Station Hill Press, 1987), 330–31.

5. Ibid., 293.

6. Ayya Khema, *Being Nobody, Going Nowhere: Meditations on the Buddhist Path* (Boston: Wisdom Publications, 1987).

CHAPTER 14: Working with the Body: Energetic States

1. Stephen Chang, *The Complete System of Self-Healing* (San Francisco: Tao Publishing, 1986), 58. Chang is a physician trained in both Western and Chinese medicine.

2. Ibid., 31–32.

3. Michael H. Sacks, "Exercise for Stress Control," in *Mind Body Medicine,* ed. Daniel Goleman and Joel Gurin (Yonkers, N.Y.: Consumer Reports Books, 1993), 315–27; and Mark Hyman, *The Ultramind Solution* (New York: Scribner, 2009), 314.

4. Kirsten K. Roessler, "Exercise Treatment for Drug Abuse—A Danish Pilot Study," *Scandinavian Journal of Public Health* 38, no. 6 (2010): 664–69.

5. Martica Hall et al., "Acute Stress Affects Heart Rate Variability during Sleep," *Psychosomatic Medicine* 66, no. 1 (2004): 56–62.
6. F. Lechin, Bertha van der Dijs, and A. E. Lechin, "Autonomic Nervous System Assessment throughout the Sleep-Wake Cycle and Stress," Letters to the Editor, *Psychosomatic Medicine* 66, no. 6 (2004): 974.

CHAPTER 15: Working with Feelings and Emotions

1. Jon Kabat-Zinn, *Full Catastrophe Living: Using the Wisdom of Your Body and Mind to Face Stress, Pain, and Illness* (New York: Dell Publishing, 1990), appendix.
2. Viktor Frankl, *Man's Search for Meaning* (Boston: Beacon Press, 2006).
3. Daniel Siegel, *Mindsight: The New Science of Personal Transformation* (New York: Bantam Books, 2010), 26.

CHAPTER 16: Working with Mind States

1. I'll admit I did not try the technique of thought stopping—"QUIET!" or "SHUT UP!" This may work for some people, but it is not the kindest approach to our natural tendency to think.
2. Byron Katie, *Loving What Is* (New York: Three Rivers Press, 2002).
3. Joseph Goldstein, *Insight Meditation* (Boston: Shambhala, 2003), 72.
4. I owe a great debt to Hal and Sidra Stone for my understanding of this subject.

CHAPTER 17: Compassion

1. Naomi Shihab Nye, "Kindness," from *Words under the Words* (Portland, Ore.: The Eighth Mountain Press, 1995), 42–43.
2. Pema Chödrön, *When Things Fall Apart* (Boston: Shambhala, 2000), 88–89.

CHAPTER 18: Addiction, Trauma, Mindfulness, and Recovery

1. Anne Wilson Schaef, *Co-Dependence* (New York: HarperCollins, 1986), 9–10.
2. Pia Mellody, Andrea Wells Miller, and J. Keith Miller, *Facing Codependence* (San Francisco: HarperSanFrancisco, 2003), 4.
3. Stephen Covey, *Seven Habits of Highly Effective People* (New York: Simon and Schuster, 2004), 69.
4. Victor Frankl, *Man's Search for Meaning* (Boston: Beacon Press, 2006), 159.
5. Anne Wilson Schaef, *When Society Becomes an Addict* (New York: Harper and Row, 1987), 3.

6. Joseph Goldstein, *Insight Meditation* (Boston: Shambhala, 2003), 3–4.

7. Fleur Adcock, "Weathering," in *Poems 1960–2000* (London: Bloodaxe Books, 2000).

8. Larry Rosenberg, *Living in the Light of Death* (Boston: Shambhala, 2000); and Ronald Siegel, *The Mindfulness Solution: Everyday Practices for Everyday Problems* (New York: Guilford Press, 2010).

9. Covey, *Seven Habits,* 151–60.

10. Sarah Lazar et al., "Meditation Experience Is Associated with Increased Cortical Thickness," *NeuroReport* 16, no. 17 (2005): 1893–97.

11. Tenzin Gyatso, *Compassion and the Individual* (Boston: Wisdom Publications, 1991), 12.

12. Larry Rosenberg, personal communication with author.

13. W. H. Murray, *The Scottish Himalayan Expedition* (London: J.M. Dent and Sons, 1951).

Acknowledgments

It has been nearly four years since I embarked on this project with the first computer I ever called my own. I have learned a great deal in that time, and during a journey that began many years ago. I recall, while I was in college, walking to the library one evening to study and coming upon a sign advertising a meeting for "Transcendental Meditation" in the dining hall. I paused for a moment and then thought, "I don't have time for that." Indeed, learning to meditate did not make sense to me then, though it was something I pursued when I was ready, which has changed my life and influenced many others. So it is with enormous gratitude and humility that I reflect on my own path to writing this book and recognize some of the many people who have helped and accompanied me along the way.

My editors at Shambhala, Eden Steinberg, Beth Frankl, and Julia Gaviria, have been extremely skillful in providing direction, support, and flexibility throughout the process. If not for Eden proposing the idea of a book, it might not have happened. My dad (and first writing teacher) had just died and my kids were off at college, so there was some space. Eden guided me in creating the book's initial vision and scope. Beth refined a sometimes unwieldy piece of work and brought it into balance, with a keen sense of what was unnecessary and what was missing. And Julia's perceptiveness and honesty about when I was not quite clear significantly improved the coherence and flow of the final product.

I thank Jean Fain for her help in approaching the book proposal. I also benefitted from the experience and skill of my writing coach, Sean LeClair, who did whatever it took—inspiring, guiding, challenging—to help me to produce a manuscript. Sean also showed me that writing is much more of an energetic than an intellectual exercise.

Throughout this process, I have thrived on a wave of support from so many friends and family who took an interest in what and how I was doing. I particularly want to express thanks for the efforts of Nancy Riemer, Suzanne Hoffman, Miles Riemer-Peltz, Abby Seixas, Lynne Diamond, and Peggy Siegel whose thoughtfulness and comments on the manuscript at various stages were both clarifying and encouraging.

Over the course of my career as a psychiatrist, I have learned and grown from the wisdom of so many teachers. I feel particularly indebted to Charles Pinderhughes, Bill Malamud, Justin Weiss, Alan Siegel, Les Havens, Margaret Frank, Marian Shapiro, Jeanne Benjamin, Barbara Green, Hal and Sidra Stone, Miriam Dyak, Cassandra Cosme, Dick Schwartz, Tony Herbine-Blank, and my early addiction mentors—Norman Zinberg, Ed Khantzian, Howard Schaeffer, Jan Kauffman, Mick Burglass, and Ken Minkoff—for their contributions to my ongoing development as a therapist and clinician.

In Massachusetts, we are blessed to have so many wonderful dharma teachers living here or who visit to speak and lead retreats at the Insight Meditation Society, Barre Center for Buddhist Studies, and Cambridge Insight Meditation Center. My own practice has been especially inspired and informed by the teaching of Larry Rosenberg, Michael Liebensen Grady, Narayan Liebensen Grady, Joseph Goldstein, Sylvia Boorstein, Sharon Salzberg, Jack Kornfield, Thich Nhat Hanh, Michelle MacDonald, Steven Smith, Tara Brach, Pema Chödrön, Bante Gunaratana, Christina Feldman, James Barasz, Andy Olendzki, Mu Soeng, and Gloria Ambrosia.

A special appreciation goes to Jon Kabat-Zinn for his seemingly limitless energy to create and develop the Stress Reduction and Relaxation Program (now the Center for Mindfulness) at the University of Massachusetts Medical School. Since 1979, the program has expanded and proliferated worldwide through the work of so many dedicated people. My personal thanks go to Saki Santorelli, Elana Rosenbaum, Ferris Urbanowski, Meg Chang, Larry Horwitz, Melissa Blacker, Fernando Torrijos, and Florence Meleo-Meyer for their determined efforts to advance an organization of vision and integrity. The Center played a seminal role in my training as a mindfulness teacher and in the book you are reading.

I also offer a deep bow to my friends and colleagues in the UMass Prison Project who taught and supported one another in learning to teach mindfulness in a rough-and-tumble environment. This wonderful group includes George Mumford, Joseph Kappel, Maddy Klyne, Anna Klegon, Ann Soulet, Diana Kamilla, Pam Erdman, Carol Lewis, and our departed, beloved buddies Uli Grossman and Karen Ryder—all of whom have gone on to teach and train others.

The Institute for Meditation and Psychotherapy has made and continues to make an enormous contribution to the field through books and workshops taught internationally. Thanks go to Phil Aranow, Stephanie Morgan, Paul Fulton, Chris Germer, Ron Siegel, and Tom Pedulla for their support and some of my early opportunities to teach on the subject of mindfulness and addiction.

Almost daily, I feel gratitude for my colleagues at Bournewood Hospital including Nasir Khan and Carmel Heinsohn, the executive management team, medical, clinical, and administrative staffs that have put the roof over our heads at the Bournewood-Caulfield Center these past fifteen years. I am deeply indebted to our patients for their courage to open themselves to healing and also to Peggy Siegel, my longtime friend and partner in exploring the challenges of dual diagnosis treatment and developing our program. I also want to recognize and thank Pat Cline, Michelle Vanas, Paula Coates, Sandy Cripps, Julie DeAngelis, and Anna Crossman for their important roles in our evolution.

My kids, Miles and Haley, were away at school during the time I was writing the book but were always interested, loving, and encouraging. I was regularly inspired by the challenging, creative work they were doing as well as their willingness to show up to learn every day. Thanks also to my dogs, Sandy and Coco, for long walks in the sun, wind, and snow, which kept my energy flowing.

The deepest appreciation goes to my wife, Nancy Riemer, whose contribution I certainly will not completely capture here. Nancy read my entire manuscript and was invariably curious, thoughtful, honest, and supportive. She has been my editor, teacher, cheerleader, and love through all of the challenges and emotions of this process. As she goes forward with her own projects and aspirations, I can only hope that she feels as helped and loved as I have.

Resources

Further Reading

MINDFULNESS AND ADDICTION

Alexander, W. *Ordinary Recovery: Mindfulness, Addiction, and the Path of Lifelong Sobriety.* Boston: Shambhala, 2010.

Bien, T., and B. Bien. *Mindful Recovery: A Spiritual Path to Healing from Addiction.* New York: Wiley, 2002.

Bowen, S., N. Chawla, and G. A. Marlatt. *Mindfulness-based Relapse Prevention for Addictive Behaviors: A Clinician's Guide.* New York: Guilford Press, 2011.

Griffin, K. *One Breath at a Time: Buddhism and the 12 Steps.* New York: St. Martin's Press, 2004.

Jacobs-Stewart, T. *Mindfulness and the 12 Steps: Living Recovery in the Present Moment.* Center City, Minn.: Hazelden, 2010.

S., Laura. *12 Steps on Buddha's Path: Bill, Buddha and We.* Somerville, Mass.: Wisdom Publications, 2006.

Williams, R., and J. Kraft. *The Mindfulness Workbook for Addiction: A Guide to Coping with the Grief, Stress, and Anger That Trigger Addictive Behaviors.* Oakland, Calif.: New Harbinger, 2012.

ADDICTION

Dodes, L. *The Heart of Addiction: A New Approach to Understanding and Managing Alcoholism and Other Addictive Behaviors.* New York: Harper Collins, 2002.

Khantzian, E., and M. Albanese. *Understanding Addiction as Self Medication: Finding Hope behind the Pain.* Lanham, Md.: Rowman and Littlefield, 2008.

Sandor, R. *Thinking Simply about Addiction: A Handbook for Recovery.* New York: Penguin, 2009.

Wilson Schaef, A. *When Society Becomes an Addict.* New York: Harper and Row, 1987.

CODEPENDENCE

Beattie, M. *Codependent No More: How to Stop Controlling Others and Start Caring for Yourself.* Center City, Minn.: Hazelden, 1987.

Mellody, P. *Facing Codependence: What It Is, Where It Comes From, How It Sabotages Our Lives.* New York: Harper Collins, 1989.

Wilson Schaef, A. *Codependency: Misunderstood—Mistreated.* New York: Harper and Row, 1986.

———. *Escape from Intimacy: Untangling the "Love" Addictions: Sex, Romance, Relationships.* San Francisco: Harper and Row, 1989.

MINDFULNESS IN DAILY LIFE

Bays, J. C. *Mindful Eating: A Guide to Rediscovering a Healthy and Joyful Relationship with Food.* Boston: Shambhala, 2009.

Fain, J. *The Self-Compassion Diet: A Step-by-Step Program to Lose Weight with Loving-kindness.* Boulder, Colo.: Sounds True, 2011.

Feldman, C. *The Buddhist Path to Simplicity: Spiritual Practice for Everyday Life.* London: Harper Collins, 2001.

Goldstein, E. *The Now Effect.* New York: Atria Books, 2012.

Harris, R. *The Happiness Trap: How to Stop Struggling and Start Living.* Boston: Trumpeter, 2008.

Joko Beck, C. *Everyday Zen: Love and Work.* San Francisco: Harper, 1989.

Kabat-Zinn, J. *Coming to Our Senses: Healing Ourselves and the World through Mindfulness.* New York: Hyperion, 2005.

———. *Wherever You Go There You Are: Mindfulness Meditation in Everyday Life.* New York: Hyperion, 1994.

Nhat Hanh, T. *Being Peace.* Berkeley Calif.: Parallax Press, 1987.

———. *Peace Is Every Step: The Path of Mindfulness in Everyday Life.* New York: Bantam, 1991.

Siegel, R. *The Mindfulness Solution: Everyday Practices for Everyday Problems.* New York: Guilford Press, 2009.

Stahl, B., and E. Goldstein. *A Mindfulness-Based Stress Reduction Workbook.* Oakland, Calif.: New Harbinger, 2010.

MEDITATION PRACTICE

Boorstein, S. *Happiness Is an Inside Job: Practicing for a Joyful Life.* New York: Ballantine, 2008.

Goldstein, J. *Insight Meditation: The Practice of Freedom.* Boston: Shambhala, 2003.

Goldstein, J., and J. Kornfield. *Seeking the Heart of Wisdom: The Path of Insight Meditation*. Boston: Shambhala, 1987.

Gunaratana, B. *Mindfulness in Plain English*. Somerville, Mass.: Wisdom Publications, 2002.

Khema, A. *Being Nobody, Going Nowhere: Meditations on the Buddhist Path*. Boston: Wisdom Publications, 1987.

Kornfield, J. *A Path with Heart: A Guide through the Perils and Promises of Spiritual Life*. New York: Bantam, 1993.

———. *The Wise Heart: A Guide to the Universal Teachings of Buddhist Psychology*. New York: Bantam Dell, 2008.

Nhat Hanh, T. *The Miracle of Mindfulness: A Manual on Meditation*. Boston: Beacon Press, 1987.

Rosenberg, L. *Breath by Breath: The Liberating Practice of Insight Meditation*. Boston: Shambhala, 1998.

Trungpa, C. *The Path Is the Goal: A Basic Handbook of Buddhist Meditation*. Boston: Shambhala, 1995.

LOVING-KINDNESS AND COMPASSION PRACTICE

Brach, T. *Radical Acceptance: Embracing Your Life with the Heart of a Buddha*. New York: Bantam Dell, 2003.

Chödrön, P. *Start Where You Are: How to Accept Yourself and Others*. London: Element/HarperCollins, 2005.

———. *When Things Fall Apart: Heart Advice for Difficult Times*. Boston: Shambhala, 1997.

Dalai Lama and H. Cutler. *The Art of Happiness: A Handbook for Living*. New York: Riverhead Books, 1998.

Germer, C. *The Mindful Path to Self-Compassion: Freeing Yourself from Destructive Thoughts and Emotions*. New York: Guilford Press, 2009.

Neff, K. *Self Compassion: Stop Beating Yourself Up and Leave Insecurity Behind*. New York: HarperCollins, 2011.

Salzberg, S. *Loving-kindness: The Revolutionary Art of Happiness*. Boston: Shambhala, 1995.

MINDFULNESS FOR MEDICAL- AND STRESS-RELATED CONDITIONS

Kabat-Zinn, J. *Full Catastrophe Living: Using the Wisdom of Your Body and Mind to Face Stress, Pain, and Illness*. New York: Dell, 1990.

Rosenbaum, E. *Being Well (Even When You're Sick)*. Boston: Shambhala, 2012.

———. *Here for Now: Living Well with Cancer through Mindfulness*. Hardwick, Mass.: Satya House, 2005.

Santorelli, S. *Heal Thy Self: Lessons on Mindfulness in Medicine*. New York: Three Rivers Press, 1999.

Siegel, R. *The Mindfulness Solution: Everyday Practices for Everyday Problems.* New York: Guilford Press, 2009.

Siegel, R., M. Urdang, and D. Johnson. *Back Sense: A Revolutionary Approach to Halting the Cycle of Back Pain.* New York: Broadway, 2001.

MINDFULNESS FOR DEPRESSION AND ANXIETY

Orsillo, S., and L. Roemer. *The Mindful Way through Anxiety: Break Free from Chronic Worry and Reclaim Your Life.* New York: Guilford Press, 2011.

Siegel, R. *The Mindfulness Solution: Everyday Practices for Everyday Problems.* New York: Guilford Press, 2009.

Williams, M., J. Teasdale, Z. Segal, and J. Kabat-Zinn. *The Mindful Way through Depression: Freeing Yourself from Chronic Unhappiness.* New York: Guilford Press, 2007.

MINDFULNESS AND PSYCHOTHERAPY

Epstein, M. *Thoughts without a Thinker.* New York: Basic Books, 1995.

Germer, C., and R. Siegel, eds. *Wisdom and Compassion in Psychotherapy: Deepening Mindfulness in Clinical Practice.* New York: Guilford Press, 2012.

Germer, C., R. Siegel, and P. Fulton, eds. *Mindfulness and Psychotherapy.* New York: Guilford Press, 2005.

Hayes, S., and S. Smith. *Get Out of Your Mind and into Your Life: The New Acceptance and Commitment Therapy.* Oakland, Calif.: New Harbinger, 2005.

Hayes, S., and K. Strosahl. *A Practical Guide to Acceptance and Commitment Therapy.* New York: Springer, 2005.

Katie, B. *Loving What Is: Four Questions That Can Change Your Life.* New York: Three Rivers Press, 2002.

Linehan, M. *Skills Training Manual for Treating Borderline Personality Disorder.* New York: Guilford Press, 1993.

Roemer, L., and S. Orsillo. *Mindfulness- and Acceptance-based Psychotherapy Practice.* New York: Guilford Press, 2008.

Siegel, D. *The Mindful Therapist: A Clinician's Guide to Mindsight and Neural Integration.* New York: Norton, 2010.

Siegel, Z., M. Williams, and J. Teasdale. *Mindfulness-Based Cognitive Therapy for Depression: A New Approach to Preventing Relapse.* New York: Guilford Press, 2002.

MINDFULNESS AND THE BRAIN

Begley, S. *Train Your Mind, Change Your Brain.* New York: Ballantine, 2007.

Davidson, R., and S. Begley. *The Emotional Life of Your Brain: How Its Unique Patterns Affect the Way You Think, Feel and Live—and How You Can Change Them.* New York: Penguin, 2012.

Goleman, D. *Social Intelligence: The New Science of Human Relationships.* New York: Bantam Dell, 2006.

Kornfield, J., and D. Siegel. *Mindfulness and the Brain: A Professional Training in the Science and Practice of Meditative Awareness* (audiobook). Boulder, Colo.: Sounds True, 2010.

Siegel, D. *The Mindful Brain: Reflection and Attunement in the Cultivation of Well-Being.* New York: Norton, 2007.

————. *Mindsight: The New Science of Personal Transformation.* New York: Bantam Books, 2010.

MINDFULNESS AND TRAUMA

Boon, S., K. Steele, and O. Van der Hart. *Coping with Trauma-Related Dissociation: Skill Training for Patients and Therapists.* New York: Norton, 2011.

Walser, R., and D. Westrup. *Acceptance and Commitment Therapy for the Treatment of Post-Traumatic Stress Disorder and Trauma-Related Problems: A Practitioners Guide to Using Mindfulness and Acceptance Strategies.* Oakland, Calif.: New Harbinger, 2007.

MINDFUL AGING

Chopra, D. *Ageless Body, Timeless Mind: The Quantum Alternative to Growing Old.* New York: Harmony Books, 1993.

Hoblitzelle, O. *Ten Thousand Joys and Ten Thousand Sorrows: A Couple's Journey through Alzheimer's.* New York: Penguin, 2010.

Rosenberg, L. *Living in the Light of Death: On the Art of Being Truly Alive.* Boston: Shambhala, 2000.

Siegel, R. *The Mindfulness Solution: Everyday Practices for Everyday Problems.* New York: Guilford, 2009.

Web Sites

Center for Mindfulness, University of Massachusetts Medical School (mindfulness-based stress reduction): www.umassmed.edu/cfm

Insight Meditation Society, Barre, Mass. (Retreat Centers, schedules): www.dharma.org

Institute for Meditation and Psychotherapy: www.meditationandpsychotherapy.org

Meditation Talks: www.dharmaseed.org

Mindfulness-based Cognitive Therapy: www.mbct.com

Mindfulness-based Relapse Prevention: www.depts.washington.edu/abrc/meditation.htm

Mindsight Institute (interpersonal neurobiology): www.mindsightinstitute.com

Spiritual Self Schema Therapy: www.3-s.us

Index

266

elements, 19–22
origins and universality, 22–24
steps to, 26–30
See also specific topics
mindfulness-based cognitive-behavioral therapy (MBCT), 108–9
mindfulness-based relapse prevention (MBRP), 109
mindfulness-based stress reduction (MBSR), 25–27, 108
mood disturbances, 120–23. *See also* bipolar disorder; depression
mortality, 245–46
Murray, W. H., 251

Neibuhr, Reinhold, 24
neurotransmitters, 145
nicotine, 9, 130, 140. *See also* smoking
nocioception, 166–67
noticing, 165
Nye, Naomi Shihab, 227

O'Keeffe, Georgia, 77
Oliver, Mary, 95–96
one moment at a time, 92–95
opiates. *See* heroin addiction

pain
and addiction, 166–68
and aversion, 169–70
mindfulness and, 167–68
vs. suffering, 21
varieties of, 162–64
working with, 165
parts and the addictive process, 82–85
parts work (psychotherapy), 111–14
Pavlov, Ivan Petrovich, 83
pity, 224
planning, 208
post-traumatic stress disorder (PTSD), 236, 238–39
posture, 59–60
powerlessness, 234
preoccupation-anticipation stage, 141

present moment, 20–21, 119. *See also* mindfulness
psychoanalysis, 40
psychoses, 123–24
psychotherapy, 101–2
mindfulness and, 40–41
psychodynamic, 40, 102–5

Rational Recovery, 95
reacting vs. responding, 29
recovery
and connection, 91
defined, 90
goals of, 117
mindful, 89–95
reflection, wise, 154
relationships, 236–37
relaxation, mindfulness as bridge to, 145–50
relaxation response, 146–47, 162
religions
mindfulness in various, 23
See also spirituality and recovery
remorse vs. guilt, 201
resolve, 249–51
respect and mindfulness, 30–31
responsibility, 5–7
freedom and, 243–45
restlessness, 175, 210
working with, 184
Rosenberg, Larry, 246, 251

sadness, 193–95
Sandor, Richard, 14–15
Schaef, Anne Wilson, 243
schizophrenia, 123
Schwartz, Richard, 114
seeing, 28. *See also* mindfulness, steps to
Segal, Zindel, 108–9
self-determination, 117
self-medication, 9
self-understanding, 28–29. *See also* mindfulness, steps to